Agua Caliente Statue

This statue can be found in Palm Springs, California. It honors American Indians. Find out more about California Communities at: www.harcourtschool.com/hss

Locate It
California

Palm Springs

Reflections

CALIFORNIA SERIES

Our Communities

Harcourt
SCHOOL PUBLISHERS

Orlando   Austin   New York   San Diego   Toronto   London
Visit *The Learning Site!*   www.harcourtschool.com

MAPQUEST

TIME
FOR KIDS

HARCOURT SCHOOL PUBLISHERS

Reflections

OUR COMMUNITIES

Senior Author

Dr. Priscilla H. Porter
Professor Emeritus
School of Education
California State University, Dominguez Hills
Center for History–Social Science Education
Carson, California

Series Authors

Dr. Michael J. Berson
Associate Professor
Social Science Education
University of South Florida
Tampa, Florida

Dr. Margaret Hill
History–Social Science Coordinator
San Bernardino County Superintendent
  of Schools
Director, Schools of California Online Resources
  for Education: History–Social Science
San Bernardino, California

Dr. Tyrone C. Howard
Assistant Professor
UCLA Graduate School of Education &
  Information Studies
University of California at Los Angeles
Los Angeles, California

Dr. Bruce E. Larson
Associate Professor Social Science Education
  Secondary Education
Woodring College of Education
Western Washington University
Bellingham, Washington

Dr. Julio Moreno
Assistant Professor
Department of History
University of San Francisco
San Francisco, California

Series Consultants

Martha Berner
Consulting Teacher
Cajon Valley Union School District
San Diego County, California

Dr. James Charkins
Professor of Economics
California State University
San Bernardino, California
Executive Director of California
  Council on Economic Education

Rhoda Coleman
K–12 Reading Consultant lecturer
California State University, Dominguez Hills
Carson, California

Dr. Robert Kumamoto
Professor
History Department
San Jose State University
San Jose, California

Carlos Lossada
Co-Director Professional Development Specialist
UCLA History–Geography Project
University of California, Los Angeles
Regional Coordinator, California Geographic Alliance
Los Angeles, California

Dr. Tanis Thorne
Director of Native Studies
Lecturer in History
Department of History
University of California, Irvine
Irvine, California

Rebecca Valbuena
Los Angeles County Teacher of the Year—2004–05
Language Development Specialist
Stanton Elementary School
Glendora Unified School District
Glendora, California

Dr. Phillip VanFossen
Associate Professor, Social Studies Education
Associate Director, Purdue Center
  for Economic Education
Department of Curriculum
Purdue University
West Lafayette, Indiana

Content Reviewers

Cynthia Delameter
Los Angeles County Teacher of the Year—2004–05
Leland Street Elementary School
Los Angeles Unified School District
Los Angeles, California

Dr. Judson Grenier
Professor of History Emeritus
California State University, Dominguez Hills
Carson, California

Lynda Lemon-Rush
Teacher
Cedargrove Elementary School
Covina, California
Teacher Consulant
California Geograhical Alliance

Classroom Reviewers and Contributors

Toni Chu
Teacher
Delevan Drive Elementary School
Los Angeles, California

Margie Clark
Teacher
Vineland Elementary School
Baldwin Park, California

David Crosson
President and CEO
History San José
San Jose, California

Mary Jew
Director of Instruction
Cupertino Union School District
Cupertino, California

Dave Kirk
Teacher
North Park Elementary School
Valencia, California

Mary Mann
Teacher
North Park Elementary School
Valencia, California

Pamela West
Teacher
North Park Elementary School
Valencia, California

Constance Cordeiro-Weidner
Teacher
Conejo Valley Unified School District
Thousand Oaks, California

Harcourt
SCHOOL PUBLISHERS

Maps
researched and prepared by
MAPQUEST.COM

Readers
written and designed by
TIME FOR KIDS

Requests for permission to make copies of any part of the work should be mailed to:

School Permissions and Copyrights
Harcourt, Inc.
6277 Sea Harbor Drive
Orlando, Florida 32887-6777
Fax: 407-345-2418

REFLECTIONS is a trademark of Harcourt, Inc. HARCOURT and the Harcourt Logos are trademarks of Harcourt, Inc., registered in the United States of America and/or other jurisdictions. TIME FOR KIDS and the red border are registered trademarks of Time Inc. Used under license. Copyright © by Time Inc. All rights reserved.

Acknowledgments appear in the back of this book.

Printed in the United States of America

ISBN 0-15-338501-4

6 7 8 9 10 032 15 14 13 12 11 10 09 08 07

Unit 1

Our Geography

CALIFORNIA STANDARDS HSS 3.1

Unit 2

American Indians

CALIFORNIA STANDARDS HSS 3.2

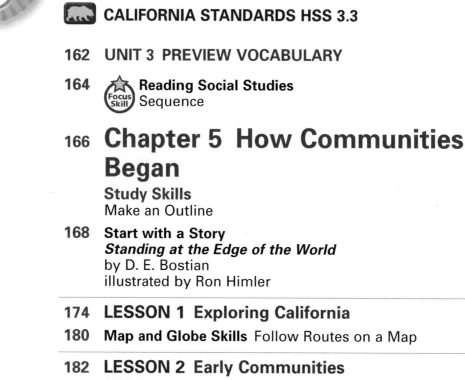

Unit 3

Community History

CALIFORNIA STANDARDS HSS 3.3

Government and Citizenship

CALIFORNIA STANDARDS HSS 3.4

Unit 6

Understanding Economics

![bear icon] **CALIFORNIA STANDARDS HSS 3.5**

Features

xvii

The Story Well Told

"All the wild world is beautiful, and it matters but little where we go . . . on the sea or land or down among the crystals of waves . . . the spot where we chance to be always seems to be the best."

—*John of the Mountains* by John Muir

This year you will be learning about many communities in California. You will read about what it was like to live in California in a **time** different from today. You will meet special **people** from communities in California, as well as from other states and countries. You will visit many **places** in California to find out how people live in different communities.

Our Communities

The Story Is About Time, People, and Place

Every community has its own history. A **history** is the story of what has happened in a place. People who study the past are called **historians**. Historians study how the past and present are linked. They look for how things change over time and how they stay the same.

Historians look at objects and documents from the past to learn about people and communities long ago. These objects used by people in the past are called **artifacts**.

Historians also study people from the past to learn more about life long ago. They often read biographies of important people from the past. A **biography** is the story of a person's life.

Historians also study the places where historical events happened. The place where an event takes place often affects how the event happens. Historians study maps from long ago to better understand the place they are studying. A **map** shows a place's location, but maps also tell historians about the land and the people who lived there.

Historians are the people who write the story of our past. They show us how time, people, and place are connected. You will learn to think like a historian as you study the history of your community in California.

Reading Your Textbook

GETTING STARTED

Unit title

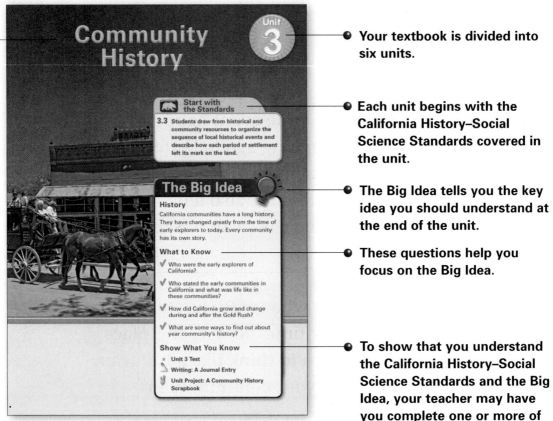

Your textbook is divided into six units.

Each unit begins with the California History–Social Science Standards covered in the unit.

The Big Idea tells you the key idea you should understand at the end of the unit.

These questions help you focus on the Big Idea.

To show that you understand the California History–Social Science Standards and the Big Idea, your teacher may have you complete one or more of these.

READING SOCIAL STUDIES

The Reading Social Studies Focus Skill will help you better understand the events you read about and make connections among them.

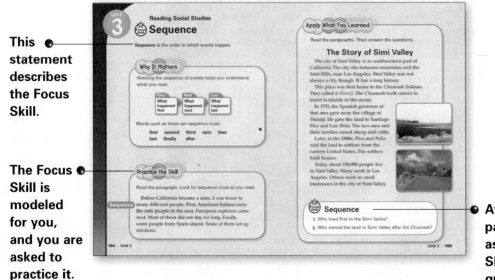

This statement describes the Focus Skill.

The Focus Skill is modeled for you, and you are asked to practice it.

After reading some paragraphs, you will be asked to apply the Focus Skill by answering these questions.

BEGINNING A CHAPTER

Each unit is divided into chapters, and each chapter is divided into lessons.

This Study Skill provides you with a strategy that you can use to remember and organize what you read.

Each chapter has a California History–Social Science Standard that is covered in the chapter.

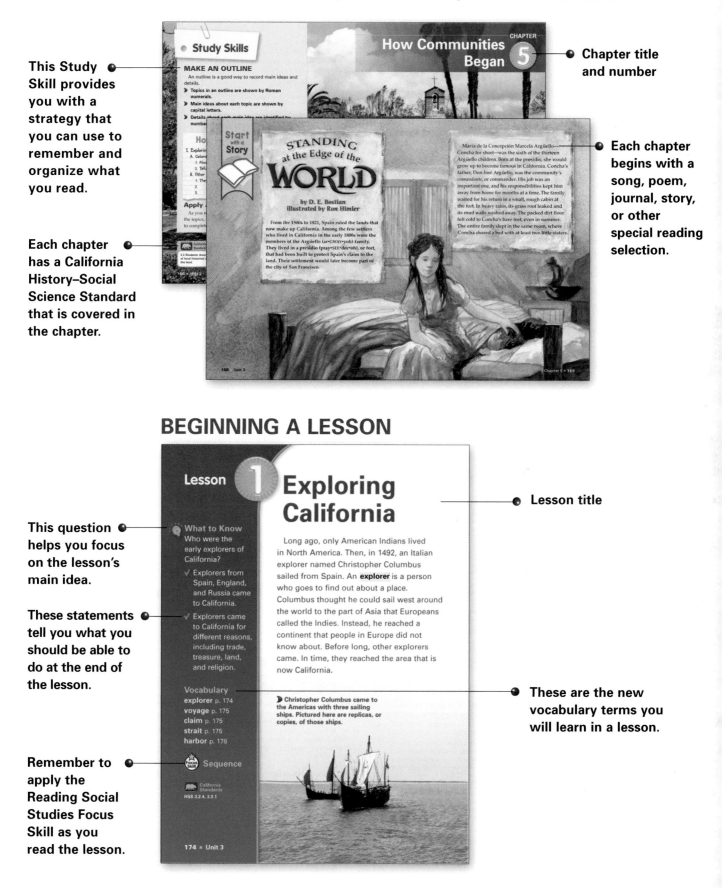

Chapter title and number

Each chapter begins with a song, poem, journal, story, or other special reading selection.

BEGINNING A LESSON

This question helps you focus on the lesson's main idea.

These statements tell you what you should be able to do at the end of the lesson.

Remember to apply the Reading Social Studies Focus Skill as you read the lesson.

Lesson title

These are the new vocabulary terms you will learn in a lesson.

READING A LESSON

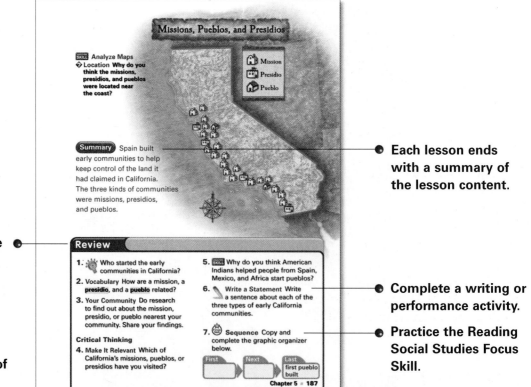

Pueblos Built in Alta California

Missions and presidios were two kinds of communities built in California. A third kind of community was a **pueblo** (PWEH•bloh), or village. Pueblos were not started by priests or soldiers. They were started by American Indians and by people from Spain, Mexico, and Africa.

Pueblos usually had adobe houses, churches, and public buildings. People in the pueblos helped supply missions and presidios with food and other goods. The first pueblo was built in 1777, near the present city of San Francisco. It became the town of San Jose. In 1781, settlers built a pueblo near the Los Angeles River. That pueblo grew to become Los Angeles.

Reading Check Compare and Contrast
How were pueblos different from missions and presidios?

Cultural Heritage

Olvera Street
In Los Angeles, you can go to Olvera Street and find Mexican food, goods, music, and dancing. Located in one of the oldest parts of the city, Olvera Street has historic buildings, a traditional Mexican-style plaza, and shops that sell Mexican crafts. Some of the buildings along Olvera Street were built when Los Angeles was a pueblo.

186 ■ Unit 3

- Vocabulary terms are highlighted in yellow.

- Each short section concludes with a **READING CHECK** question, which helps you check whether you understand what you have read. Be sure that you can answer this question correctly before you continue reading the lesson.

Some lessons have special features where you can read about Cultural Heritage, Geography, and Children in History.

Missions, Pueblos, and Presidios

SKILL Analyze Maps
◆ Location **Why do you think the missions, presidios, and pueblos were located near the coast?**

🗺️ Mission
🏛️ Presidio
🏠 Pueblo

Summary Spain built early communities to help keep control of the land it had claimed in California. The three kinds of communities were missions, presidios, and pueblos.

- Each lesson ends with a summary of the lesson content.

Review

1. Who started the early communities in California?

2. Vocabulary How are a mission, a **presidio**, and a **pueblo** related?

3. Your Community Do research to find out about the mission, presidio, or pueblo nearest your community. Share your findings.

Critical Thinking

4. Make It Relevant Which of California's missions, pueblos, or presidios have you visited?

5. **SKILL** Why do you think American Indians helped people from Spain, Mexico, and Africa start pueblos?

6. Write a Statement Write a sentence about each of the three types of early California communities.

7. Sequence Copy and complete the graphic organizer below.

First → Next → Last first pueblo built

Chapter 5 ■ 187

Each lesson, like each chapter and unit, ends with a review. Questions and activities help you check your understanding of the standards covered by the lesson.

- Complete a writing or performance activity.

- Practice the Reading Social Studies Focus Skill.

LEARNING SOCIAL STUDIES SKILLS

Your textbook has lessons that help you build your Participation Skills, Map and Globe Skills, Chart and Graph Skills, and Critical Thinking Skills.

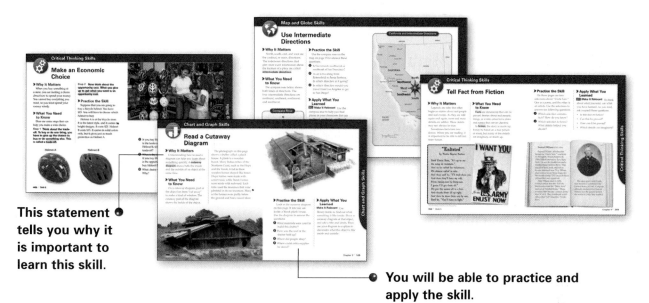

This statement tells you why it is important to learn this skill.

You will be able to practice and apply the skill.

SPECIAL FEATURES

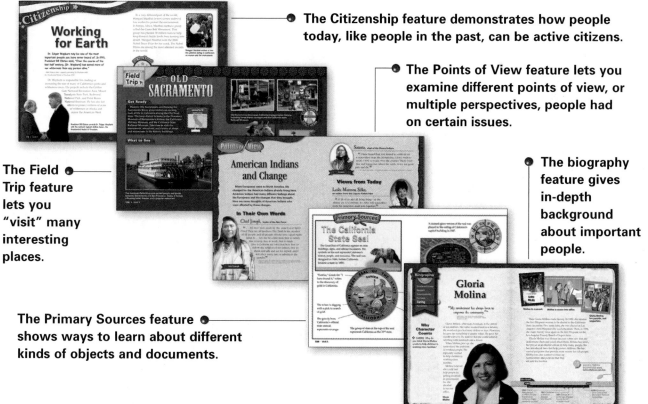

The Citizenship feature demonstrates how people today, like people in the past, can be active citizens.

The Points of View feature lets you examine different points of view, or multiple perspectives, people had on certain issues.

The Field Trip feature lets you "visit" many interesting places.

The biography feature gives in-depth background about important people.

The Primary Sources feature shows ways to learn about different kinds of objects and documents.

FOR YOUR REFERENCE

At the back of your textbook, you will find different reference tools, such as the Atlas, Research Handbook, Biographical Dictionary, Gazetteer, Glossary, and Index. You can use these tools to look up words or to find out information about people, places, and other topics.

The Five Themes of Geography

Learning about places is an important part of history and **geography**—the study of Earth's surface and the ways people use it. Geographers often think about five main themes, or topics, when they study Earth and its geography. Keeping these themes in mind as you read will help you think like a geographer.

GEOGRAPHY

Location

Everything on Earth has its own **location**—the place where it can be found.

Place

Every location has physical and human features that make it different from all other locations. **Physical features** are formed by nature. **Human features** are created by people.

Human-Environment Interactions

The environment may affect people, causing them to **adapt**, or adjust, to their surroundings.

Movement

Each day, people in different parts of our state and country and around the world exchange products and ideas.

THEMES

Regions

Areas of Earth that share features that make them different from other areas are called **regions**. A region can be described by its physical features or human features.

Looking at Earth

A distant view from space shows Earth's round shape. You probably have a globe in your classroom. A globe is a sphere, or ball. It shows Earth's major bodies of water and its **continents**. Continents are the largest land masses. Earth's continents, from the largest to the smallest, are Asia, Africa, North America, South America, Antarctica, Europe, and Australia. Because of its shape, a **globe** can only show one half of Earth at a time.

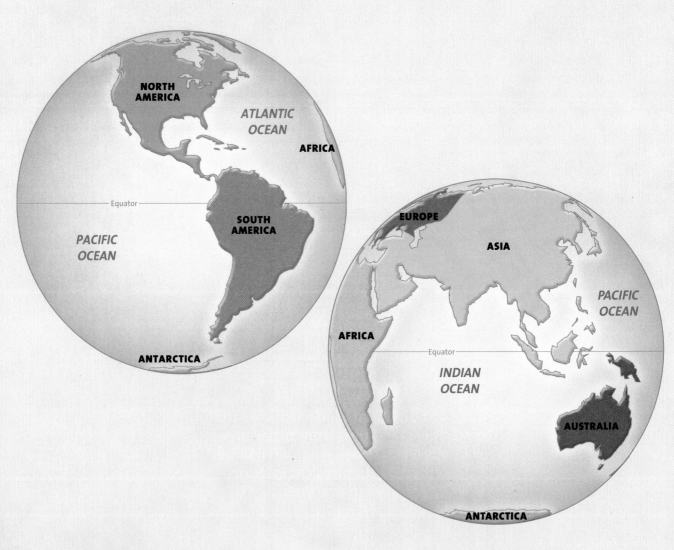

Halfway between the North and South Pole on a globe is a line called the **equator**. It divides Earth into two equal halves, or **hemispheres**. The Northern Hemisphere is north of the equator, and the Southern Hemisphere is south of it. Another line, the **Prime Meridian**, divides Earth into the Western Hemisphere and the Eastern Hemisphere.

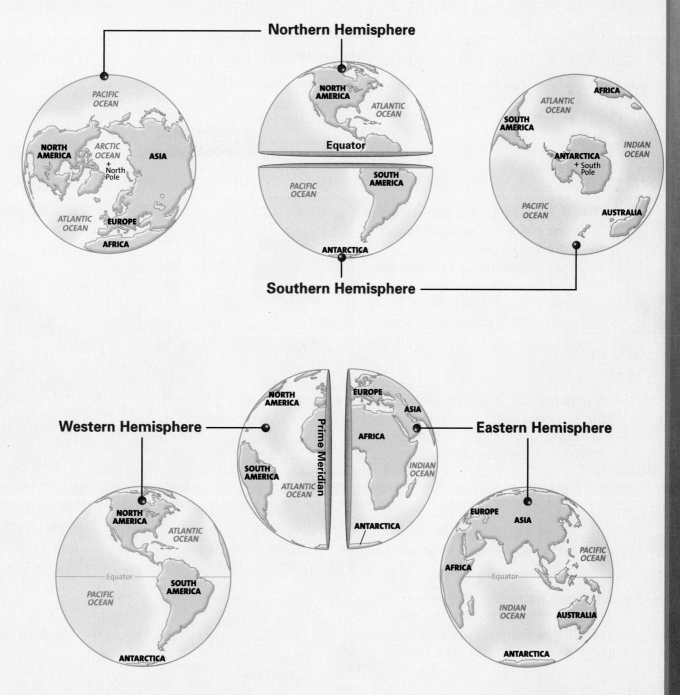

Reading Maps

Maps can provide you with many kinds of information about Earth and the world around you. A map is a drawing that shows on a flat surface all or part of Earth. To help you read maps more easily, mapmakers add certain features to most maps they draw. These features usually include a title, a map legend or key, a compass rose, a locator, and a map scale. These things help you find the **relative location** of a place, or the location of a place, in relationship to another place.

A **locator** is a small map or globe that shows where the place on the main map is located within a larger area.

The United States

A **map title** tells the subject of the map. It may also identify the kind of map.
- A political map shows cities, states, and countries.
- A physical map shows kinds of land and bodies of water.

A **map legend**, or key, explains the symbols used on a map. Symbols may be colors, patterns, lines, or other special marks.

- ⊛ National capital
- ★ State capital
- — National border
- — State border

An **inset map** is a smaller map within a larger one.

A **map scale** compares a distance on the map to a distance in the real world. It helps you find the real distance between places on a map.

ARCTIC OCEAN

ALASKA

CANADA

Anchorage

Juneau

0 250 500 Miles
0 250 500 Kilometers

PACIFIC OCEAN

Seattle
Olympia
WASHINGTON
Portland
Salem
OREGON
IDAHO
WEST
Boise

Helena ★ MONTANA
Billings

WYOMING
Pocatello
Casper
Ogden
NEVADA
Cheyenne
Carson City
Salt Lake City
Sacramento
UTAH
Denver
Colorado Springs
COLORADO
CALIFORNIA
Las Vegas

PACIFIC OCEAN

Los Angeles

SOUTHWEST Santa Fe
Albuquerque
ARIZONA
NEW MEXICO
Phoenix
Tucson

PACIFIC OCEAN
Honolulu
HAWAII
Hilo

0 100 200 Miles
0 100 200 Kilometers

MEXICO

0 250 500 Miles
0 250 500 Kilometers

Mapmakers sometimes need to show places marked on a map in greater detail or places that are located beyond the area shown on the map. Find Alaska and Hawaii on the map of the Western Hemisphere: Political on page R6. This map shows the location of these two states in relation to the rest of the country.

Now find Alaska and Hawaii on the map below. To show this much detail for these states and the rest of the country, the map would have to be much larger. Instead, Alaska and Hawaii are shown in separate inset maps, or a small map within a larger map.

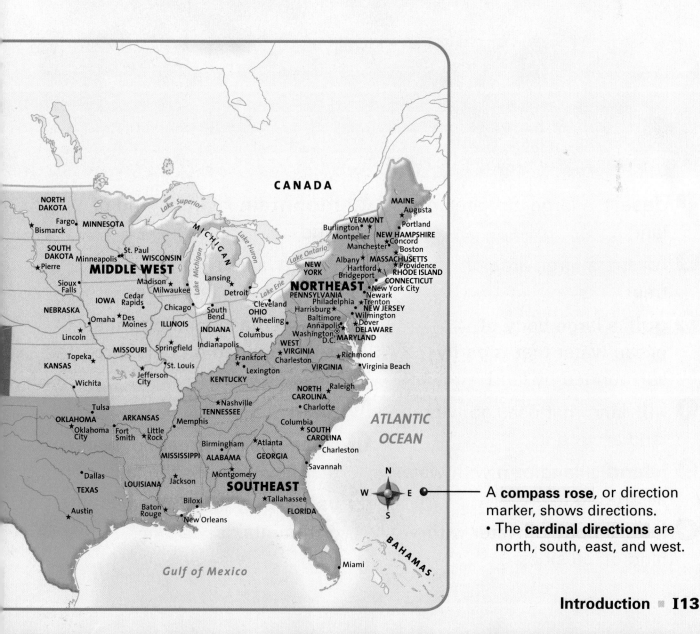

A **compass rose**, or direction marker, shows directions.
• The **cardinal directions** are north, south, east, and west.

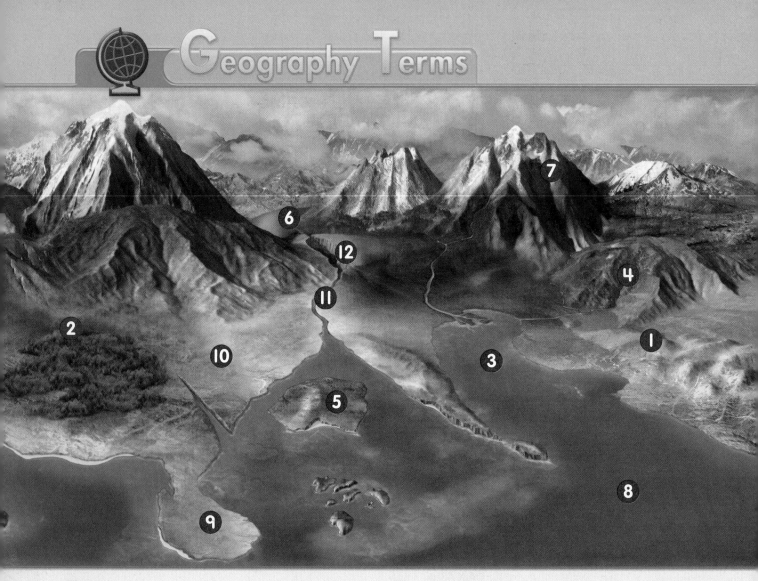

1. **desert** a large, dry area of land

2. **forest** a large area of trees

3. **gulf** a large body of ocean water that is partly surrounded by land

4. **hill** land that rises above the land around it

5. **island** a landform with water all around it

6. **lake** a body of water with land on all sides

7. **mountain** highest kind of land

8. **ocean** a body of salt water that covers a large area

9. **peninsula** a landform that is surrounded on only three sides by water

10. **plain** flat land

11. **river** a large stream of water that flows across the land

12. **valley** low land between hills or mountains

Our
Geography

Start with the Standards

3.1 Students describe the physical and human geography and use maps, tables, graphs, photographs, and charts to organize information about people, places, and environments in a spatial context.

The Big Idea

Geography
California has a variety of landforms and waterways. People change the landscape with the structures they build.

What to Know

✔ How would you describe where you live?

✔ What are the physical features of California?

✔ What are some ways in which people use the natural resources of their area every day?

✔ How have people changed the physical environment?

Show What You Know

★ Unit 1 Test

✎ Writing: A Narrative

✐ Unit Project: A Community Atlas

Our Geography

Talk About

Geography

" A map can help me find my location. "

"It's fun to explore the many landforms of my state."

"People use natural resources every day."

Vocabulary

community A group of people who live and work in the same place. (page 10)

location The place where something is found. (page 11)

physical feature Something found in nature, such as weather, plant life, water, and land. (page 16)

human-made feature Something people have built, such as a building, a bridge, or a road. (page 26)

natural resource Something from nature that people can use. (page 46)

GO ONLINE Visit INTERNET RESOURCES at **www.harcourtschool.com/hss** to view Internet Resources.

Reading Social Studies

⭐ Focus Skill Compare and Contrast

When you **compare** things, you think about how they are alike. When you **contrast** things, you think about how they are different.

Why It Matters

Knowing how to compare and contrast will help you better understand how things, people, and ideas are alike and different.

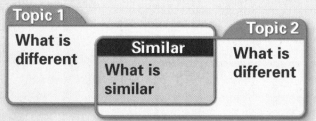

Topic 1
What is different

Similar
What is similar

Topic 2
What is different

Watch for these words and phrases that tell you how things are alike and different:

the same as	**different from**	**similar**	**but**
although	**like**	**unlike**	**in contrast**	**however**

Practice the Skill

Read the paragraphs. Compare and contrast the two lakes.

Compare   California has 8,000 lakes. Lake Tahoe and the Salton Sea are two of the largest. Both lakes are used for recreation and fishing.

Contrast   However, these lakes are quite different. Lake Tahoe is located high in the Sierra Nevada and was formed by nature. In contrast, the Salton Sea is in the desert region of southeastern California. It is a human-made lake.

Read the paragraphs. Then answer the questions.

California's Largest Lakes

Two of the largest lakes in California are the Salton Sea and Lake Tahoe. These lakes are alike in some ways, but they are very different in others.

Lake Tahoe is a very old lake located in the Sierra Nevada. Water flowing down rivers in the mountains formed the lake in a valley below. The water in Lake Tahoe is fresh water, not salty.

In contrast, the Salton Sea is a new lake. It was formed when people built dams on the Colorado River in the desert. Water overflowed the dams in 1905 and flooded the land. After the flood, a huge lake had formed in a low area. This lake became known as the Salton Sea. At first, the water in the Salton Sea was fresh water. However, over time the water changed and became salty.

Focus Skill

Compare and Contrast

1. How do the sizes of the lakes compare?

2. How is the water different in the two lakes?

Study Skills

USE A KWL CHART

A KWL chart can help you focus on what you already know about a topic and what you want to learn about it.

- ❯ **Use the K column to list what you know about a topic.**
- ❯ **Use the W column to list what you want to know about the topic.**
- ❯ **Use the L column to list what you have learned about the topic after reading.**

Physical and Human Geography

What I Know	What I Want to Know	What I Learned
I live in a house and in a city. The name of my state is California.	What else should I know about where I live? What is physical and human geography?	_____ _____ _____ _____

Apply As You Read

Complete your own KWL chart as you read this chapter.

California History-Social Science Standards, Grade 3

3.1 Students describe the physical and human geography and use maps, tables, graphs, photographs, and charts to organize information about people, places, and environments in a spatial context.

Physical and Human Geography

Mount Shasta in California

Walk Lightly

Geographic Travels in Verse and Rhyme

by J. Patrick Lewis
illustrated by Alison Jay

Author J. Patrick Lewis likes to travel and write
poetry for children. In this poem, he suggests how
to think about some of the places he has visited.

Make the Earth your companion.
Walk lightly on it, as other creatures do.
Let the Sky paint her beauty—she is always
watching over you.

Learn from the Sea how to face harsh forces.
Let the River remind you that everything will pass.
Let the Lake instruct you in stillness.
Let the Mountain teach you grandeur.
Make the Woodland your house of peace.
Make the Rainforest your house of hope.
Meet the Wetland on twilight ground.
Save some small piece of Grassland for a red kite
   on a windy day.
Watch the Icecaps glisten with crystal majesty.
Hear the Desert whisper hush to eternity.
Let the Town bring you togetherness.
Make the Earth your companion.
   Walk lightly on it, as other creatures do.

Response Corner

1. Why does the author repeat the same two lines at the beginning and end of the poem?

2. What do you think it means to "walk lightly" upon the Earth?

Lesson 1

Finding Your Location

What to Know

How would you describe where you live?

✓ People live in communities.

✓ Your community is part of a state, a country, and a continent.

Vocabulary

community p. 10
location p. 11
border p. 11

Focus Skill Compare and Contrast

California Standards
HSS 3.1

People live just about everywhere on Earth. Some people live near mountains, and some live on flat lands. Some people live where it is very cold. Others live where it is hot, even in winter. No matter where they live, most people are part of a community. A **community** is a group of people who live in the same place.

Analyze Illustrations

❖ Which covers a larger area, California or Oregon?

Where on Earth?

Communities are different in many ways. One way is their **location**, or the place where they are found. What is your community's location, or place on Earth?

You can say that your community is on the continent of North America. Your community is also in one of the 50 states of the United States. If you look at a map of the United States, you will see the borders of each state. A **border** is a line that shows where a state or nation ends. The state where you live is called California. California shares part of its border with the states of Arizona, Nevada, and Oregon. California is also bordered by the country of Mexico and by the Pacific Ocean.

Reading Check ☼ **Compare and Contrast**
How does the size of California compare with that of other states in the United States?

The United States

California

Your Own Community

You have located your continent, your country, and your state. Now you are ready to locate your community within the state of California. If your community is a city, it might be on a map of the United States or even on a globe of the world. If your community is small, you may have to look instead at a map showing only California. A map showing only California has room to show some small towns.

Reading Check **Main Idea and Details**
How would you describe the location of your community?

Geography

Weaverville, California

Weaverville is a community in northern California, in the Trinity Mountains. It is close to the Trinity River, where gold was discovered in 1848. Right away a gold rush brought many new people to the town. Men, women, and children came from as far away as China, hoping to get rich. By 1854, about 2,500 Chinese people were working in the mines and living in Weaverville. The Chinese set up their own small community, called Chinatown. At its center was the joss house, or temple, which is still used today.

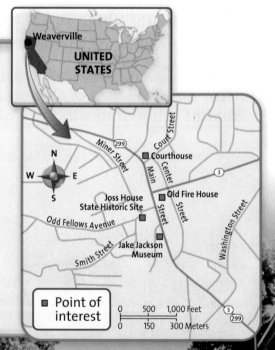

Weaverville

UNITED STATES

Courthouse
Miner Street
Court Street
Center Street
Main Street
Old Fire House
Joss House State Historic Site
Washington Street
Odd Fellows Avenue
Smith Street
Jake Jackson Museum

■ Point of interest

| 0 | 500 | 1,000 Feet |
| 0 | 150 | 300 Meters |

Name Lily Tanner
Street 123 Jasper Court
City Weaverville
State California
Country The United States
Continent North America

Summary Communities are located in many places. Your community is located in the state of California, in the country of the United States, and on the continent of North America.

Review

1. How would you describe where you live?

2. **Vocabulary** What states share a **border** with California?

3. **Your Community** Which of California's bordering states is closest to your community?

Critical Thinking

4. **Make It Relevant** What would you include on a map of your city or town?

5. **ANALYSIS SKILL** Why is it important to know how to read and interpret information on a map?

6. **Make a Flip Book** Make a flip book called "Where I Live." On each page, draw a picture and write the names of your continent, country, state, and city or town.

7. **Focus Skill Compare and Contrast** On a separate sheet of paper, copy and complete the graphic organizer about California's location.

Topic 1
California's location

Similar

Topic 2

Use Intermediate Directions

▶ Why It Matters

North, south, east, and west are the cardinal, or main, directions. The in-between directions that give more exact information about the location of a place are called **intermediate directions**.

▶ What You Need to Know

The compass rose below shows both kinds of directions. The four intermediate directions are northeast, southeast, northwest, and southwest.

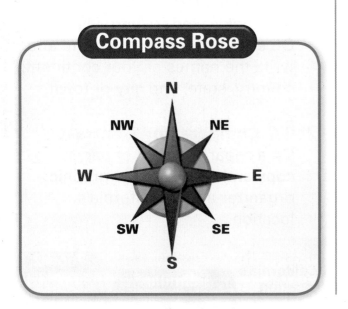

Compass Rose

▶ Practice the Skill

Use the compass rose on the map on page 15 to answer these questions.

1 Is Sacramento northwest or northeast of San Francisco?

2 A car is traveling from Bakersfield to Santa Barbara. In which direction is it going?

3 In which direction would you travel from Los Angeles to get to San Diego?

▶ Apply What You Learned

ANALYSIS SKILL **Make It Relevant** Use the compass rose to help you find places in your classroom that are northeast, southeast, southwest, and northwest of where you sit. List the objects in a four-column chart. Use the intermediate directions as headings.

Practice your map and globe skills with the **GeoSkills CD-ROM**.

California and Intermediate Directions

OREGON

IDAHO

Crescent City

Yreka

Alturas

Eureka

Redding

Susanville

UTAH

Chico

Fort Bragg

CALIFORNIA

NEVADA

★Sacramento

North

Stockton

San Francisco   Oakland

Northwest

Northeast

San Jose

West

East

Monterey

Fresno

Southwest

Southeast

South

Ridgecrest

Bakersfield

Barstow

Needles

Lancaster

Santa Barbara

San Bernardino

Los Angeles

PACIFIC OCEAN

Long Beach

Palm Springs

ARIZONA

San Diego

MEXICO

0   50   100 Miles
0   50   100 Kilometers

Physical Features

What to Know
What are the physical features of your state?

✔ Communities have different types of physical features.

✔ Land, water, climate, and plant life are physical features.

Compare and Contrast

California Standards
HSS 3.1, 3.1.1

All places on Earth have features, or things that are special about them. You can describe a place by telling about its **physical features**—its land, water, climate, and plant life. Physical features are sometimes called geographical features.

Highlands

To describe the physical features of a place, you might talk about its landforms. A **landform** is a feature such as a mountain, a valley, a plain, or a hill. California has all of these landforms.

If you live in the highlands, you may live in the mountains, on a hill, or on a plateau. A **plateau** (pla•TOH) is a landform with steep sides and a flat top that rises high into the air.

Mount Whitney, the highest mountain in California, is part of the Sierra Nevada (see•ER•uh nuh•VA•duh) mountain range. A **mountain range** is a large chain of mountains. The Sierra Nevada is California's largest mountain range. It stretches north and south across much of the eastern part of the state.

Not all mountains are the same, though. For example, the mountain peaks, or tops, of the Coast Ranges are rounded, not pointed like those of the Sierra Nevada. Even the two sides of the Sierra Nevada range are very different.

Reading Check ☼ **Compare and Contrast** How are the Sierra Nevada and the Coast Ranges different?

❯ Over time, water, ice, and wind have worn down the peaks of California's Coast Ranges.

❯ Some peaks of the Sierra Nevada are covered with snow even in summer.

Lowlands

Large areas of flat, low land are called lowlands. If you live in the lowlands, you might live in a valley, on a plain, or on the coast. A **valley** is a lowland that lies between hills or mountains. Rain and melting snow run down the mountains and keep the valleys watered. Plants grow well in the valley's soil.

Valleys can be narrow or wide. A wide valley shaped like a bowl is known as a basin. A canyon is a very narrow valley with steep sides.

A plain is a flat, rolling stretch of land. A lowland plain that lies along a seacoast or an ocean is called a **coastal plain**. Plants usually grow well on coastal plains.

Reading Check ○ **Compare and Contrast**
What is the difference between a valley and a plain?

A Closer Look

Landforms and Bodies of Water

Earth has many different kinds of landforms and bodies of water. Look at this drawing to see how they are alike and different.

❶ A desert is very dry land with few plants.

❷ An island is land that has water on all sides.

❸ A peninsula is a place that is surrounded by water on three sides.

❹ The mouth of a river is the place where the river empties into another body of water.

❺ Land along the side of a river is a riverbank.

❻ A peak is the top of a mountain.

◆ Which of these landforms or bodies of water are near your community?

desert   plateau

❶

valley

hill

❷ island

Bodies of Water

Bodies of water are another physical feature of Earth. Many communities are built near bodies of water. You may be able to describe your community as being near an ocean, a lake, or a river.

Earth's largest bodies of water are its oceans. Oceans cover more than half of Earth. All ocean water is salty.

On the continents are many smaller bodies of water, such as lakes, ponds, rivers, and streams. Most of these contain fresh water, or water that is not salty. Fresh water is the kind of water we drink and use in our homes.

Reading Check ✪ **Compare and Contrast**
How are lakes, ponds, rivers, and streams alike?

❱ **Yosemite Falls is one of many waterfalls in Yosemite National Park.**

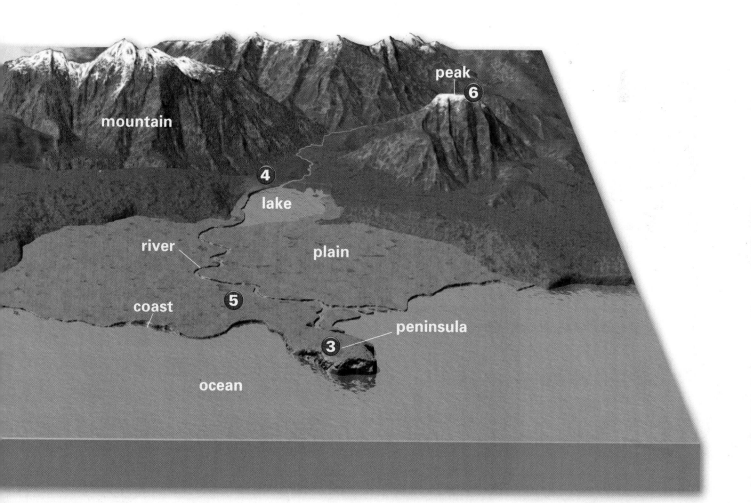

peak
6

mountain

4

lake

river

plain

coast

5

peninsula

3

ocean

Climate and Plant Life

Climate is also a physical feature. **Climate** is the weather that a place has over a long period of time. A place's climate is affected by how close the place is to the equator and to a large body of water. Climate includes how hot or cold the temperatures are and how much rain or snow falls. Because the United States is so large, it has many different climates. A large state such as California has more than one climate.

Earth's physical features can also affect climate. California's Sierra Nevada gives a good example of how mountains affect climate. Places between the Sierra Nevada and the ocean, on the western side of the mountain, get enough rain to grow crops. Places on the eastern side of the mountains have hot, dry air and little rain.

Locate It

CALIFORNIA

Joshua Tree National Park

❱ Joshua trees grow among the rocks in the desert area of Joshua Tree National Park.

Plant life is another physical feature. Some plants grow well in the hot, dry places called **deserts**. Other plants, such as trees in forests, need more rain or a wetter climate. Climate also affects how long plants can grow during each season. The growing season is longer in places with short, warm winters.

Reading Check **Generalize**
Why don't forest trees grow well in the desert?

Summary You can describe a place by telling about its physical, or geographical, features.

❯ Rock climbers learn to trust each other on this ropes course at Joshua Tree National Park.

Review

1. What are the physical features of your state?

2. **Vocabulary** Use the vocabulary word **desert** to describe where Joshua trees grow.

3. **Your Community** What are the geographical features of your community?

Critical Thinking

4. **Make It Relevant** What kinds of plants grow in your community?

5. **ANALYSIS SKILL** How do the physical features of your community affect its character?

6. **Write a Description** Choose a physical feature of your community. Write a paragraph to identify and describe the physical feature.

7. **Focus Skill** **Compare and Contrast** On a separate sheet of paper, copy and complete the graphic organizer about physical features.

Topic 1
Highlands
Similar
Topic 2
Lowlands

Read a Landform Map

❱ Why It Matters

There are many kinds of maps, each with a special use. For example, to find where a friend lives, you can use a street map. If you want to know about the geography of a place, you can use a **landform map**. This kind of map shows a place's physical features, such as mountains, hills, plains, plateaus, lakes, rivers, and oceans.

❱ What You Need to Know

A landform map uses different colors and patterns to show the different physical features.

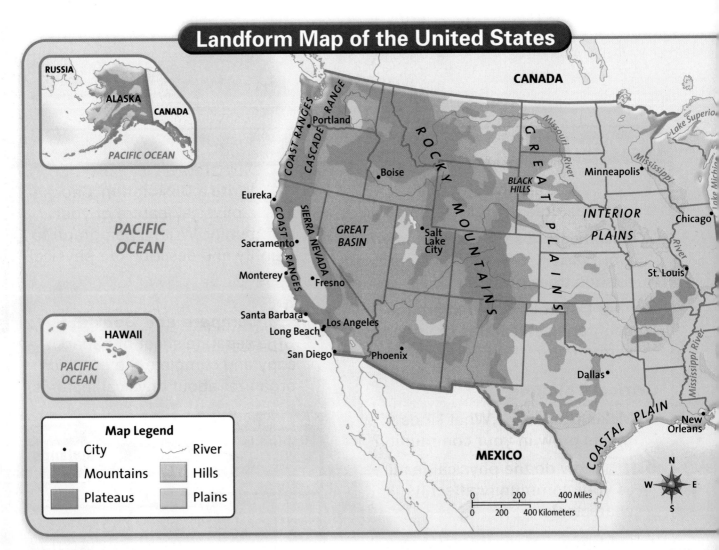

Landform Map of the United States

RUSSIA

ALASKA

CANADA

PACIFIC OCEAN

CANADA

COAST RANGES
CASCADE RANGE
Portland
Boise
ROCKY MOUNTAINS
GREAT PLAINS
Missouri River
Minneapolis
Lake Superior
Mississippi
Lake Michigan

PACIFIC OCEAN

Eureka
SIERRA NEVADA
COAST RANGES
Sacramento
Monterey
Fresno
GREAT BASIN
Salt Lake City
BLACK HILLS
INTERIOR PLAINS
Chicago
St. Louis
Mississippi River

Santa Barbara
Long Beach
Los Angeles
San Diego
Phoenix
Dallas

HAWAII
PACIFIC OCEAN

MEXICO
COASTAL PLAIN
New Orleans

Map Legend

- • City
- 〜 River
- ▮ Mountains
- ▮ Hills
- ▮ Plateaus
- ▮ Plains

0   200   400 Miles
0   200   400 Kilometers

N
W   E
S

The map legend, or map key, tells you what color, pattern, or symbol stands for each kind of physical feature.

❯ Practice the Skill

Use the map and the map legend on these pages to answer the following questions.

1 What bodies of water do the coastal plains border?

2 Which city is on higher ground—Monterey, California, or Fresno, California?

3 On what landform is the city of Sacramento, California, built?

4 What body of water is near Eureka, California?

❯ Apply What You Learned

ANALYSIS SKILL **Make It Relevant**
Using the map, look at the landforms of California and a bordering state. Write a paragraph to describe the landforms of California. In a second paragraph, compare California's landforms with those of the bordering state you chose.

Practice your map and globe skills with the **GeoSkills CD-ROM**.

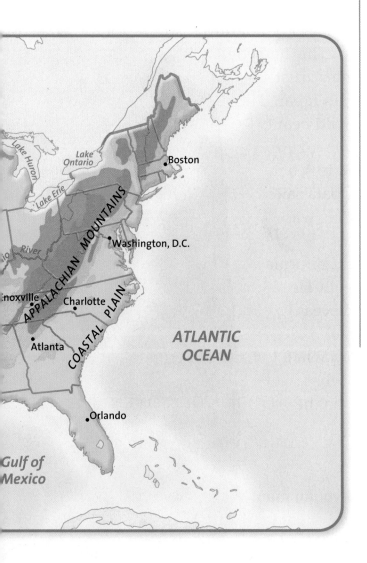

Trustworthiness

Respect

Responsibility

Fairness

Caring

Patriotism

Chiura Obata

"Listen to what nature tries to tell you in its quietness, [so] that you can learn and grow."*

Why Character Counts

? **How did Chiura Obata show his respect for the beauty of the natural world?**

When he was 5 years old, Chiura Obata began drawing. He drew trees, mountains, and things he saw around him. He learned to love and respect nature. He observed nature with all his senses. This helped him become a better artist.

Obata grew up in Japan. He heard about the wild beauty of nature in the United States. He wanted to see it. In 1903, Chiura Obata sailed to San Francisco. He was 17 years old.

Obata thought California was wild and lovely. He walked along the ocean cliffs. He hiked the forests. He painted what he saw. He liked what he saw so much that he stayed.

Chuira Obata as a young man

* Chiura Obata. *Nature Art* by Michael Elsohn Ross. Carolrhoda, 2000.

Obata teaching painting

Eagle Peak Trail, **painted by Chiura Obata in 1930**

Obata wanted art to bring people together. He helped form the East West Art Association. This group included artists from Japan, China, Russia, and the United States.

In 1932, Obata began working as an art teacher at the University of California at Berkeley. He showed his students how to use stones, shells, and other things in nature to make art supplies.

Obata led tour groups of Americans to Japan. He taught them about Japanese culture, art, and love of nature. At the age of 80, Obata received the Order of the Sacred Treasure from the emperor of Japan. The award honored Obata for helping create understanding and peace between Japan and the United States. Today, Obata's paintings still help people learn to respect and understand nature and each other.

GO ONLINE Visit MULTIMEDIA BIOGRAPHIES at www.harcourtschool.com/hss

Bio Brief

1885 Born

1903 Moves to California from Japan

1932 Becomes art teacher at University of California at Berkeley

1965 Receives Order of the Sacred Treasure from the emperor of Japan

1975 Died

3 Human-Made Features

What to Know

How do people change the places where they live?

✓ Communities have been built in certain locations.

✓ People add human-made features in many different ways.

Vocabulary
human-made
feature p. 26
trade p. 27
transportation p. 29

Focus Skill Compare and Contrast

 California Standards
HSS 3.1, 3.1.2

When you look outdoors, what features of your community do you see? You may notice some physical features—a hill or a river. You might also see things people have made, such as a bridge or a building. Things that people add to a landscape are called **human-made features**. Your school, your home, and the street you live on are all human-made features.

Locate It

Vallejo

CALIFORNIA

Where People Build

When people first came to California, they built communities in places that had fresh water and good soil. They traded with the people around them. To **trade** means to exchange one thing for another. Over time, these communities grew. To see where communities in California are today, look at the photograph to the right, taken from space. The lights show where people have built towns and cities. Notice that many communities are near the ocean.

Reading Check ⚬ **Compare and Contrast**
What do you think is different about the main landforms found in the light and dark areas on the photograph taken from space?

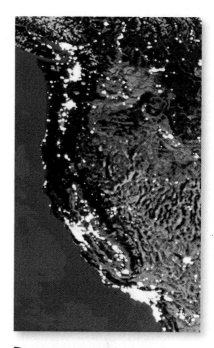

❯ This photograph, taken from space, shows California at night.

❯ Three bridges carry traffic across the Carquinez Strait in Vallejo, California. New lanes for pedestrians and bicycles opened in 2004.

Buildings and Roads

When people move to a place, they add buildings to it. Perhaps they want to live near a river or a particular landform, so they decide to build their homes there. New towns begin with homes for people to live in and buildings to work in. In time, some communities also build parks and other places where people can have fun.

▶ *Urban Freeways* is the name of a painting by California artist Wayne Thiebaud (TEE·boh).

Today, much of California is covered with roads, bridges, and railroad tracks. These paths between one place and another make **transportation**, the movement of people, goods, and ideas, possible.

Reading Check **Generalize**
Why did people build roads, bridges, and railroad tracks in California?

Summary Human-made features are things that people add to a landscape. Buildings, roads, bridges, and railroad tracks are some human-made features.

⚡Fast Fact

Lombard Street in San Francisco is very steep and crooked. Tourists travel many miles to drive on the street.

Review

1. How do people change the places where they live?

2. **Vocabulary** What clues can you use to remember the meaning of the term **human-made features**?

3. **Your Community** What are some human-made features in your community?

Critical Thinking

4. **Make It Relevant** What jobs are associated with the human-made features in your community?

5. **ANALYSIS SKILL** Explain how building a road can help a community grow.

6. **Make a Mural** Choose a human-made feature in your community. Draw a picture of it for a classroom mural.

7. **Focus Skill** **Compare and Contrast** On a separate sheet of paper, copy and complete the graphic organizer about human-made features.

Topic 1
Bridges
Similar
Human-Made Features
Topic 2

4 California's Regions

Geographers who study Earth often divide countries and states into regions. A **region** is an area with at least one feature that makes it different from other areas.

The Regions

One way to divide the United States is into five regions—the Northeast, the Southeast, the Middle West, the Southwest, and the West. States in each region may have a similar climate and other similar features. California is a state in the West.

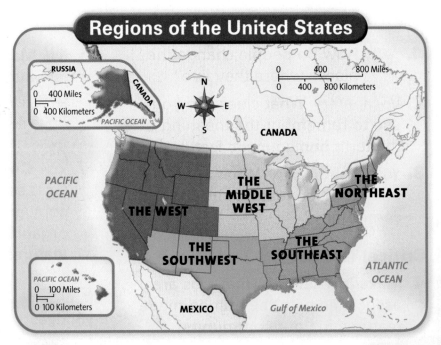

Regions of the United States

ANALYSIS SKILL **Analyze Maps**
◈ **Regions** In which region is California located?

California can be divided into four regions, too. They are the Coast Region, the Central Valley Region, the Mountain Region, and the Desert Region.

Reading Check ○ **Compare and Contrast**
How are states in each region of the United States alike?

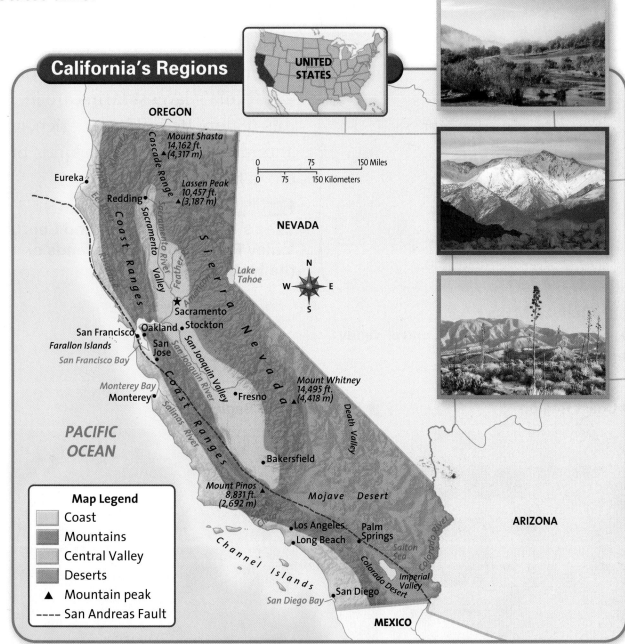

California's Regions

UNITED STATES

OREGON

Mount Shasta
14,162 ft.
▲(4,317 m)

Eureka

Redding

Lassen Peak
10,457 ft.
▲(3,187 m)

Cascade Range

Coast Ranges

Sacramento River

Sacramento Valley

Feather River

American River

Sierra Nevada

NEVADA

Lake Tahoe

N
W   E
S

Sacramento ★

Oakland • Stockton

San Francisco

Farallon Islands

San Jose

San Francisco Bay

San Joaquin River

San Joaquin Valley

Monterey Bay

Monterey

Coast Ranges

Salinas River

PACIFIC OCEAN

• Fresno

Mount Whitney
14,495 ft.
▲(4,418 m)

Death Valley

• Bakersfield

Mount Pinos
8,831 ft. ▲
(2,692 m)

Mojave   Desert

ARIZONA

Channel Islands

• Los Angeles
• Long Beach

Palm Springs

Salton Sea

Colorado River

Colorado Desert

Imperial Valley

San Diego •

San Diego Bay

MEXICO

Map Legend
- Coast
- Mountains
- Central Valley
- Deserts
- ▲ Mountain peak
- ---- San Andreas Fault

ANALYSIS SKILL **Analyze Maps** The San Andreas Fault is an area where earthquakes often occur.
◈ **Regions** In which regions of California does the San Andreas Fault begin and end?

Coast and Central Valley Regions

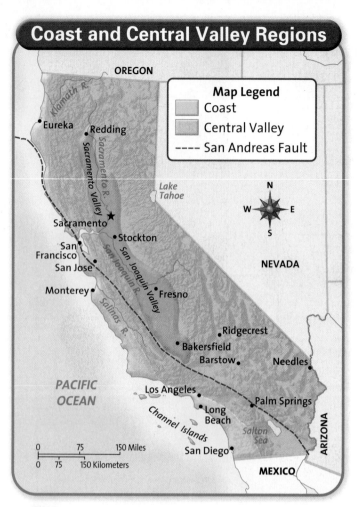

Coast and Central Valley Regions

Map Legend
- Coast
- Central Valley
- ---- San Andreas Fault

OREGON

Klamath R.

Eureka
Redding
Sacramento R.
Sacramento Valley
Sacramento ★
Lake Tahoe
Stockton
San Francisco
San Jose
San Joaquin R.
San Joaquin Valley
Monterey
Salinas R.
Fresno

NEVADA

Ridgecrest
Bakersfield
Barstow
Needles

PACIFIC OCEAN

Los Angeles
Long Beach
Palm Springs
Channel Islands
Salton Sea
San Diego

ARIZONA

MEXICO

0   75   150 Miles
0   75   150 Kilometers

N W E S

Coast and Central Valley Regions

California's Coast Region touches the border of Oregon in the north. It reaches Mexico in the south. All along the western side is the Pacific Ocean.

The Central Valley Region is in the middle of the state. Many of California's largest farms are in this region. Its soil is very rich, and farmers grow many kinds of crops there.

Reading Check **Categorize and Classify** Are the Coast and Central Valley Regions in the lowlands or the highlands?

ANALYSIS SKILL **Analyze Maps**

◈ Regions Where is the Central Valley Region located?

❱ Coast Region

❱ Central Valley Region

Mountain and Desert Regions

The Mountain Region is made up of California's mountain ranges. These include the Cascade Range, the Sierra Nevada, and the Coast Ranges.

The Desert Region includes Death Valley, the lowest point in the Western Hemisphere. Other deserts in the region are the Sonoran (suh•NOHR•uhn) Desert, the Mojave (moh•HAH•vee) Desert, and the Colorado Desert. Some mountains and plateaus are also in this region.

Reading Check ⚲ **Compare and Contrast** How are the Mountain and Desert Regions alike?

Desert and Mountain Regions

Map Legend
- Mountains
- Deserts
- ▲ Mountain peak
- ---- San Andreas Fault

OREGON

Mount Shasta 14,162 ft. (4,317 m)

Lassen Peak 10,457 ft. ▲ (3,187 m)

Eureka
Redding

Klamath
Cascade Range
Coast Ranges
Sacramento R.
Sierra Nevada
Lake Tahoe

Sacramento ★

San Francisco
San Jose
Stockton

Monterey

San Joaquin R.
Coast Ranges
Salinas R.

Fresno

Mount Whitney 14,495 ft. (4,418 m) ▲

NEVADA

Death Valley

Ridgecrest
Bakersfield

Mount Pinos 8,831 ft. ▲ (2,692 m)

Barstow
Mojave Desert
Needles

PACIFIC OCEAN

Los Angeles
Long Beach

Sonoran Desert
Palm Springs
Salton Sea
Imperial Valley
Colorado Desert

San Diego

ARIZONA

MEXICO

0   75   150 Miles
0   75   150 Kilometers

ANALYSIS SKILL **Analyze Maps**
❖ **Regions** In which California region is Palm Springs located?

▶ **Desert Region**

▶ **Mountain Region**

People and Regions

Today, most of the Coast Region has a large **population**, or number of people. It has more cities and people than the other regions in the state. The physical features of the region—the weather, the ocean, and the beaches—have caused many people to move to its urban and suburban areas. An **urban** area is a city. The smaller communities near the cities are **suburban** areas. Most Californians live in the suburban areas around Los Angeles, San Diego, and San Francisco.

The next-most-populated region is the Central Valley Region. Most of California's farms and many of its cities can be found in this region.

▶ Below is a view of the suburban area around Los Angeles. Urban Los Angeles is shown in the smaller photograph.

Some of the Central Valley Region is rural. A **rural** area has fields, woods, farms, and small towns. It has far fewer people than urban and suburban areas have.

The Mountain Region and the Desert Region have the fewest people. Large parts of these regions have no people at all.

Reading Check ⚡ **Compare and Contrast**
How are the populations of the Mountain Region and the Desert Region alike?

Summary Geographers divide places into regions. California is divided into four regions. These are the Coast Region, the Central Valley Region, the Mountain Region, and the Desert Region. Californians live in urban, suburban, and rural areas.

❯ This flower field is in rural Santa Paula, California.

Review

1. 💡 What are the four regions of California?

2. **Vocabulary** How are the words **urban** and **suburban** the same, and how are they different?

3. **Your Community** In which region of California is your community located?

Critical Thinking

4. **Make It Relevant** Do you live in an urban, a suburban, or a rural area of California? How do you know?

5. **ANALYSIS SKILL** Why do you think a physical feature is used to name each of California's regions?

6. 🖌 **Make a Map** Draw a large outline map of California. Draw pictures of the state's regions. Cut out the pictures, and paste them on the map in the regions where they belong.

7. ⭐**(Focus Skill)** **Compare and Contrast** On a separate sheet of paper, copy and complete the graphic organizer about California's regions.

Topic 1		Topic 2
Coast and Central Valley	Similar	Mountain and Desert

Use a Map Grid

▶ Why It Matters

To find the **exact location** of a place, you can use a map that has a **grid system**. A grid system is a set of lines that cross each other to form boxes. Knowing how to use a grid makes it easier to find locations on a map quickly. For example, you can find the exact location of a street or a park on a city map by using a grid.

▶ What You Need to Know

Look at the grid on this page. Find the row labels—the letters along the sides of the grid. Now look for the column labels—the numbers at the top and at the bottom of the grid.

Put a finger on the purple box. Now slide your finger to the left side of the grid. You will see that the purple box is located in row C. Go back to the purple box. Slide your finger to the top of the grid. The purple box is in column 3. To describe the exact location of the purple box, you would say that it is at C-3.

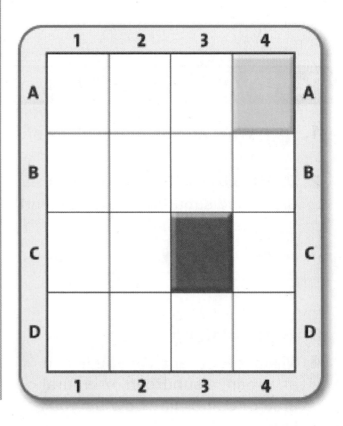

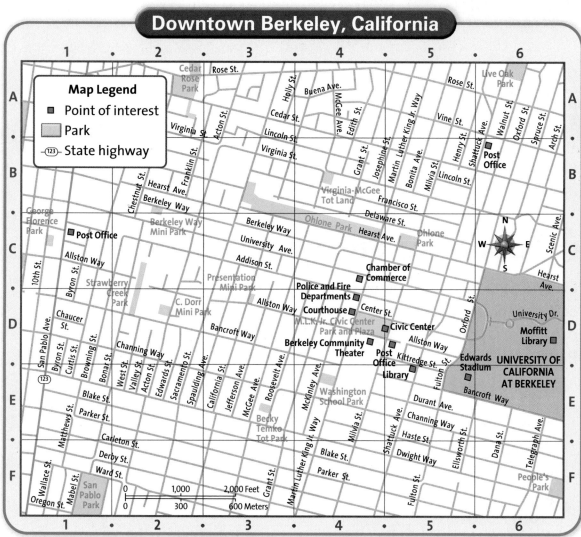

Downtown Berkeley, California

Map Legend
- Point of interest
- Park
- ⟨123⟩ State highway

▶ Practice the Skill

Look at the map above. Use the map and its grid to answer the following questions. Give a letter and a number when you are asked for a location.

1 Where is Live Oak Park?

2 What point of interest do you see in the box at D-6?

3 Where is the Berkeley Community Theater?

▶ Apply What You Learned

ANALYSIS SKILL **Make It Relevant** Draw a map of a place you know, such as your neighborhood, your school, or your classroom. Add a grid, and label places on your map. Then share your map with a classmate.

Practice your map and globe skills with the **GeoSkills CD-ROM**.

Reading Social Studies

To **compare** is to think about how two or more things are alike. To **contrast** is to think about how two or more things are different.

(Focus Skill) Compare and Contrast

Copy and complete this graphic organizer to compare and contrast two of California's regions. A copy of a graphic organizer appears on page 11 of the Homework and Practice Book.

Physical and Human Geography

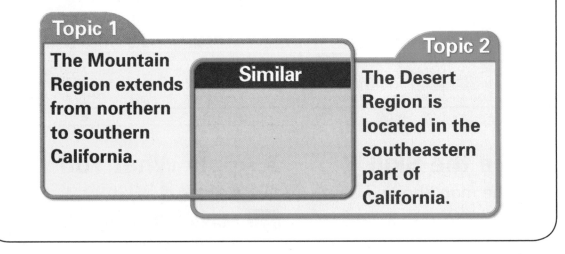

Topic 1

The Mountain Region extends from northern to southern California.

Similar

Topic 2

The Desert Region is located in the southeastern part of California.

California Writing Prompts

Write a Postcard Imagine you are touring California. Write about one special place in a postcard to a friend. Describe the physical features, including land, water, climate, and plant life.

Record a Diary Entry Choose one of the California landforms you read about in this chapter. Write about an adventure you might have had while exploring the landform.

Use Vocabulary

Write the correct word from the list to complete each sentence.

location, p. 11   **region,** p. 30
border, p. 11   **population,** p. 34
plateau, p. 17

1. A landform with steep sides and a flat top is called a ____.

2. An area with at least one feature that makes it different from other areas is a ____.

3. If you find where a place is on Earth, you find its ____.

4. The number of people living in one place is its ____.

5. A line that shows where a state or a nation ends is called a ____.

Recall Facts

Answer these questions.

7. What country does California border?

8. What is the lowest point in the Western Hemisphere?

Write the letter of the best choice.

9. Which of California's regions is known for its large farms?
   A the Central Valley Region
   B the Coast Region
   C the Mountain Region
   D the Desert Region

10. Which of the following would you expect to find in a rural area?
   A a skyscraper
   B a city
   C a small town
   D a large town

Apply Skills

Read a Landform Map Use the landform map on pages 22 and 23 to answer the question.

6. **ANALYSIS SKILL** What landforms lie along California's eastern border?

Think Critically

11. **ANALYSIS SKILL** Why do you think your community was started where it was? Does the location still have the same advantages it once did?

PREVIEW AND QUESTION

Previewing a lesson to identify main ideas and asking yourself questions about these ideas can help you read to find important information.

▶ **To preview a passage, read the lesson title and the section titles. Try to get an idea of the main topic. Think of questions you have about the topic.**

▶ **Read to find the answers to your questions. Then recite, or say, the answers aloud. Finally, review what you have read.**

People and Their Environment

Preview	Questions	Read	Recite	Review
Lesson 1 California has many natural resources.	How do people use natural resources in California?	✓	✓	✓
Lesson 2				

Apply as You Read

In a chart, identify the topic you will be reading about. Then write down questions about it. Read, recite, and review to be sure that you understand the information.

California History-Social Science
Standards, Grade 3

3.1 Students describe the physical and human geography and use maps, tables, graphs, photographs, and charts to organize information about people, places, and environments in a spatial context.

People and Their Environment

Canal in Venice, California

JOHN MUIR

America's Naturalist

BY THOMAS LOCKER

This is the story of a naturalist, John Muir. He was born in Scotland in 1838. When he was eleven years old, his family came to the United States and settled in the wilderness of Wisconsin. John became interested in preserving nature at a very early age. He once said, "All that the sun shines on is beautiful, so long as it is wild." After an accident in the factory where he worked, he left to travel the world. He took notes in his journal about the plants and animals he saw along the way.

John's travels led him to California. He found a job herding sheep in the high meadows near the Yosemite Valley. When the sheep entered Yosemite, John saw "the unforgettable skyline of sculptured domes and spires." The beauty took his breath away.

Yosemite had a powerful effect on John Muir. He moved to the valley and for years took odd jobs, which left him plenty of time to hike and explore. He went up into the mountains in search of glaciers and into the groves of gigantic and ancient trees. Yosemite became his home.

In the groves of ancient trees, John studied the ways of the animals: the bears, deer, squirrels, and even the tiny ants. He called the soaring trees the "tree people." He identified the different kinds of pines and fir trees and made drawings of the noble redwoods and ancient Sequoia. Some of the Sequoia were thousands of years old.

When it came time for John to settle down, he married and became the father of two girls. John ran a farm in the valley, but continually returned to his beloved Yosemite. He became upset when lumber interests and cattlemen began closing in. At the urging of his friends, John started writing to encourage the preservation of the wilderness.

John Muir talked with the legislators in California and Washington, D.C. He wrote books and articles. John won many battles and lost some. Still, he found time to explore the glaciers of Alaska and other wilderness areas all over the world.

John Muir's years of wandering in the wilderness led him to a deeper way of seeing Nature. Everything from the smallest snowflake to the farthest star were part of Nature, and man was not its master. Because of John Muir's gifts, people today can see Nature with new eyes.

Response Corner

1 Why did Muir start writing about the wilderness?

2 What do you think Muir meant when he said, "All that the sun shines on is beautiful, so long as it is wild"?

Many Natural Resources

What to Know

What natural resources does Earth provide?

✔ Natural resources are found on the land.

✔ Natural resources are found inside Earth.

✔ Water is an important natural resource.

Vocabulary

natural resource p. 46
agriculture p. 47
mineral p. 48
fuel p. 49
aqueduct p. 50
canal p. 50
irrigation p. 51

Focus Skill
Compare and Contrast

California Standards
HSS 3.1, 3.1.2

The naturalist John Muir wrote, "So extraordinary [amazing] is Nature with her choicest [best] treasures. . . ."* The treasures that Muir wrote about are Earth's natural resources. A **natural resource** is something from nature that people can use, such as trees, water, animals, and soil. Many of Earth's "choicest treasures" are found in California.

*John Muir. *Nature Writings: The Story of My Boyhood and Youth.* Penguin Books. 1997.

▶ **Trees are cut down near Redding, California.**

> Soil is an important resource used to grow artichokes in this field in Castroville, California.

> Almost all the artichokes sold in the United States are grown in California.

On the Land

Forests cover much of California's land. The state tree, the redwood, grows along California's northern coast. Trees, a natural resource, are used to build houses, to make furniture and paper, and to burn for heat.

Another natural resource that is a California treasure is the land itself. The soil of the Central Valley and other valleys is very rich. The rich soil makes these areas good for agriculture. **Agriculture** is the growing of crops and the raising of farm animals for sale. Some crops that grow well in California are almonds, lettuce, oranges, artichokes, tomatoes, walnuts, peaches, grapes, and cotton. Turkeys, sheep, dairy cattle, and beef cattle are also raised in California.

Reading Check 🖑 Compare and Contrast
How are trees and soil alike?

Inside Earth

In the 1800s, the discovery of gold made California famous. Thousands of people came to California to search for gold and to get rich.

Gold is a **mineral**, a kind of natural resource found inside Earth. Gold is still found in California. Many other minerals are also found in the state. They include iron, copper, salt, silver, talc, boron, and tungsten. People use salt to make some foods taste better. Gold and silver are used in making jewelry. People use boron to make soap, medicine, and cleaning products. Tungsten is used in electric lights and television sets.

▶ These workers are using gold to manufacture headphones.

Children in History

Children of the Gold Rush

Children growing up during the gold rush in California spent much time doing chores. They collected firewood, cared for the family's animals, helped their parents pan for gold, and worked in family restaurants by washing dishes or serving the miners. They also helped make money for their families by running a wet pin along the cracks in the floorboards to pick up any gold dust spilled by miners. However, there were few children in gold rush towns. Most miners had left their families behind.

Fuels are also mined in California. A **fuel** is a natural resource that is burned to make heat or electricity. People and businesses buy fuel.

Fuels found in California include oil and natural gas. These fuels come from inside Earth. Deep wells are drilled to get the oil. Oil and natural gas wells are found in the Central Valley and along much of the California coast. Oil is also found under the waters of the Pacific Ocean, off the coast. Special machines drill for oil in the ground under the water.

Reading Check ⚙ **Compare and Contrast**
How are gold and boron different in the way they are used?

▶ Some oil-drilling platforms, like these off the California coast, are taller than city skyscrapers.

The Importance of Water

Water is one of California's most important natural resources. Like many other natural resources, water is not found in the same amount in all parts of the state. The mountain areas have a lot of water from rain and melted snow. However, California's deserts and southern valleys are mostly dry.

Because many of California's people and farms are in the dry southern valleys, water must be brought from other parts of the state. Many **aqueducts** (A•kwuh•duhkts), or large pipes, and canals carry water from one place to another. A **canal** is a waterway dug across land.

Water in California

Klamath River
Trinity River
Pit River
Eel River
Sacramento River
Feather River
Russian River
American River
Lake Tahoe
Mono Lake
San Francisco
Merced River
San Joaquin R.
Owens River
Pacific Ocean
Kings River
Salinas River
Kern River
N
W E
S
Cuyama R.
Mojave River
Santa Ynez River
Santa Ana R.
Los Angeles
Salton Sea
Colorado River
San Diego

Map Legend
— Aqueduct
— Canal
— River

ANALYSIS SKILL Analyze Maps

◈ Human-Environment Interactions

Why are California's aqueducts located mostly in the southern part of the state?

For example, water from the Colorado River is brought to farms and cities in southern California by aqueducts. Aqueducts and canals are ways to provide **irrigation**, or the moving of water to dry areas.

Some of California's fresh water comes from its lakes. Fresh water is also found underground. Spring water comes to Earth's surface through natural openings. People also dig wells to bring up underground water.

Reading Check 🐚 **Compare and Contrast**
What parts of California have lots of water? What parts are mostly dry?

Summary California has many natural resources. These include trees, soil, minerals and fuels, and water.

▶ **The water between these plants comes from springs that run into Hot Springs Creek in Lassen Volcanic National Park.**

Review

1. 💡 What natural resources does Earth provide?

2. **Vocabulary** What **minerals** are found in California?

3. **Your Community** What is grown on farms near your community?

Critical Thinking

4. **Make It Relevant** How have people changed the land in your community?

5. 🔲 **ANALYSIS SKILL** What natural resources are needed near where people live? Why?

6. ✏️ **Make a Web** Make a word web with the words *Natural Resources* in the middle. Write the names of resources found in your community. Draw a picture of each resource, and label each.

7. ⭐**Focus Skill** **Compare and Contrast** On a separate sheet of paper, copy and complete the graphic organizer below.

Read a Picture Graph

Why It Matters

When you need to compare sets of numbers, a graph can often make the job easier. Graphs are drawings that show how numbers of things compare.

What You Need to Know

There are different kinds of graphs. A **picture graph** uses small pictures as symbols to stand for the numbers of things. Picture graphs have a title and a key that explains what the pictures show.

For example, in the picture graph on page 53, a bucket stands for 5 gallons of water. Washing dishes by hand uses two times 5 gallons—or 10 gallons—of water.

Practice the Skill

Use the picture graph to answer these questions.

1 What does the graph show?

2 How many gallons of water do you use to brush your teeth?

3 Which uses less water— washing dishes in a sink or using a dishwasher?

4 Which activity uses the most water?

Apply What You Learned

ANALYSIS SKILL **Make It Relevant** Find out about other natural resources in or near your community. Then make a picture graph to show the information. Share your finished graph with a family member or classmate.

Picture Graph of Water Usage

ACTIVITY	NUMBER OF GALLONS USED
Brush your teeth	🪣
Take a bath	🪣🪣🪣🪣🪣🪣🪣
Take a shower	🪣🪣🪣🪣🪣🪣🪣🪣🪣🪣
Wash dishes in dishwasher	🪣🪣🪣
Wash dishes by hand	🪣🪣
Wash the car	🪣🪣🪣🪣🪣🪣🪣🪣🪣
Wash the dog	🪣🪣🪣🪣🪣🪣🪣🪣🪣🪣🪣🪣
Wash your hands	🪣

🪣 = 5 gallons of water

2 Using Our Resources

People who come to California find a beautiful state rich in natural resources. People use natural resources to meet their needs. Communities are often built to be near certain natural resources.

❱ **Morro Bay and other seaport towns are good places for shopping, fishing, and enjoying nature.**

Locate It

CALIFORNIA

Morro Bay

Communities Built Near Water

Many people choose to live on California's coast, in communities like Morro Bay. A **bay** is a body of water that is part of a sea or an ocean and is partly enclosed by land. Each morning, fishing boats go out into the Pacific Ocean's waters. They come back with mackerel, tuna, crabs, and other shellfish. Tourists also come to Morro Bay and its waters. They come to scuba dive, to surf, and to watch whales or birds.

❯ Morro Bay workers unload their day's catch of shrimp.

Reading Check ⚙**Compare and Contrast**
Why might people settle near Morro Bay instead of an inland community?

Communities Built Near Resources

Some communities grew up around bodies of water. Other communities developed because of other natural resources.

Early logging towns, such as Eureka, were built near forests. Logging is still important near the Sierra Nevada and in northwestern California. Douglas fir and ponderosa pine trees are cut and sold as lumber. Lumber is wood that has been cut into boards to be used for building.

1 Workers pick the fruit from tomato plants in Fresno fields.

2 Just-picked tomatoes are sent by truck to be processed.

Communities also developed near good farmland. Cities such as Fresno are important places for farmers. Some of the food grown on nearby farms is processed—dried, frozen, or canned—in Fresno.

Still other towns developed because of minerals found nearby. Sacramento was settled soon after gold was found in the area. Thousands of people came to find gold or start shops there. The town grew to 10,000 people in just seven months.

Another town that developed because of a mineral is Brea (BRAY•uh). In 1898, people began drilling for oil in the area near Brea. Many people moved there to work in the oil fields. Soon a town grew up there.

Reading Check **☆Compare and Contrast**
Near what resources were Eureka and Fresno built?

❸ The tomatoes are washed in a processing plant.

❹ A machine puts a label on each tomato.

Californians Use Resources

Californians have found new ways to use their resources. They have learned to use the wind's power. They get energy from wind, just as they get energy from natural resources such as oil and gas. **Energy** is the power that makes electricity. It gives us light and makes some engines run.

The wind's power is turned into energy by thousands of modern windmills, called wind turbines. Most of California's wind turbines are in Altamont Pass near San Francisco, and in Tehachapi (tih•HA•chuh•pee) Pass and San Gorgonio (gawr•GOH•nee•oh) Pass near Palm Springs.

> ❯ In the early 1980s, California became the first state to build large wind farms for wind turbines.

Californians also use solar, or sun, power for energy. Some people put solar panels on their roofs. The sun's energy heats the house or heats water for bathing and cleaning.

Reading Check **Main Idea and Details**
How do Californians use solar power to get energy?

Summary Many communities in California grew up near resources. Californians continue to find new ways to use natural resources.

▶ Solar panels provide power for some of California's streetlights and traffic signals.

Review

1. What are some ways in which people use the natural resources of their area every day?

2. **Vocabulary** How do people in California get **energy**?

3. **Your Community** What important natural resources are found in or near your community?

Critical Thinking

4. **Make It Relevant** Which resources in your community help provide jobs?

5. **ANALYSIS SKILL** Why do you think it is important to find new ways to get energy?

6. **Write a Paragraph** Write a paragraph about the water resources in or near your community. Explain how you use water in your everyday life.

7. **Focus Skill** **Compare and Contrast** On a separate sheet of paper, copy and complete the graphic organizer below.

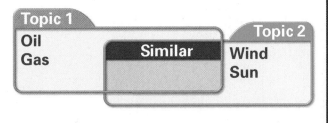

Topic 1
Oil
Gas

Similar

Topic 2
Wind
Sun

Read a Resource Map

❯ Why It Matters

Where are California's forests, oil, water, and other natural resources? Where are the state's farms? You can find answers to questions like these by looking at a map that shows where resources are found and used.

❯ What You Need to Know

On a **resource map**, symbols show where different natural resources are found. Colors show land use, or how most of the land in an area is used. A land use and resource map does not show every forest or farming area. It shows only the main ones.

A map legend shows which color stands for each kind of land use. It also shows what resource each picture symbol stands for.

❯ Practice the Skill

Use the map and the map legend on the next page to answer these questions.

1 What color shows the location of most of California's forests?

2 Along which river are oil and natural gas found?

3 What color shows land on which cattle graze?

4 Where is most of the state's little-used land?

❯ Apply What You Learned

ANALYSIS SKILL **Make It Relevant** Make a resource map of the area where you live. Find how people use the land there. Find out, too, what natural resources are nearby. Use reference materials to find the information you need. Make a map legend to explain the colors and symbols on your map.

 Practice your map and globe skills with the **GeoSkills CD-ROM**.

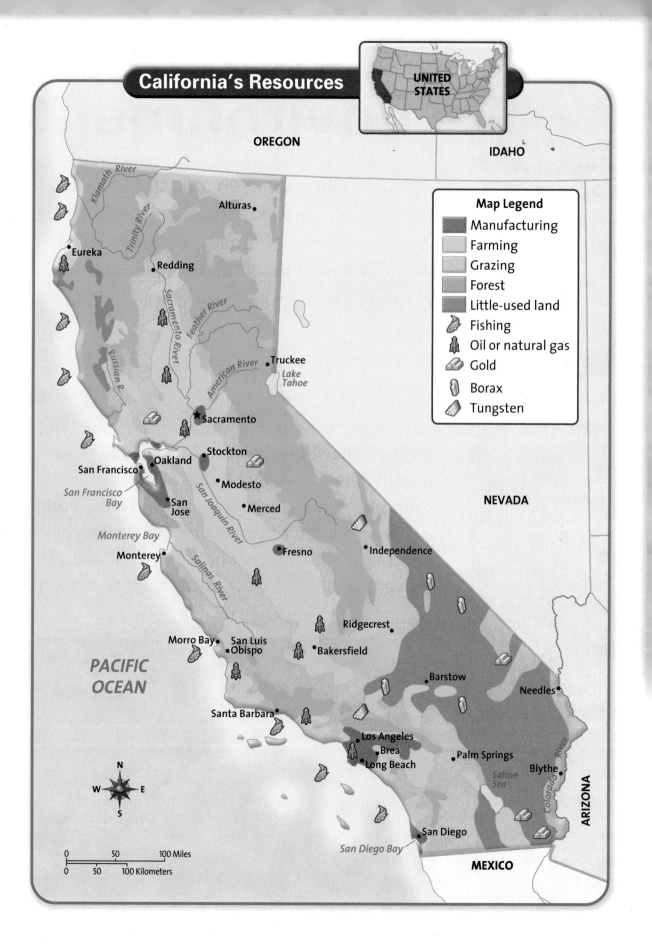

California's Resources

UNITED STATES

OREGON

IDAHO

Map Legend
- Manufacturing
- Farming
- Grazing
- Forest
- Little-used land
- Fishing
- Oil or natural gas
- Gold
- Borax
- Tungsten

Klamath River

Trinity River

Alturas

Eureka

Redding

Sacramento River

Feather River

Russian R.

American River

Truckee

Lake Tahoe

Sacramento

Stockton

Oakland

San Francisco

San Francisco Bay

San Jose

Modesto

San Joaquin River

Merced

NEVADA

Monterey Bay

Monterey

Salinas River

Fresno

Independence

PACIFIC OCEAN

Morro Bay

San Luis Obispo

Ridgecrest

Bakersfield

Barstow

Needles

Santa Barbara

Los Angeles

Brea

Long Beach

Palm Springs

Blythe

Salton Sea

Colorado River

ARIZONA

San Diego

San Diego Bay

MEXICO

N W E S

0   50   100 Miles
0   50   100 Kilometers

A Changing Environment

What to Know

How have people changed the physical environment?

✓ A dam changes the environment.

✓ Bridges change people's lives.

✓ People adapt to a changing environment.

Vocabulary
environment p. 62
dam p. 62
reservoir p. 63
adapt p. 66
disaster p. 66

Focus Skill **Compare and Contrast**

California Standards
HSS 3.1, 3.1.2

People continue to change the physical features of places where they live. Such changes affect the area's environment. An **environment** is made up of the physical features and human features of a place.

Changing Physical Features

People have found ways to change, or modify, the physical features of Earth. For example, many communities near rivers build dams across the rivers. **Dams** are earthen or concrete structures that hold back water and prevent floods.

Locate It

CALIFORNIA

Oroville Dam

Today

In 1957, people began building a dam on the Feather River, in northern California. They finished it in 1968. It is the tallest dam made of earth in the United States. The builders named it Oroville Dam after a nearby city.

Oroville Dam changed the environment in central and southern California. It brought electricity to many towns and farms there. It also made a **reservoir**, a lake used for collecting and storing water. Part of the Feather River turned into a huge lake, called Lake Oroville. Today, Lake Oroville is a popular place for boating, fishing, swimming, and waterskiing. People also hike along its 167 miles of shoreline.

Reading Check ♂ **Compare and Contrast**
How was California different after the Oroville Dam was built?

❯ Oroville Dam is 770 feet high and 7,600 feet long.

❯ Oroville Dam (above) under construction

Building a Bridge

▶ Workers attach cables to the bridge's two towers.

▶ Visitors walk across the bridge on opening day.

The Golden Gate Strait is a short waterway between the Pacific Ocean and San Francisco Bay. For many years, people hoped to build a bridge across the strait. Such a bridge would connect the city of San Francisco with the lands across the strait to the north.

The building of a bridge across the strait began on January 5, 1933. The bridge, called the Golden Gate Bridge, finally opened on May 27, 1937. People were allowed to walk on its roadway that first day.

The day after the bridge opened, cars and trucks were allowed on it. Since then, more than 1.5 billion cars and trucks have crossed the Golden Gate Bridge.

▶ The Golden Gate Bridge today

All those cars, of course, meant that more and bigger roads had to be built. Having so many cars also made the air dirtier. The environment was being changed.

Because of the bridge, people today can work in San Francisco but live outside the city. They can drive to work from the northern suburbs. Houses, stores, and schools are still being built in the suburbs. The environment continues to change.

Reading Check **Cause and Effect**
What effect did the building of the Golden Gate Bridge have on San Francisco?

Adapting to a Changing Environment

> The Transamerica Building in San Francisco has been specially designed to withstand earthquakes.

People **adapt**, or change, when their environment changes. Some events, such as earthquakes, floods, powerful storms, and forest fires, can change an area in only a few days. These events are called natural disasters. A **disaster** is an event that causes great harm or damage. In 1906, a powerful earthquake hit San Francisco. After the earthquake, Californians began to change their buildings, using materials that were stronger and would also bend without breaking.

Today, there are laws that make sure new buildings are made strong. Communities also teach people ways to be safe if an earthquake takes place.

> The 1906 earthquake greatly damaged much of San Francisco.

Some people live in places where there are snowstorms, floods, and mudslides. Their communities have plows and equipment for removing the snow and mud. Other people live where there are forest fires. To protect their homes, they cut down dry brush around the homes.

Reading Check ⟲ **Compare and Contrast** What has changed in California since the 1906 earthquake?

Summary The environment of California continues to change. People change the land's physical features, and natural disasters also cause change. People adapt when their environment changes.

▶ **A forest fire in Los Padres National Forest**

Review

1. 💡 How have people changed the physical environment?

2. **Vocabulary** How have people adapted to natural **disasters**?

3. **Your Community** How has your community prepared for earthquakes?

Critical Thinking

4. **Make It Relevant** Do you think people in your community like change? Why or why not?

5. **ANALYSIS SKILL** What are some changes caused by building large bridges?

6. ✏️ **Draw a Picture** With your classmates, list ways in which people have changed the environment where you live. Then make a picture of one of the changes. Write a caption for your picture.

7. **Focus Skill** **Compare and Contrast** On a separate sheet of paper, copy and complete the graphic organizer below.

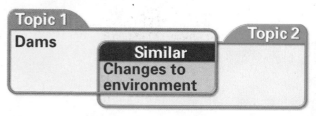

Topic 1
Dams
Similar
Changes to environment
Topic 2

Caring for Our Resources

What to Know
What can people do to take care of their environment?

✔ Humans affect the environment.

✔ Some people work to protect our resources.

Vocabulary
pollution p. 69
conservation p. 70
hybrid p. 70
recycle p. 71

Compare and Contrast
Focus Skill

California Standards
HSS 3.1, 3.1.2

People use Earth's land, water, and air in many ways. They set up farms to grow food and start ranches to raise animals. They use some land for factories and other land for homes and shopping centers. They make some land into places where people can have fun. All of these changes to the land can cause problems.

❯ Palm Springs, California, is part of Coachella Valley.

Humans Affect the Land

To get the things they need, people often use up most or all of the nearby natural resources. They cut down forests to get wood to use as fuel, to build houses, and to make furniture. It takes many years for a forest to grow again.

People also cause pollution. **Pollution** is anything that makes a natural resource dirty or unsafe to use. If water is polluted, it is not safe to drink.

Factories and cars sometimes cause air pollution. The smoke-filled air can mix with fog. This kind of pollution is called smog.

> Smog over the city of San Diego

Reading Check ŏ**Compare and Contrast**
What is the difference between clean air and air that is polluted?

Fast Fact

Palm Springs was first known as *Agua Caliente*, which is Spanish for "Hot Water." Palm Springs is in an area that has water. However, to meet their water needs, the people of Palm Springs must also get water from Mount San Jacinto and from the Colorado River.

Ways to Protect Our Resources

People can prevent pollution. They can also protect natural resources through conservation. **Conservation** means working to save resources and make them last longer.

People can replace some resources that they use. Many lumber companies now plant a tree for every tree they cut down.

Carmakers have invented hybrid cars that harm the environment less than regular cars do. **Hybrid** cars conserve resources by using less gas. They have both a gasoline engine and an electric motor with batteries. Hybrids cause less air pollution.

▶ Communities all over California celebrate Earth Day each April 22.

Cultural Heritage

Earth Day

The first Earth Day was held on April 22, 1970. Since then, Earth Day has become a time to celebrate nature and learn how to protect the environment. Every year, people in Sacramento, California, plan an Earth Day program of special activities.

Children and adults can learn ways to take care of our planet. Guest speakers teach about topics such as using energy from the sun to cook. The whole day focuses on taking care of Earth and making it a better place to live.

Recycling is another way in which people can protect the environment. When people **recycle**, they use resources over again. Glass bottles and jars, newspapers and cardboard, many plastics, and aluminum from cans can be reused. By recycling, people add less trash to landfills. Landfills are places where trash is dumped.

Reading Check ☼ **Compare and Contrast**
What are some differences between hybrid cars and regular cars?

Summary Some of the changes that people make to Earth can cause problems. Many people in California work to protect the environment.

❯ Hybrid cars produce less smog than regular cars.

Review

1. ☀ What can people do to take care of their environment?

2. **Vocabulary** What are some kinds of **pollution**?

3. **Your Community** What are some ways people in your community protect the environment?

Critical Thinking

4. **Make It Relevant** How do you practice conservation?

5. **ANALYSIS SKILL** Without conservation, what do you think would happen to the environment?

6. 🖌 **Make a Poster** Make a poster that shows your support for protecting the environment. Include a catchy slogan.

7. **Focus Skill** **Compare and Contrast** On a separate sheet of paper, copy and complete the graphic organizer below.

Topic 1		Topic 2
Replace	Similar	Conserve

Working for Earth

Dr. Edgar Wayburn may be one of the most important people you have never heard of. In 1999, President Bill Clinton said, "Over the course of the last half century, [Dr. Wayburn] has saved more of our wilderness than any person alive."

—Bill Clinton, from a speech presenting Dr. Wayburn with the Presidential Medal of Freedom, 1999

Dr. Wayburn is responsible for creating or increasing the size of many of California's parks and wilderness areas. His projects include the Golden Gate National Recreation Area, Mount Tamalpais State Park, Redwood National Park, and Point Reyes National Seashore. He has also led efforts to protect millions of acres of wilderness in Alaska and across the American West.

President Bill Clinton awards Dr. Edgar Wayburn the nation's highest civilian honor, the Presidential Medal of Freedom.

In a very different part of the world, Wangari Maathai (wan•GAH•ree mah•DY) has worked to protect the environment. In Kenya, Africa, Maathai started a group called the Green Belt Movement. That group has planted 30 million trees to help keep Kenya's fertile lands from turning into desert. Wangari Maathai won the 2004 Nobel Peace Prize for her work. The Nobel Prizes are among the most admired awards in the world.

Wangari Maathai waters a tree she planted during a conference on women and the environment.

Did You Know?

An organization of California young people works to help the environment. The group, called the Tree Musketeers, organizes tree-planting projects. They started a recycling program in their community of El Segundo. Today, the Tree Musketeers teach people across the United States how to care for the environment.

Think About It!

Make It Relevant What can you do to help care for the environment in your community?

Reading Social Studies

To **compare** is to think about how two or more things are alike. To **contrast** is to think about how two or more things are different.

(Focus Skill) Compare and Contrast

Copy and complete this graphic organizer to compare and contrast types of energy. A copy of a graphic organizer appears on page 20 of the Homework and Practice Book.

People and Their Environment

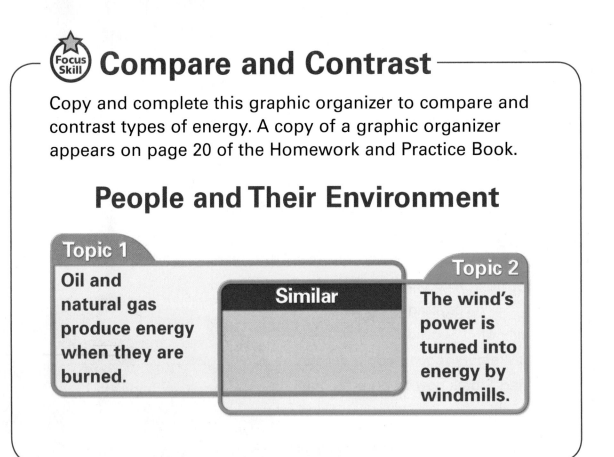

Topic 1
Oil and natural gas produce energy when they are burned.

Similar

Topic 2
The wind's power is turned into energy by windmills.

California Writing Prompts

Write About a Resource Write a paragraph about a natural resource that interests you. Tell at least two ways that the resource can be used. Start with a topic sentence.

Write Words for a Song "America the Beautiful" names some of the many resources in the United States. Write words for a song about California's resources.

Use Vocabulary

Write the word that correctly matches each definition.

aqueduct, p. 50   **disaster,** p. 66
bay, p. 55   **pollution,** p. 69
dam, p. 62

1. a body of water that is part of a sea or an ocean and is partly enclosed by land

2. earthen or concrete structure that holds back water and prevents floods

3. a large pipe that carries water from one place to another

4. anything that makes a natural resource dirty or unsafe to use

5. an event that causes great harm or damage

Apply Skills

Read a Resource Map Use the resource map on page 61 to answer the question.

6. **ANALYSIS SKILL** Is most of California's farmland in the center of the state or along the eastern border of the state?

Recall Facts

Answer these questions.

7. Why is the rich soil in California's valleys a valuable resource?

8. Where does California's fresh water come from?

Write the letter of the best choice.

9. What did the Oroville Dam give California?
   A a place for fishing
   B electricity
   C a lake
   D all of the above

10. What is smog?
    A a mineral
    B a type of air pollution
    C a hybrid car
    D a type of energy

Think Critically

11. **ANALYSIS SKILL** What are some ways people have changed the physical features of your community?

12. **ANALYSIS SKILL** Why should someone buy a hybrid car?

Field Trip

Oakland Museum

Get Ready

Since 1969, the Oakland Museum of California has showcased California's natural wonders, its historic events, its arts, and many people who have left their mark on the state. Visitors enjoy exciting exhibits, performances, and hands-on activities about everything Californian, from bats to buildings, people to photography, and the gold rush to global warming.

Locate It

California

Oakland

What to See

CALIFORNIA COMMUNITIES AND ECOSYSTEMS

THE COASTLINE

THE COASTAL MOUNTAINS

At the Hall of Ecology, visitors take a virtual walk through California's geographic regions.

Displays re-create native plants and animals of the desert (left), and the coast (below).

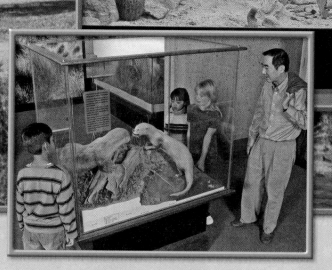

Exhibits also include the sounds of birds, insects, and other animals of each region.

Young people enjoy searching the exhibits of animals that have camouflaged, or hidden, themselves in their environments.

A Virtual Tour

GO ONLINE

Visit VIRTUAL TOURS at www.harcourtschool.com/hss

Review

THE BIG IDEA

Geography California has a variety of landforms and waterways. People change the landscape with the structures they build.

Summary ## Our Geography

Every place has <u>physical features</u>. These include land, water, climate, and plant life. People sometimes change physical features. They add buildings, roads, bridges, and other human-made features.

California has four <u>regions</u>. They are the Coast, the Central Valley, the Mountain, and the Desert regions. Each region has natural resources. Californians try to use these resources without harming the environment.

Main Ideas and Vocabulary

Read the summary above. Then answer the questions that follow.

1. Which of the following is a <u>physical feature</u>?
   A a bridge
   B a tunnel
   C a road
   D a mountain

2. Which of the following is one of California's <u>regions</u>?
   A the Northeast Region
   B the Middle West Region
   C the Mountain Region
   D the Southern Region

3. How do people change places?
   A They add physical features.
   B They add human-made features.
   C They divide places into regions.
   D They name the places where they live.

Answer these questions.

4. What is the highest mountain in California?

5. What regions of California have the fewest people?

6. What crops grow well in California?

7. How do Californians use solar power?

8. What type of disaster caused change in California in 1906?

Write the letter of the best choice.

9. Which landform is found in the highlands?
   - **A** a coastal plain
   - **B** a canyon
   - **C** a plateau
   - **D** a basin

10. Which of the following is the least populated area?
    - **A** urban
    - **B** rural
    - **C** community
    - **D** suburban

11. What are boron, talc, and salt?
    - **A** fuels
    - **B** minerals
    - **C** vegetables
    - **D** landforms

12. **ANALYSIS SKILL** What is one physical or human-made feature in your region that makes it different from another region?

13. How can you and your family help protect the environment?

Read a Landform Map

ANALYSIS SKILL Use the map below to answer the following questions.

14. What color shows where mountains can be found?

15. Which city is on lower ground—San Francisco or Modesto?

Landform Map of Central California

Chico
Yuba City
Sacramento ★
Oakland
San Francisco
Santa Cruz
Stockton
Modesto
San Jose
Madera
Monterey
Fresno

PACIFIC OCEAN

N W E S

Map Legend
- Mountains
- Hills
- Plateaus
- Plains

0 50 100 Miles
0 50 100 Kilometers

Read More

■ *Where Water Comes From,* by Dan Ahearn.

■ *How Glaciers Changed Our Planet,* by Alan M. Ruben.

■ *California's Land and Water,* by Bill Doyle.

Unit Writing Activity

Write a Narrative Write a narrative story about a community that worked together to protect its environment. It can be a place that you imagine or one that really exists. Include any physical features or resources that are special to the community. Tell why and how the community saved its natural treasures.

Unit Project

Community Atlas Work in a small group to make an atlas of your community. Include maps and information about the different physical features found in your community. Refer to other atlases for ideas.

GO ONLINE Visit ACTIVITIES at www.harcourtschool.com/hss

American Indians

Start with the Standards

3.2 Students describe the American Indian nations in their local region long ago and in the recent past.

The Big Idea

California Indians

Long ago, American Indians developed cultures in which they used the land to meet their needs. Indian groups differed in their languages and customs. Many of their traditions survive today.

What to Know

✔ Who were the early American Indians in California and how did geography affect the way they lived?

✔ How did early American Indians trade, and how were they governed?

✔ What were some beliefs, customs, and stories of early California Indians?

✔ How has life changed for the California Indians and how do they preserve their culture?

Show What You Know

★ Unit 2 Test

✏ Writing: An Article

🖌 Unit Project: California Indian Cultures Fair

Unit 2 American Indians

Talk About

American Indians of California

" California Indians used natural resources to make the things they used every day. "

"California Indians have used stories and songs to keep their traditions alive."

"California Indians dress in traditional clothing on special days."

FIRE RACE
A Karuk Coyote Tale

Vocabulary

tribe A group of American Indians that shares some common ways of life. (page 92)

government A group of people that solves problems and makes rules for a community. (page 112)

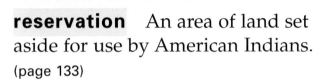

reservation An area of land set aside for use by American Indians. (page 133)

economy The way a country or community produces and uses goods and services. (page 110)

culture A way of life shared by members of a group. (page 142)

Visit INTERNET RESOURCES at **www.harcourtschool.com/hss** to view Internet Resources.

Reading Social Studies

★ Focus Skill — Cause and Effect

A **cause** is something that makes something else happen. An **effect** is what happens as a result of a cause.

Why It Matters

Understanding causes and effects can help you see why things happen.

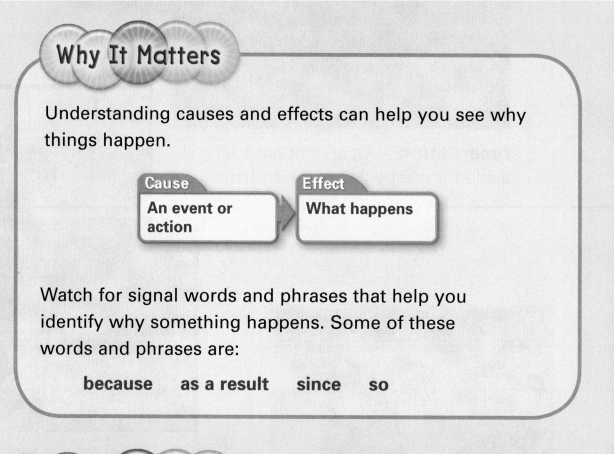

Cause		Effect
An event or action	➤	What happens

Watch for signal words and phrases that help you identify why something happens. Some of these words and phrases are:

because   as a result   since   so

Practice the Skill

Read the paragraph. Find one effect.

Cause
Effect

The Yurok Indians lived along the Pacific Coast in what is now northern California. Heavy rains caused trees and plants to grow tall. In the thick forests, the Yurok found berries and nuts, and they hunted wild animals. There were clams and shellfish in the ocean. Each spring, salmon swam up the rivers from the ocean. The Yurok had a plentiful food supply.

Read the paragraphs. Then answer the questions.

The Mojave Solve a Problem

The Mojave Desert in southern California gets only from two to six inches of rain each year. As a result, not many plants or animals can live there. The Mojave Indians, who lived in the desert long ago, had a difficult time finding enough food to eat.

The Colorado River flows through the Mojave Desert. Long ago, the river flooded the land each year. The flood water carried rich soil from farther up the river and dropped it near the river. Because of this, the land along the river had fertile soil.

The Mojave needed a way to get more food. Therefore, they learned to do something that most other California Indians did not need to do. They learned to farm. In the fertile soil near the river, they planted squash, pumpkins, beans, and corn.

Focus Skill

Cause and Effect

1. What is one effect of the low rainfall in the Mojave Desert?

2. What caused the land near the Colorado River to become good for farming?

TAKE NOTES

Taking notes can help you remember important ideas.

➤ **Write only important facts and ideas. Use your own words. You do not have to write in complete sentences.**

➤ **Organize your notes in a way that will make them easy to reread. One way to organize notes is in a chart. Write down the main ideas in one column and facts and details in another.**

The Land and the First People

Main Ideas	Facts
Lesson 1: • Tribes of California • How They Lived • _____	• Many American Indians lived in California long ago. • Indians belonged to different tribes. • _____

Apply As You Read

As you read this chapter, use a chart to take notes about each lesson.

California History-Social Science Standards, Grade 3

3.2 Students describe the American Indian nations in their local region long ago and in the recent past.

The Land and the First People

A Hupa Indian fishes on California's Trinity River.

FIRE RACE

A Karuk Coyote Tale of How Fire Came to the People

by Jonathan London
illustrated by Sylvia Long

People from all cultures tell legends. A **legend** is a story that helps explain something. Read this American Indian legend from the Karuk tribe to find out how fire came to the people.

Long ago, the animal people had no fire. Then one day a wise old Coyote heard about fire. But the fire was guarded by three Yellow Jacket sisters and they did not want to share it. They lived high on top of a snowy mountain. Coyote went to the sisters' house and was able to sneak out with a charred oak branch in his teeth. The Yellow Jacket sisters came after him and tried to sting him. Coyote was able to pass the fire to Eagle, who passed it on to Mountain Lion. Then Mountain Lion passed the coal to Fox, and then the coal was passed to Bear.

As Bear fell, Measuring Worm, the Long One, took the fire. The Long One stretched way out over three ridges, yet the Yellow Jackets were there, waiting, ready to strike. Somehow, right under the Yellow Jackets's eyes, Turtle sneaked in, grabbed the fire, and scrambled off. But of course Turtle was slow, and one of the Yellow Jacket sisters stung him on his tail. *Akee! Akee! Akee!*

Turtle pulled in his head and legs and flip-flopped down the hill. *Fallumph. Fallumph. Fallumph.* The Yellow Jackets were swarming all over Turtle, when Frog leaped out of the river and swallowed the fire. *Gulp!*

Then Frog hopped back into the river—
plog—and sat on the bottom. The Yellow Jackets
stormed the river, circling once, circling
twice, circling three times, buzzing the
surface. They waited and they waited and
they waited, but Frog held the fire, and his
breath. Finally, the Yellow Jackets gave up, and flew
back home.

As soon as the Yellow Jacket sisters were gone,
Frog burst out of the water, and spat the hot coal into
the roots of the willow growing along the river. The
tree swallowed the fire, and the animal people didn't
know what to do.

Then once again Coyote came along, and the
animal people said, "Grandfather, you must show
us how to get the fire from the willow." So Old Man
Coyote, who is very wise and knows these things,
said, "Hah!" and showed them how to rub two willow
sticks together over dry moss to make fire.

From that time on the people have known how to
coax fire from the wood in order to keep warm and
to cook their food. And at night in the seasons of the
cold, they have sat in a circle around the fires and
listened as the elders told the old stories. And so it is,
even to this day. *Kupanakanakana.*

Response Corner

1 Why do you think people create legends?

2 Use the illustrations to retell the story of how fire came to the people.

Tribes of California

Hundreds of years ago, only American Indians lived on the land that would become California. When people from Europe first arrived, about 300,000 American Indians were living in what is now California.

Four Geographical Groups

American Indians in many parts of North America lived in groups called tribes. A **tribe** is an Indian group that shares some common ways of life. In California, however, Indian tribes were smaller than in other places.

▶ This 1857 painting shows American Indians fishing on the Noyo River in Mendocino County.

California Indians lived in small villages. Several villages made up each tribe. Some villages were long-lasting. Other villages were used for only a short time before the Indians had to move to look for food.

Most California tribes belonged to one of four main geographical groups. They were California's Northern Coastal group, Central Valley and Mountain group, Southern Coastal group, and Desert group.

Because the tribes in each group lived in the same type of environment, their lives were alike in some ways. For example, tribes in the Desert group ate the same kinds of foods, because they found the same kinds of plants and animals near them. Since they had the same climate, their homes and their clothes were nearly alike.

Each tribe had its own language. A **language** is the group of sounds and words people use to communicate.

(Reading Check) ŏ **Cause and Effect**
Why were the lives of Indians in a geographical group alike in many ways?

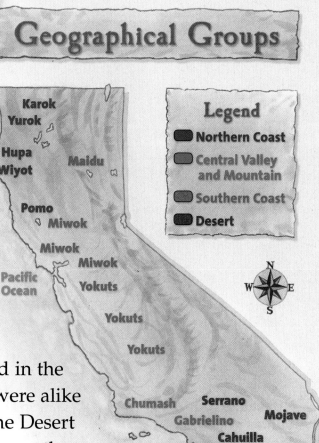

Geographical Groups

Karok
Yurok
Hupa
Wiyot
Maidu
Pomo
Miwok
Miwok
Miwok
Pacific Ocean
Yokuts
Yokuts
Yokuts
Chumash
Serrano
Gabrielino
Mojave
Cahuilla
Chumash
Gabrielino

Legend
- Northern Coast
- Central Valley and Mountain
- Southern Coast
- Desert

ANALYSIS SKILL **Analyze Maps**
❧ **Regions** Where in California did the Yurok and Mojave Indians live?

Indians of the Northern Coast

The Northern Coastal people survived by using the area's rich natural resources. The forests were full of animals and were thick with cedar and redwood trees. The rivers and the Pacific Ocean had lots of fish. People used the rivers and oceans for travel, too.

The Northern Coastal lands have much rain and cool weather. For this reason, the people built strong **shelters**, or homes and buildings that protected them from the weather. Women wore tightly woven basket caps. People wrapped themselves in capes or blankets made of animal skins. Among the Indians of the Northern Coastal area are the Yurok (YOOR•ahk), Hupa (HOOP•uh), Karuk (KAHR•uhk), Pomo, and Wiyot (WEE•ot).

Reading Check ŏ **Cause and Effect**
Why did Indians of the Northern Coastal group build strong shelters?

❱ Because food sources were plentiful, year-round village life was possible for the Indians of the Northern Coast.

Indians of the Central Valley and Mountain group lived in the valleys, foothills, and mountains of the Sierra Nevada.

Indians of the Central Valley and Mountains

The Central Valley and Mountain tribal group had the most land in what is today California. This group also had the largest population.

People living in California's valleys enjoyed a mild climate. Because they needed little protection from the weather, their clothes and homes were simple.

These Indians traveled from the valleys during hot summer months to the cooler regions of the foothills. In the winter, they moved back to the valleys. In both places, they found plenty of food. They hunted animals for food and gathered seeds, nuts, acorns, and berries. The rivers had plenty of fish. The Indians of this region include the Miwok (MEE•wahk), Maidu (MY•doo), and Yokuts (YOH•kuhts).

Reading Check ○̆ **Cause and Effect**
Why was the Central Valley and Mountain tribal group the largest in California?

Indians of the Southern Coast

People of the Southern Coastal group lived in the southwestern part of what is today California. They lived inland, along the coast, and on islands near the coast. They built strong canoes for traveling by water. Some of these tribes lived in large villages. A village might have as many as 2,000 people!

People of the Southern Coast hunted and fished. They gathered acorns as one of their main foods. Among the Indians of the Southern Coastal area are the Chumash (CHOO•mash) and Gabrielino (gah•bree•uh•LEEN•yoh) tribes. The Gabrielino are also known as the Tongva (TONG•vuh).

Reading Check **Compare and Contrast**
How were the Indians of the Southern Coastal group like those of the Central Valley and Mountain tribal group?

❯ **Many Indians of the Southern Coastal group lived along the Pacific coast.**

Indians of the Desert

The Desert tribal group lived to the east of the Southern Coastal Indians. They had a small population. Life for Desert tribes was very hard. The California desert is hot and dry in summer, and few plants grow in its sandy soil.

Most Desert people survived by eating insects, seeds, and beans. A smaller number of the Desert people lived along the Colorado River and farmed. Some tribes in the Desert tribal group are the Mojave (moh•HAH•vee), Cahuilla (kuh•WEE•yuh), and Serrano.

▶ Desert Indians adapted to the climate of the Mojave Desert.

Reading Check Ŏ**Cause and Effect**
Why was it hard to live in the desert?

Summary   Many Indian tribes lived in California before Europeans came. The tribes can be divided into four major groups, based on where they lived.

Review

1. Who were the early American Indians in California?

2. **Vocabulary** Use **shelter** in a sentence about California Indians.

3. **Your Community** What tribal group lived in or near your community?

Critical Thinking

4. **Make It Relevant** How is your life similar to the lives of Indians who lived in your part of California?

5. **Make a Map** Make a map showing which California Indian tribe or tribes once lived where your community is now.

6. (Focus Skill) **Cause and Effect** Copy and complete the graphic organizer below.

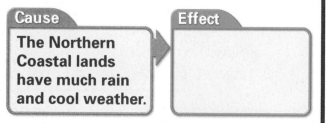

Cause	Effect
The Northern Coastal lands have much rain and cool weather.	

Read a Table

▶ Why It Matters

A **table** is a graphic organizer that shows information in columns and rows. Knowing how to use a table will help you compare numbers and other kinds of information easily.

▶ What You Need to Know

Like charts and graphs, tables have titles that describe what they show. Below the title, headings give the topics. The information is organized into columns and rows.

Columns go up and down, and rows go across. In the table on this page, there are four columns and three rows.

The table on page 99 gives information about different groups of California Indian tribes. It lists the names of the main tribal groups, some of the tribes that were part of each group, the places the groups lived, and the geography of each group's area.

To find information about each tribal group, look for its name in the first column. Then read across that row.

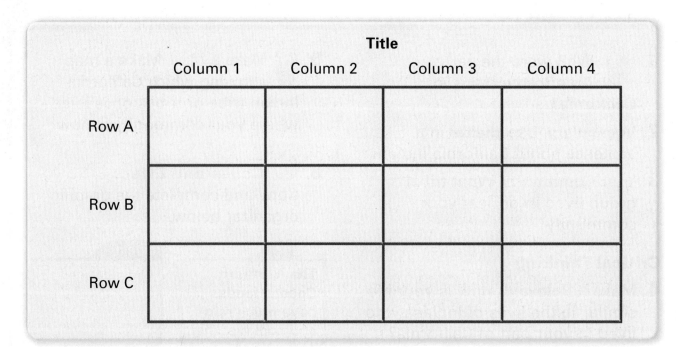

Title

	Column 1	Column 2	Column 3	Column 4
Row A				
Row B				
Row C				

Tribal Groups in California

TRIBAL GROUP	TRIBES INCLUDED	WHERE THEY LIVED	GEOGRAPHY OF THEIR AREA
Northern Coastal	Yurok, Hupa, Karuk, Pomo, Wiyot	northern coastal California	forests, rivers; rainy, mild climate
Central Valley and Mountains	Miwok, Maidu, Yokuts	Central Valley and mountains of California	valley, foothills, mountains, hills, rivers; mild climate
Southern Coastal	Chumash, Gabrielino	southern coastal California	sunny plains, valleys, rivers, mountains; warm climate
Desert	Mojave, Cahuilla, Serrano	southeastern California	desert, mountains, rivers; hot climate

❯ Practice the Skill

Use the table on this page to help you answer these questions.

1 Where did the Indians of the Desert tribal group live?

2 Which main tribal group were the Gabrielino Indians part of?

3 Where did the Miwok, Maidu, and Yokuts live?

4 Which main tribal group lived in a wet area of thick forests?

❯ Apply What You Learned

Make It Relevant Work with a partner to list the titles of tables you find in the newspaper. Cut out three tables that interest you. Share your list and the tables with your class.

What to Know
How did geography affect the ways early American Indians lived?

✓ Early California Indians got their food, clothing, shelter, and tools from their environment.

✓ Geography and climate affected what California Indians ate, what they wore, and what kind of shelters they built.

Vocabulary
tool p. 101

Cause and Effect
Focus Skill

California Standards
HSS 3.2, 3.2.2

Like people today, American Indians used California's rich natural resources. They treated the land and its plants and animals with respect. Like all American Indians, the Pomo, the Maidu, the Gabrielino, and the Mojave used natural resources for food, clothing, shelter, and tools.

The Pomo

California's Pomo Indians lived along the north-central coast in what are today Mendocino, Sonoma, and Lake Counties. The Pomo group had more than 70 villages.

❯ The Pomo hunted and fished from boats made of bundled grass.

Locate It

Pomo

⟩ Pomo Indians made their homes, boats, and baskets from plants that grew around them.

The Pomo lived in small, bowl-shaped shelters. In the rainy season, groups lived in villages. These were often built on the side of a hill to stay safe from flooding rivers. When the rains ended, people burned their winter shelters and moved closer to a river, lake, or the ocean. There they used many **tools** to do their work. These tools included nets, spears, and traps for fishing, and the bow and arrow for hunting birds, deer, and other animals. Food was so plentiful that the Pomo languages had no word for famine, or starvation.

The Pomo were expert basket makers. They used baskets for gathering, storing, and cooking food. Other baskets, decorated with feathers and shells, were used in special ceremonies.

Reading Check Ŏ**Cause and Effect**
Why did the Pomo build their villages on hillsides?

The Maidu

California's Maidu Indians lived in the north-central part of the state, from the Sierra Nevada west to where Sacramento is today. The Maidu often built their villages on high ground so that they could see strangers coming.

A Maidu lodge, or home, looked like a big, rounded mound of earth with a hole in the top. The floor and first few feet of the walls were dug into the ground. Inside, log poles held up the frame for the roof, which was covered with a heavy layer of earth. The hole in the roof was the doorway. The Maidu built these lodges mainly to keep warm in the winter. Several families might share one lodge.

In warm weather, the Maidu built open-air shelters. They cut branches to support a roof of sticks, grass, or dirt. The roof blocked the sun's heat but still let the breeze through.

◗ Maidu feast basket

Locate It

Maidu

◗ **Maidu woman preparing acorns to eat**

▶ Maidu summer shelter

In cooler seasons or high in the mountains, the Maidu sometimes wore tall moccasins stuffed with grass to protect their feet from the snow. They tied animal skins around their legs. Blankets of deerskin or rabbit fur also provided warmth.

Maidu men made knives and arrowheads from flint. They hunted deer, elk, rabbits, birds, and sometimes even bears! They fished for salmon, trout, and eels in nearby rivers and streams.

The Maidu also gathered much of their food. In the spring, Maidu groups might travel for weeks gathering wild plants, seeds, roots, insects, and berries. In the fall, the Maidu gathered acorns. The Maidu carried, stored, and cooked food in baskets woven from reeds and grasses.

Reading Check **Summarize**
Why did the Maidu use different shelters at different times?

The Gabrielino

The lands of the Gabrielino Indians stretched from Topanga south to Laguna Beach and included what is today Los Angeles. They built villages near the Los Angeles River and on the nearby Channel Islands. Like other Indians in the area, the Gabrielino built strong plank boats. They used the boats to carry people and goods to and from the islands. Men also fished for swordfish and hunted seals and sharks from their boats. They used hooks and nets to catch smaller fish. They hunted rabbits, squirrels, deer, and ducks.

Women ground acorns into flour. They boiled the flour to make a hot cereal called mush. The Gabrielino also ate pine nuts, seeds, and fruits.

❯ A Gabrielino woman

❯ A Gabrielino shelter made of bent tree saplings covered with tule mats

Locate It

Gabrielino

Like many other California tribes, the Gabrielino were expert basket makers. Gabrielino women wove so tightly that they could carry water and cook liquid foods in their baskets! To cook acorn mush, for example, they heated rocks in a fire. Then they dropped the rocks into the mush in the basket. Skillful stirring with long sticks kept the rocks from burning the basket before the mush was cooked.

Gabrielino women wore skirts woven of tule (TOO•lee). Tule is a tall, reedlike grass that grows in wet, marshy areas. Young tule shoots are tender enough to eat. Fully grown shoots are very strong. When woven together, they can be used as a building material.

Reading Check **Sequence**
What steps were used to cook acorn mush?

❱ Gabrielino women were expert basket makers.

❱ Wicker seed-beating tool

❱ Purse or bag woven from plant fibers

The Mojave

The Mojave tribe lived in the Mojave Desert, in southeastern California. Unlike other California tribal groups, the Mojave were farmers. Yearly floods left rich soil on both sides of the Colorado River. In this rich soil, the Mojave planted beans, corn, and pumpkins.

The Mojave gathered wild plants, seeds, and roots. They also fished in the Colorado River with traps and nets. They trapped small animals, such as rabbits, skunks, and beavers.

The clothes of the Mojave were suited for a hot climate. Sometimes, the men wore cloth tied around their hips. Women sometimes wore knee-length skirts of woven willow bark. The women also wore shirts of beaver and rabbit skins in winter months.

▶ A Mojave clay pitcher

Locate It

Mojave

▶ A Mojave camp from the late 1800s

The Mojave did not live in villages. Instead, they built simple shelters where they found good land for farming. They made their shelters from willow poles covered with grasses. Unlike most California tribes, the Mojave lived where the clay was good for making pots. They also wove baskets, but they used clay pots for cooking and storing food.

Reading Check ŏ **Cause and Effect**
Why were the Mojave able to farm in their desert environment?

Summary California tribes used the natural resources of the land. The Pomo hunted and fished. The Maidu built lodges and gathered acorns. The Gabrielino built boats and cooked in baskets. The Mojave grew crops and made clay pots.

⚡ Fast Fact

Mojave Indians, like this woman with a pot of water, often carried things on their heads.

Review

1. 💡 How did geography affect the ways early American Indians lived?

2. **Vocabulary** What types of **tools** did early American Indians make?

3. **Your Community** How did geography and climate affect the way American Indians lived in or near what is now your community?

Critical Thinking

4. **Make It Relevant** How does geography affect your life?

5. **ANALYSIS SKILL** Why do you think early California Indians depended on the land for their way of life?

6. ✎ **Write a Paragraph** Write a paragraph about a California Indian tribe that lived near your community. How did they get their food, clothing, shelter, and tools from the environment?

7. (Focus Skill) **Cause and Effect**

On a separate sheet of paper, copy and complete the graphic organizer below.

Cause	Effect
	The Gabrielino could carry water in their baskets.

Read a Cutaway Diagram

❱ Why It Matters

Understanding how to read a diagram can help you learn about something quickly. A **cutaway diagram** shows both the inside and the outside of an object at the same time.

❱ What You Need to Know

On a cutaway diagram, part of the object has been "cut away" to make a kind of window. The cutaway part of the diagram shows the inside of the object.

The photograph on this page shows a shelter called a plank house. A plank is a wooden board. Many Indian tribes of the Northern Coast, such as the Hupa and the Yurok, lived in these wooden homes shaped like boxes. Hupa homes were made with cedarwood, while Yurok homes were made with redwood. Each tribe used the resources that were plentiful in its environment. Many of the houses were partly below the ground and had a round door.

❯ Practice the Skill

Look at the cutaway diagram on this page. It lets you see inside a Yurok plank house. Use the diagram to answer the questions.

1 What materials were used to build this shelter?

2 How was the roof of the shelter held up?

3 Where did people sleep?

4 Where could extra supplies be stored?

❯ Apply What You Learned

Make It Relevant Use library books to find out what something is like inside. Draw a cutaway diagram of that object, and add a title and labels. Then use your diagram to explain to classmates what the object is like inside and outside.

3

Trade and Government

What to Know

How did early American Indians trade, and how were they governed?

✓ Early Indians bartered and shared resources with one another.

✓ Early American Indian tribes had different kinds of governments.

Vocabulary

economy p. 110
barter p.110
government p. 112

Focus Skill

Cause and Effect

California Standards
HSS 3.2, 3.2.3

Countries and communities have different ways of making and using goods and services. These ways make up an **economy**. The economy of early California Indians included trading, gift-giving, and sharing.

Sharing Resources

California Indians gathered food and other things they used from the land around them. Tribes also bartered with one another for things they could not find in their area. To **barter** is to trade without using money.

❱ Indian man, woman, and child with a trader showing a blanket

Tribes from the Northern Coast had plenty of fish, shells, and salt to barter. Inland tribes bartered the skins of animals or pine nuts. These things could not be found in the coastal areas of California. Most Indians bartered with members of their own or neighboring tribes.

In addition to bartering, exchanges were made during gift-giving ceremonies. Gift-giving was also done within tribal groups. If a tribe had extra food, the leader might invite a neighboring tribe to a feast. The leader would expect the other tribe to invite his or her tribe to a feast in the future.

Indians valued foods, baskets, weapons, and canoes. The people traded these items or gave them as gifts. Indians also traded rocks and minerals for making tools and arrowheads. Obsidian (uhb•SID•ee•uhn), a shiny black glass, was always needed. It could be chipped and made into arrowheads and other sharp tools. California Indians used shells and beads as money.

Reading Check ÖCause and Effect
Why did Indian tribes barter with one another?

❱ Wearing many beads and shells was a sign of honor.

❱ Thin, tubelike shells called dentalium were used as money. Some Indians carried their shells and beads in boxes or purses.

Government

A **government** is a group of people that makes rules and solves problems for a community. In early California, different Indian tribes had different kinds of governments. Some Indian tribes had very little government.

For Indians of the Northern Coast, the chief, or leader, was often the richest man in the village. Because his wealth would pass on to his oldest son, that son was likely to become chief one day.

Often, Indian chiefs had little real power. They gave advice instead of orders. In some tribes, women were the chiefs. Other tribes were led by a group of elders instead of a chief.

❯ **This painting by Albert Bierstadt shows Indians meeting.**

The Serrano and Mojave tribes were divided into family groups called clans. Each clan had its own chief, who got his role from his father. The people could replace a chief if they did not think he was a good leader. The Mojave also had war chiefs who led them into battle.

Reading Check ŏ **Cause and Effect**
Why was a Northern Coast chief's son likely to become chief some day?

Summary California Indians bartered and gave gifts. Tribes had different kinds of governments and were often led by chiefs.

❯ **Washoe chief and his family**

Review

1. 💡 How did early American Indians trade, and how were they governed?

2. **Vocabulary** What kinds of items did California Indians **barter**?

3. **Your Community** What items did the tribe that lived near your community probably barter?

Critical Thinking

4. **Make It Relevant** What items have you traded by bartering?

5. **ANALYSIS SKILL** Why were chiefs important even though they sometimes had no official power?

6. ⚜ **Make a Poster** Make a poster about the American Indian tribe you are studying for the unit project. On your poster, tell about how tribe members bartered and about the tribe's government.

7. **Focus Skill** **Cause and Effect** On a separate sheet of paper, copy and complete the graphic organizer below.

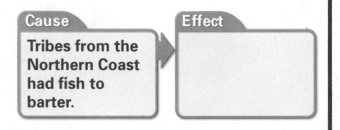

Cause	Effect
Tribes from the Northern Coast had fish to barter.	

Customs and Folklore

Each of California's Indian tribes had its own **customs**, or ways of doing things. Many of those customs showed people's shared respect and love for the land.

Celebrations

Celebrations were important in the lives of California Indians. Celebrations were often part of a tribe's **religion**, or beliefs about gods and spirits. Many tribes believed that different spirits had control of different parts of nature. In many villages, a **shaman** (SHAH•muhn), or curing doctor, was said to help cure the sick. Both men and women could be shamans.

▶ Five Kumeyaay (kuh•mee•AY) shamans wave eagle feathers in a special ceremony.

What to Know

What were some beliefs, customs, and stories of early California Indians?

✔ Indians had their own ceremonies and customs.

✔ Indians passed down beliefs and culture through storytelling.

✔ Folklore includes many different types of games, stories, and art.

Vocabulary

custom p. 114
religion p. 114
shaman p. 114
folklore p. 116
oral history p. 117

Focus Skill

Cause and Effect

California Standards
HSS 3.2, 3.2.1

▶ American Indian bird singers gather at the Kumeyaay powwow near San Diego.

Locate It

CALIFORNIA

Sycuan Indian Reservation

Some ceremonies marked special times in people's lives, such as a marriage. Other ceremonies marked special times of the year. These special times included the beginning of a hunting or fishing season or the start of the acorn harvest.

For example, the Yurok had a ceremony to give thanks for the year's first salmon catch. They said prayers over the first fish that was caught, and every man in the village ate one bite of it. No other fishing was done until this ceremony was finished.

Reading Check ŏ **Cause and Effect**
Why did tribes have special ceremonies?

⟩ A storyteller shares his tales with a group of American Indian children on the Barona Indian Reservation.

Storytelling

Early American Indians did not have written languages. Instead, children learned nearly everything by listening to the adults around them. Children learned especially about the folklore of their own tribes. **Folklore** is the history, beliefs, and customs of a group as told in its stories. Indians shared a great deal through the telling of stories. Adults told stories of the history of the tribe or the village. They also told about the lives of older people. Some stories taught children lessons about how to act. Other stories explained the tribe's beliefs about how the world and humans came to be. Still others told why things in the world are the way they are.

One Maidu woman remembers sitting with a group of children as her grandfather told stories. "'All of you, listen very closely,' he would say to us, 'I am talking in the ancient manner.' Then he would talk and tell us many things of long ago."

Because this kind of sharing is done through spoken words instead of written words, it is called **oral history**. *Oral* means "spoken."

Reading Check ☼ Cause and Effect
Why did American Indians share their histories through storytelling?

How Eagle and Crow Made Land
A Yokuts Tale

Long ago a flood covered Earth. Eagle and Crow flew over the water looking for a place to land. Finally, they found a tree stump sticking out of the water. The two birds stayed there, eating fish. Sometimes they flew around looking for land, but they couldn't find any.

One day, the birds asked, "How can we make land?" They were watching Duck dive into the water for fish. They noticed that Duck sometimes brought up more mud than fish.

"If we give Duck some fish, maybe she will bring us mud," the birds agreed. So each bird caught fish for Duck in exchange for mud. Each bird piled the mud on his side of the tree stump.

Once, Eagle noticed that Crow had piled more mud on his own side of the stump. Eagle started to give Duck twice as many fish. Duck gave Eagle twice as much mud. Soon, Eagle's mud pile was much higher than Crow's.

One morning, the birds noticed that the water level was going down. Soon their huge piles of mud were surrounded by land. A hot sun baked the two mud piles. Crow's mud pile became the Coast Ranges. Eagle's mud pile was taller. It became the mighty Sierra Nevada.

Art

California Indians from very long ago painted and carved art into rocks. Some rock art shows shapes of things such as people and animals. Other rock art shows designs of circles, lines, and dots.

California Indians used art in their everyday lives as well. They carved furniture and tools from wood and bone. They made pottery dolls and musical instruments. They wove beautiful baskets with detailed patterns. Some clothes and head coverings were also brightly colored works of art. These objects were used every day, but were also beautiful and full of special meaning.

Reading Check **Summarize**
How did California Indians use art in their everyday lives?

▶ **California Indians weave beautiful zigzag patterns into their famous baskets.**

Children in History

George Blake, Hupa and Yurok Artist

Artist George Blake belongs to both the Hupa and the Yurok tribes. He was born in 1944 in the Hupa Valley, near the Trinity River. He began carving acorn spoons when he was still in high school. He said he knew at the time that his hands were gifted for making this type of art.

Today, Blake's elk antler purses, silver jewelry, traditional bows, and redwood dugout canoes are on display in museums around the United States. Blake has received important awards for his art.

Games

Among the California Indians, both adults and children played many games. In one popular game, players holding nets chased a ball across a field. In another, a player rolled a hoop. Other players tried to catch the hoop on the ends of poles. Some games helped young people gain skills, such as shooting arrows or caring for children. These were skills they would need as adults.

Reading Check **Summarize**
How did playing games prepare children for adulthood?

Summary California's Indians showed a respect for the land. Tribes had different ways of life, including different religious beliefs, ceremonies, stories, art, and games. Together, these ways of life were part of each tribe's customs and folklore.

▶ A Mojave clay doll

Review

1. 💡 What were some beliefs, customs, and stories of early California Indians?

2. **Vocabulary** How is **oral history** related to **folklore**?

3. **Your Community** What are some traditions of your community's American Indian tribe?

Critical Thinking

4. **Make It Relevant** What are some customs of your family? How did you learn about them?

5. **ANALYSIS SKILL** How is listening to storytelling a good way to learn about history?

6. ✏️ **Write a Story** Find a story that comes from the California tribe you are studying. Retell the story to your class in your own words.

7. **Focus Skill** **Cause and Effect** On a separate sheet of paper, copy and complete the graphic organizer below.

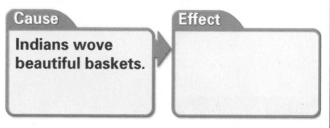

Cause	Effect
Indians wove beautiful baskets.	

American Indians and Change

When Europeans came to North America, life changed for the American Indians already living here. American Indians had many different feelings about the Europeans and the changes that they brought. Here are some thoughts of American Indians who were affected by these changes.

In Their Own Words

Chief Joseph, leader of the Nez Perce

" . . . All men were made by the same Great Spirit Chief. They are all brothers. The Earth is the mother of all people, and all people should have equal rights upon it. . . . Let me be a free man, free to travel, free to stop, free to work, free to trade . . . [free to] choose my own teachers, free to follow the religion of my fathers, free to think and talk and act for myself, and I will obey every law, or submit to the penalty. "

— from Chief Joseph's "An Indian's Views of Indian Affairs" speech given to cabinet members in Washington, D.C., in 1879. *Indian Oratory: Famous Speeches by Noted Indian Chieftains*, Norman University of Oklahoma Press, 1971.

Chief Joseph

Satanta, chief of the Kiowa Indians

"I have heard that you intend to settle us on a reservation near the mountains. I don't want to settle. I love to roam over the prairies. There I feel free and happy, but when we settle down we grow pale and die."

— from a speech at a meeting in 1876 between American Indians and people sent from the U.S. Congress.

Satanta

Views from Today

Leslie Marmon Silko,
an author from the Laguna Pueblo tribe

"If all of us and all living things on the planet are to continue, we, who still remember how we must live, must join together."

— from *Enduring Wisdom: Sayings from Native Americans,* selected by Virginia Driving Hawk Sneve. Holiday House, 2003.

Leslie Marmon Silko

Buffalo Tiger, Miccosukee leader

"Think like Indians, be like Indians, but learn English, learn how to write, be educated. You have two minds and you can work with both. We do not want to lose out on being Indians."

— from *Enduring Wisdom: Sayings from Native Americans,* selected by Virginia Driving Hawk Sneve. Holiday House, 2003.

Buffalo Tiger

It's Your Turn

ANALYSIS SKILL **Analyze Points of View** Work with a partner. Reread the quotations on these pages. What are the different ways the Indians looked at change? Explain why you think each person said what he or she said.

Reading Social Studies

A **cause** is an event or an action that makes something happen. An **effect** is what happens as a result of that event or action.

(Focus Skill) Cause and Effect

Copy and complete this graphic organizer to show that you understand the causes and effects of how California Indians used natural resources. A copy of a graphic organizer appears on page 30 of the Homework and Practice Book.

The Land and the First People

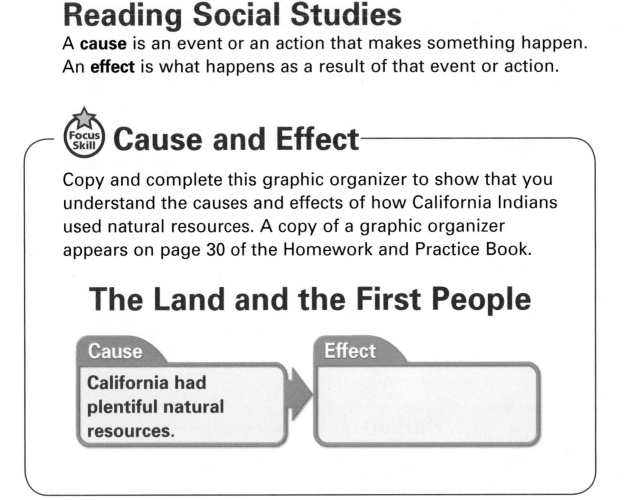

Cause
California had plentiful natural resources.

Effect

California Writing Prompts

Write a Report Select one of the American Indian tribes that you read about in this chapter. Write a report, telling what you learned about their way of life.

Write a Description Recall one of the Indian shelters you read about in this chapter. Describe the shelter and how it was suited to the environment.

Use Vocabulary

Write the word that correctly matches each definition.

shelter, p. 94   **barter,** p. 110
tool, p. 101   **folklore,** p. 116
economy, p. 110

1. to trade without using money

2. homes and buildings that protect people from the weather

3. ways of making and using goods and services

4. an item used to get work done

5. the history, beliefs, and customs of a group as told in its stories

Apply Skills

Read a Table Use the table shown on page 99 to answer the question.

6. Which main tribal group were the Karuk part of?

Recall Facts

Answer these questions.

7. How many major tribal groups were found in California?

8. Which group was the only tribal group that farmed?

Write the letter of the best choice.

9. For which tribe was food so plentiful that they had no word for starvation?
   A the Serrano
   B the Yurok
   C the Cahuilla
   D the Pomo

10. Which tribe lived where Los Angeles is today?
    A the Mojave
    B the Gabrielino
    C the Maidu
    D the Pomo

Think Critically

11. **ANALYSIS SKILL** Why do you think California Indians lived in different ways?

Study Skills

ORGANIZE INFORMATION

A graphic organizer can help you make sense of the facts you read.

- ▶ **Webs, charts, and tables are graphic organizers that can show main ideas and important details.**
- ▶ **A graphic organizer can help you classify and categorize information. It can also help you understand the relationship between the subject of the chapter and each lesson.**

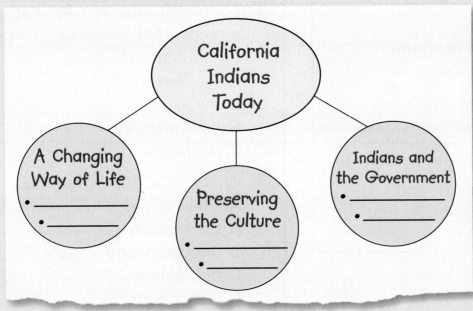

California Indians Today

A Changing Way of Life
- _____
- _____

Preserving the Culture
- _____
- _____

Indians and the Government
- _____
- _____

Apply As You Read

As you read this chapter, fill in each part of a web like the one above with facts from each lesson.

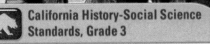

California History-Social Science Standards, Grade 3

3.2 Students describe the American Indian nations in their local region long ago and in the recent past.

California Indians Today

A Chumash Indian powwow in Santa Ynez Valley, California

The Yurok of Northern California

by Diane Hoyt-Goldsmith

photographs by Lawrence Migdale

Some stories we read are about real people and real places. These stories are called nonfiction. They help us to learn about the world we live in. Read this nonfiction selection to find out how Yurok children live today.

Many hundreds of years ago, the Yurok settled in villages along the Pacific Ocean where the Klamath River runs into the sea. They also built settlements up the river along its banks. The Yurok fished in the river for salmon. They traveled on it in canoes to trade with other tribes further to the east. Even the name Yurok means "downriver." For these reasons, the Klamath River in Northern California has always been the center of Yurok life. It is no different today.

A Yurok girl wears a ceremonial dress made from deerskin. Her hat is a finely woven basket. ▶

▲ Yurok children help their parents fish for salmon. They use nets as their ancestors once did.

▲ This map shows the location of Yurok lands and bodies of water.

Now, many of the ancestral villages are gone. The Yurok still live near them, however, in small towns like Hoopa and Weitchpec, and in rural areas that are so remote that many Yurok families have no electricity or telephones in their homes. The Yurok lands stretch from the mouth of the Klamath and then along its banks on both sides for a distance of forty miles. Surrounded by forest, many Yurok people live close to the river. They see it every day as they come and go to school and to work. They hear its music when they fall asleep at night.

Each summer, the Yurok tribe sponsors a cultural camp for kids at one of the ancestral village sites. During week-long sessions, kids between the ages of 7 and 12 can learn what it was like to live as their ancestors did. The campers board jet boats at the mouth of the river. With a loud roar, the engines start up and the boats fly over the water. After an hour, the boats arrive at a site many miles upstream where the children will camp.

During the week, the campers have the opportunity to learn about their culture. Elders from the tribe visit the camp, bringing legends, memories, and stories from the past. They play drums and sing about a time long ago.

In the Yurok tribe, there are only a few elders who still remember how to speak the Yurok language. They visit the camp to teach the children. Theirs is a precious heritage and each Yurok word a camper learns is a way to preserve it. Campers visit Sumeg, a place where they can see an old Yurok-style dwelling.

Like children everywhere, the Yurok love games. At the cultural camp, Yurok kids learn to play a traditional game called stick ball. The flat, sandy beach along the river makes an excellent playing field.

Stick ball is a fast-moving, exciting game that combines running and wrestling with the skill to use a driving stick to capture and throw a tossel. The driving stick is carved from a three- or four-foot length of wood and has a hook on one end. The tossel is made from two wooden pegs that are tied together.

▲ Campers head upriver in powerful jet boats.

The game starts with the tossel in the center of the playing field. Two equal teams, usually with two to four players, face off. Each team tries to capture the tossel and get it into the opponent's goal. As players rush for the tossel, it becomes a wild free-for-all. A player hooks the tossel and lobs it to a teammate. The defense wrestles the player to the ground and steals the tossel. The odds shift back and forth between the teams until someone scores.

Stick ball is popular today because it is so much fun. Some experts think that long ago playing stick ball may have been a way of settling disputes between individuals or families.

▲ A stick ball player holds a driving stick and the tossel.

◀ The Yurok Brush Dance is performed by people wearing ceremonial dress, decorated with beads and shells.

▲ At camp, Yurok children learn how to make baskets.

Examples of Yurok baskets
▼

In ancient times, the Yurok were known for the excellent baskets they made. An important part of the Yurok diet was acorns. Ground into a meal, acorns provided the Yurok with a healthy and tasty food. Baskets were needed to collect and store the acorns. They were also used as cooking utensils and to carry and store water. The Yurok also traded their baskets with other tribes for items that they needed.

A dwelling at Sumeg ▶

Campers learn to prepare smoked salmon as their ancestors did. Salmon that has been threaded on long redwood sticks is set in the sand around the coals of a hot fire. The stakes are turned, cooking the salmon evenly.

At camp, Yurok children learn to weave the grasses that grow along the river into baskets. Using materials from nature, they make something as useful as it is beautiful. Because of the cultural camp, each Yurok child can touch the past— experiencing a little of how their ancestors lived along the Klamath River so long ago.

After setting up the tents, children have a lunch of salmon, bread, and salad. ▼

Response Corner

1 Why was the Klamath River important to Yurok people in the past?

2 What do Yurok children learn at Yurok cultural summer camp?

A Changing Way of Life

When the first Europeans came to California, it was the start of many changes for California Indians.

Newcomers Bring Change

Each group of newcomers to California wanted something different from the Indians. Some wanted to hunt on the Indians' lands. Some wanted to trade. The Spanish wanted Indians' lands and resources. They also wanted to change the Indians' way of life. In the 1700s, the Spanish began to build religious communities called **missions** in California. There Indians learned to follow the Catholic religion.

▶ Mission San Gabriel Arcangel, near Los Angeles, was the fourth of 21 Spanish missions built in California.

What to Know
How has life changed for California Indians?

✔ The lives of California Indians today are both the same as and different from the lives of Indians long ago.

✔ Many Indians now live on Indian reservations or in cities in California.

Vocabulary
mission p. 132
reservation p. 133
rancheria p. 135

Focus Skill
Cause and Effect

California Standards
HSS 3.2, 3.2.1, 3.2.3, 3.2.4

California Indians outside a house on the Tejon Reservation in Kern County

At first, the newcomers respected the Indians' right to their lands. However, as more people moved into California, the Indians' rights were treated as less important. Many people from the eastern United States began to move into the area in 1848 to search for gold. The newcomers fought with the Indians over land. Many Indians died. Many who were left were treated badly and had their land taken away.

The United States hoped to end the fighting by setting up **reservations** (reh•zer•VAY•shunz). These were areas of land reserved, or set aside, for the Indians. Some California Indians were forced to move to reservations away from the land where they had always lived. Some were left with no land at all. All of this was difficult for a people whose ways of life were linked to their lands.

Reading Check ♂ **Cause and Effect**
Why did the United States government create reservations?

Tule River Indian Reservation

California's Central Valley is home to the Tule River Indian Reservation. The reservation includes some 55,000 acres, almost 85 square miles, of mountainous land along the southern end of the Sierra Nevada. The land includes giant sequoia redwood trees. It is beautiful, but it is not an easy place to live or work. Members of the Tule River tribe who live there hope to buy flatter land nearby that is better for homes and farming.

Life on a Reservation

Until very recently, Indians living on reservations in California were very poor. Most reservation land was not good for farming. The people could not live off the land as they once had. They did not have the natural resources they needed to make goods to trade.

Today, many California Indians still live on reservations. Some reservations have post offices, stores, and government buildings. Many people who live on reservations are poor. However, more and more are finding ways to create jobs and make money.

The Tule River Indian Reservation is home to many Yokuts Indians. Members of the Tule River tribe have built an entertainment center. Near the airport, they have also built a place where airplanes are built and repaired. In addition, they have built a food distribution center. There is also a company that tests soil and water. All of these places provide jobs.

Today, California's Indian reservations and **rancherias**, or small reservations, run many companies. These range from hotels and golf courses to power plants and sawmills. California is home to more than 50 rancherias. Rancherias began as small Indian villages that were later made reservations by the United States government.

Reading Check **Compare and Contrast**
How are reservations like cities?

▶ This American Indian man works on airplanes at the Tule River Indian Reservation.

▶ Robinson Rancheria, a Pomo community in Lake County

Locate It

CALIFORNIA

Robinson Rancheria

Many American Indians live in Pasadena (above) and other California cities. Their lives are much like the lives of other Americans.

Life in the City

Today, California Indians dress, eat, live, and travel in the same ways that most other Americans do. Many have moved to large cities instead of living on reservations. However, most still learn the old ways in order to honor their past. They learn the art forms, dances, and languages of the past. Some also wear the kind of clothing that California Indians of the past wore. However, they do these activities mainly on special days.

American Indians from other parts of the United States have moved to California's cities. They are meeting each other and learning about the ways of different tribes.

One way to learn about different tribes in California is to attend a powwow. At a powwow, American Indians from many tribes gather to dance, sing, and learn about different tribes. Powwows were started by American Indians who came to California from other places. Some powwows are held on reservations. Others are held near large cities, such as the Stanford University Powwow. It is held near the city of San Francisco.

Reading Check **Summarize**
How do today's American Indians honor their past?

Summary California newcomers changed the way American Indians lived. Today, Indians live on reservations, on rancherias, and in cities.

❱ **Pomo Indians celebrate their heritage by wearing traditional clothing.**

Review

1. 💡 How has life changed for California Indians?

2. **Vocabulary** What is an Indian **reservation**?

3. **Your Community** Find out about a powwow or other American Indian event that takes place in or near your community. Share with your classmates what you find out.

Critical Thinking

4. **Make It Relevant** What missions are located nearest you? what reservations or rancherias?

5. **ANALYSIS SKILL** How might life be different for California's Indians if they had not lost their land?

6. ✏ **Do Research** Do research to find out about the reservation closest to your community. Share with your classmates everything you learn, and use it to complete the unit project.

7. **(Focus Skill)** **Cause and Effect** On a separate sheet of paper, copy and complete the graphic organizer below.

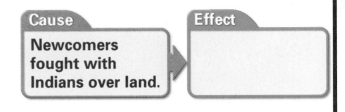

Cause	Effect
Newcomers fought with Indians over land.	

Compare History Maps

▶ Why It Matters

The maps on page 139 show California at two different times in its history. By comparing these history maps, you can see what has changed and what has stayed the same. A **history map** shows how a place looked at an earlier time.

▶ What You Need to Know

Colors are often used as map symbols. They can help you tell water from land and show you the areas of states and countries. On these two maps, color is used to help you locate each southern California tribal group.

▶ Practice the Skill

Look at the map legend to see what each color shows. Then use the maps to answer these questions.

1 What were some of the American Indian groups in California long ago? What are some groups in California today?

2 Where would you have gone to visit the Chumash long ago? Where would you go today?

▶ Apply What You Learned

ANALYSIS SKILL **Make It Relevant** Find an old map and a new map of your community. Compare the two maps. What things have changed? What things have stayed the same?

 Practice your map and globe skills with the **GeoSkills CD-ROM**.

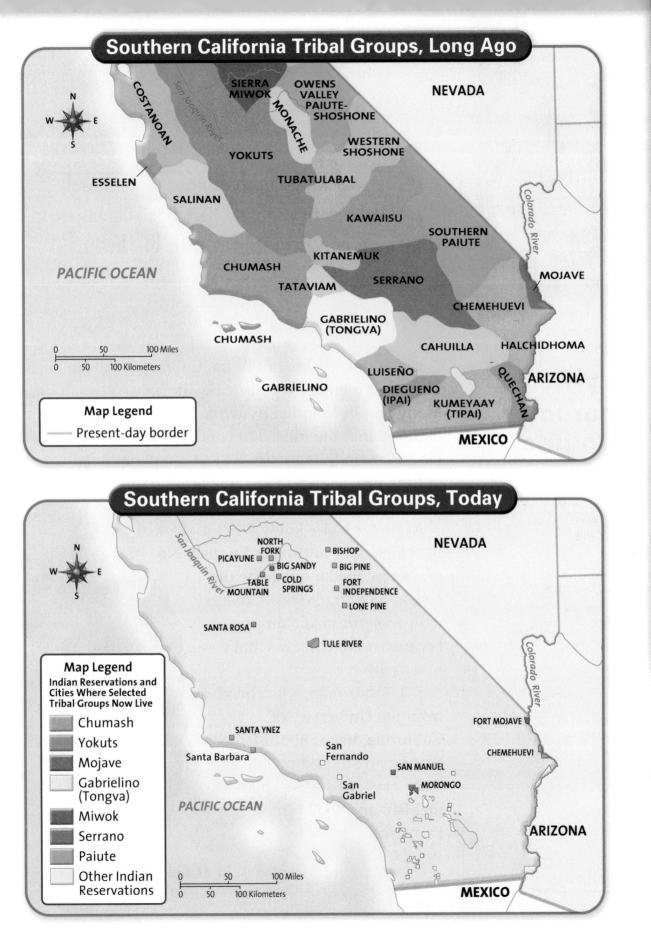

Southern California Tribal Groups, Long Ago

NEVADA

COSTANOAN

SIERRA MIWOK

OWENS VALLEY PAIUTE-SHOSHONE

San Joaquin River

MONACHE

YOKUTS

WESTERN SHOSHONE

ESSELEN

TUBATULABAL

SALINAN

KAWAIISU

SOUTHERN PAIUTE

Colorado River

PACIFIC OCEAN

CHUMASH

KITANEMUK

TATAVIAM

SERRANO

MOJAVE

CHEMEHUEVI

CHUMASH

GABRIELINO (TONGVA)

CAHUILLA

HALCHIDHOMA

0   50   100 Miles

0   50   100 Kilometers

LUISEÑO

GABRIELINO

DIEGUENO (IPAI)

KUMEYAAY (TIPAI)

QUECHAN

ARIZONA

MEXICO

Map Legend

—— Present-day border

Southern California Tribal Groups, Today

NEVADA

San Joaquin River

NORTH FORK

PICAYUNE

BISHOP

BIG SANDY

BIG PINE

TABLE MOUNTAIN

COLD SPRINGS

FORT INDEPENDENCE

LONE PINE

SANTA ROSA

TULE RIVER

Colorado River

FORT MOJAVE

SANTA YNEZ

CHEMEHUEVI

Santa Barbara

San Fernando

SAN MANUEL

San Gabriel

MORONGO

PACIFIC OCEAN

ARIZONA

0   50   100 Miles

0   50   100 Kilometers

MEXICO

Map Legend
Indian Reservations and Cities Where Selected Tribal Groups Now Live

- Chumash
- Yokuts
- Mojave
- Gabrielino (Tongva)
- Miwok
- Serrano
- Paiute
- Other Indian Reservations

Trustworthiness

Respect

Responsibility

Fairness

Caring

Patriotism

Ishi

"He was kind; he had courage and self-restraint, and though all had been taken from him, he had no bitterness in his heart."*

–Dr. Saxton Pope, Ishi's friend

Why Character Counts

? How did Ishi show fairness to the people around him?

Ishi walked alone out of the California hills in 1911. The other members of his tribe, the Yahi, were all dead. Many had been killed by white settlers. A few had fled into the hills. Ishi was one of these. He had been living with the last members of his tribe. Then all the Yahi except Ishi died. Ishi walked until he found a town.

At first, no one knew what to do with Ishi. He could not speak English. No one knew the language he did speak. At first, the tired, hungry man was put in jail simply because no one knew what else to do with him.

T. T. Waterman, a teacher from the University of California, heard about Ishi. Waterman studied people as parts of groups. Waterman met Ishi and took him to San Francisco.

Ishi in 1911 at the time of his capture.

* Dr. Saxton Pope. *Encyclopedia of North American Indians*. Frederick E. Hoxie, ed. 1996.

Sam Batwi, Alfred
Kroeber, and Ishi

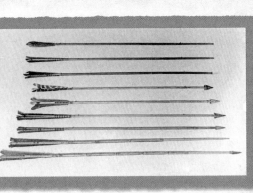

Arrows made by Ishi

Ishi in 1914

Once there, Alfred Kroeber tried to talk with Ishi. He knew a language much like the one Ishi spoke. Finally, Ishi could tell a little about his life. He did not tell his real name. That was against the laws of his people. The teachers called him *Ishi*. That means "man" in the Yahi language.

Ishi lived at a museum. People came to see him make the crafts of his people. He made arrow points and bows. Ishi also cleaned the museum. People talked about his friendly ways.

In December 1914, Ishi became sick. He died two years later. Ishi was about 56 years old. He had lived in the city a little more than four years.

Ishi had seen most of his friends and family die. Ishi was not angry, though. Ishi treated the people around him fairly. He proudly told them about Yahi ways.

GO ONLINE Visit MULTIMEDIA BIOGRAPHIES at www.harcourtschool.com/hss

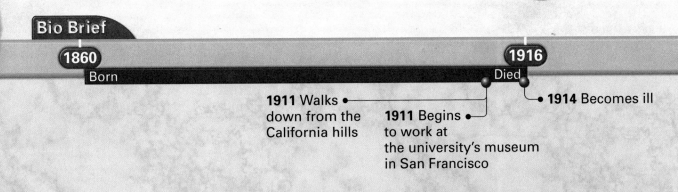

Bio Brief

1860 • Born

1911 Walks down from the California hills

1911 Begins to work at the university's museum in San Francisco

1914 Becomes ill

1916 • Died

Preserving the Culture

California's Indians think it is important to remember their ways of life. Many of them have passed on their customs to their children and grandchildren. Today, the Indians of California work to keep the old ways of life alive.

Keeping Culture Alive

Culture is a way of life shared by members of a group. Since today's California Indians live as most other Americans do, they have to find special ways to remember their cultures.

Cause and Effect

California Standards
HSS 3.2, 3.2.1

❯ Chumash historian and storyteller Julie Tumamait helps keep her culture alive.

Many attend celebrations at which Indian dances and songs are performed. They also hold ceremonies and festivals like those of the past. Some Indians teach their children their languages and customs.

Artists **preserve** their cultures, or keep them alive, by painting pictures that show how things were done in the past. Artists also make baskets and crafts in the old ways and teach their skills to others.

Many people who work in museums preserve Indian clothing, artwork, and tools so the objects will last a long time. A **museum** is a place to keep and display objects. Many cities and reservations in California have museums that show objects from American Indian cultures.

Reading Check ŏ **Cause and Effect**
What is one effect of keeping objects in museums?

Cultural Heritage

California Native American Day

California Native American Day became an official state holiday in 1998. It is celebrated on the fourth Friday of September. It is set aside as a day for people to learn more about American Indian cultures and traditions. Special events are planned at which people are taught American Indian songs and dances. Other activities include making pottery and preparing and eating foods.

Oroville Salmon Festival

One example of a festival celebrated by an Indian tribe is the Oroville Salmon Festival. Each year, salmon swim up rivers in northwestern California to lay their eggs. In the past, Maidu tribes held ceremonies to celebrate this event. Today, the Maidu continue the tradition. A **tradition** is a way of doing something that is passed on to others.

The festival is held in Oroville. It begins when an elder of the tribe spears the first salmon. An **elder** is an older, respected member of the tribe. The salmon is dried over a smoky fire and shared with the elders of other tribes. Drumming, dancing, and singing follow this ceremony. Then everyone enjoys a meal of salmon.

Reading Check **Summarize**
What event does the Oroville Salmon Festival celebrate?

⚡ Fast Fact

Long ago Maidu Indians began catching salmon from the Feather River. Now the Maidu are an important part of the Oroville Salmon Festival. The festival has been held every September since 1994.

▶ **This Maidu man is holding salmon. Below, this dam on the Feather River directs salmon to a nearby fish hatchery.**

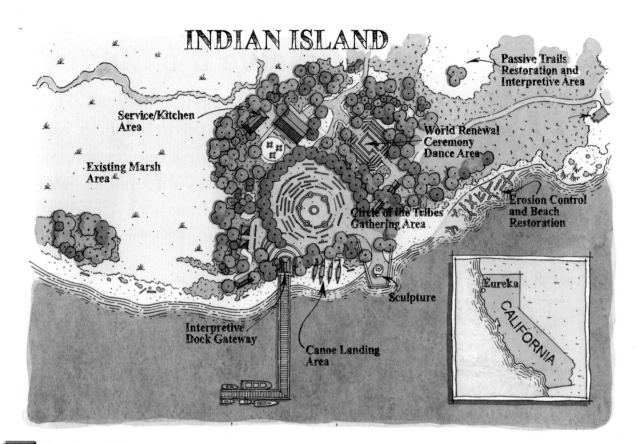

INDIAN ISLAND

Passive Trails Restoration and Interpretive Area

Service/Kitchen Area

World Renewal Ceremony Dance Area

Existing Marsh Area

Erosion Control and Beach Restoration

Circle of the Tribes Gathering Area

Eureka

CALIFORNIA

Sculpture

Interpretive Dock Gateway

Canoe Landing Area

ANALYSIS SKILL **Analyze Maps**

❖ **Human-Environment Interactions** What places do the Wiyot plan to build for holding ceremonies and gatherings?

Indian Island

Long ago, Indian Island was very important to the Wiyot Indians. Wiyot tribes gathered there each year for special ceremonies. But in 1860, many Wiyot were killed on the island. Others were moved to a reservation.

Today, members of the Wiyot tribe live at the Table Bluff Reservation, south of Eureka, California. In 2000, they bought some of the island's land. They are cleaning up the land and plan to rebuild a ceremonial dance area.

▶ Eureka Mayor Peter LaVallee and Wiyot tribal leader Cheryl Seidner sign Indian Island land documents.

Reading Check **Main Idea and Details**
Why is Indian Island important to the Wiyot?

Learning to Preserve the Culture

▶ **Students at D-Q University**

In 1971, D-Q University opened in Davis, California. It became the first college run by Indians on land outside a reservation. Since then, several California universities have created special departments of American Indian studies. At these schools, experts learn more about American Indian cultures and teach what they know to others.

Katherine Siva Saubel is one of these experts. She is a Cahuilla who helped start the Malki Museum at the Morongo Indian Reservation near Banning. To do this, she worked with others, including her husband, Mariano Saubel, and her friend, Jane Penn. Katherine Siva Saubel is also the last native speaker of the Cahuilla language.

▶ **Students learn about American Indian cultural arts in this building at D-Q University.**

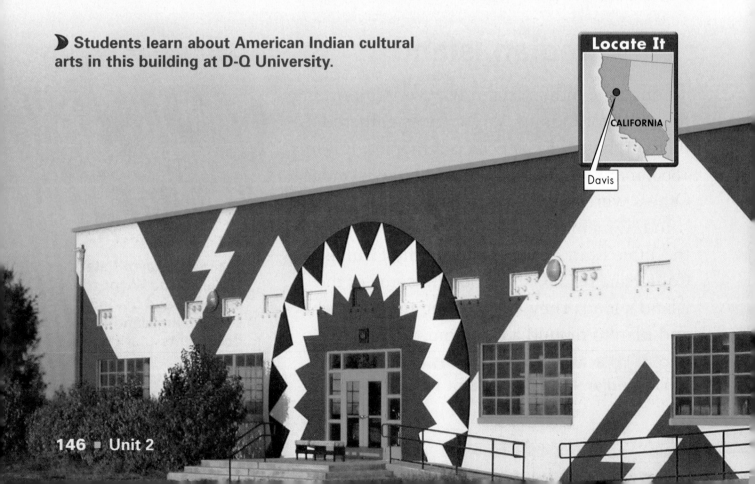

Locate It

CALIFORNIA

Davis

Saubel has written a Cahuilla dictionary and made recordings to show how the words are spoken. She has also recorded many Cahuilla tribal songs and worked with researchers to name many of the plants that the Cahuilla used as medicine.

For her work, Saubel has been named to the National Women's Hall of Fame. She was also named Elder of the Year by the State Indian Museum in Sacramento.

▶ Katherine Siva Saubel

Reading Check **Summarize**

What work has Katherine Siva Saubel done to preserve the Cahuilla way of life?

Summary American Indians are preserving their cultures so that they will be remembered in the future. They hold festivals and teach their traditions to young people.

Review

1. 💡 How have American Indian cultures been preserved?

2. **Vocabulary** Explain the difference between **culture** and **tradition**.

3. **Your Community** Where can you learn about the American Indians who live in or near your community?

Critical Thinking

4. **Make It Relevant** How do members of your family or community preserve their culture?

5. **ANALYSIS SKILL** Why is it important to preserve culture?

6. 🖌 **Make a Cultural Object** For the Cultural Fair, make a cultural object, such as a basket or drum, that represents a tribe.

7. **Focus Skill** **Cause and Effect** On a separate sheet of paper, copy and complete the graphic organizer below.

Cause	Effect
	Members of the Wiyot tribe are cleaning up Indian Island.

Cultural Objects and Artifacts

For many years, people have admired the expert arts and crafts of California's American Indians. California's Indians used materials from nature to make their homes, tools, clothing, and jewelry.

necklace of magnetite and clamshell beads

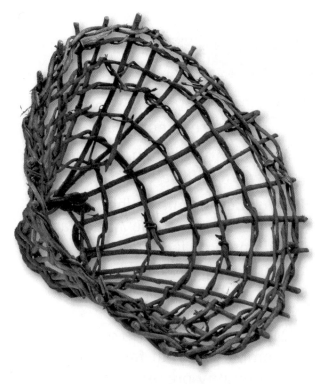

fish trap basket

ceremonial headroll

skirt made of
shredded bark

woven seed beater

ANALYSIS SKILL **Analyze Artifacts**

1. What do the trap basket and seed beater tell you about what California Indians ate?

2. What items did American Indians wear?

3. Which item do you think was the hardest to make? Why?

GO ONLINE Visit PRIMARY SOURCES at www.harcourtschool.com/hss

Indians and Government

Many Indian tribes today have their own governments. They are also able to take part in the United States government.

Indian Government Today

Tribal government is separate from the federal, or national, government. It is also separate from state and local governments. This kind of government is called a **sovereign** (SAH•vruhn) government. A tribe with a sovereign government is like a separate nation in many ways. It may have its own **constitution**, or written set of laws that tell how a government is to work.

> The tribal council of the Agua Caliente Band of Cahuilla Indians

What to Know
How do American Indian tribes organize their governments?

✔ Indian tribes have their own governments and constitutions.

✔ Indian tribal leaders work with the state and federal government.

Vocabulary
sovereign p. 150
constitution p. 150
tribal council p. 151
treaty p. 152

Focus Skill
Cause and Effect

California Standards
HSS 3.2, 3.2.3, 3.4.5

▶ Richard Milanovich, tribal chairperson of the Agua Caliente Band of Cahuilla Indians, talks about his tribe's plans.

Most reservations are run by tribal councils. A **tribal council** is a group of leaders elected by tribe members. It represents its tribe in the state and national government. The council also manages the tribe's economy.

The Konkow Valley Band of Maidu has its own government. Its tribal council includes a chairperson and three other members. Each tribal council member serves for two years. Then he or she may be reelected.

Many tribal governments offer special services to tribe members. For example, the Wiyot tribe at Table Bluff Reservation provides a community meal one day each week. It also offers child-care services and programs in which children can get help with their schoolwork.

(Reading Check) ŎCause and Effect
What effect do tribal governments have on Indians?

Taking Part in State and Federal Government

The United States Constitution gives power in Indian affairs to the federal government, not to state governments. Many of the treaties made in the past between the United States federal government and Indian tribes are still in effect today. A **treaty** is an agreement between groups or countries. In exchange for the tribes' land, the United States promised to provide education, health care, and other services.

The main branch of the federal government that works with Indian tribes is the Bureau of Indian Affairs (BIA). The BIA provides many services on reservations, such as job training, medical care, and education.

▶ These California tribal leaders are filing a claim to be recognized by the federal government.

The BIA also helps tribes run their own governments. It encourages tribes to provide services for themselves as much as possible.

In general, state governments have no control over tribal governments. Instead, the tribal and state governments most often cooperate with each other.

Reading Check **Summarize**
How are the federal and state governments related to tribal government?

Summary Tribes have their own constitutions and govern themselves through tribal councils. Indian treaties are still in effect today. The federal government provides services to Indian reservations. State and tribal governments work together.

▶ **Governor Arnold Schwarzenegger and five California tribal leaders sign new statewide cooperation agreements.**

Review

1. How do American Indian tribes organize their governments?

2. **Vocabulary** Explain the relationship between a **tribal council** and its **constitution**.

3. **Your Community** How is a reservation like your community?

Critical Thinking

4. **Make It Relevant** What news related to American Indians can you find in your local newspaper?

5. **ANALYSIS SKILL** What is the relationship between tribal government and state government?

6. **Make a T-Chart** Make a T-chart. On one side, tell what you know about tribal government. On the other side, tell what you know about the federal government.

7. **Focus Skill** **Cause and Effect** On a separate sheet of paper, copy and complete the graphic organizer below.

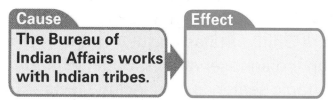

Cause
The Bureau of Indian Affairs works with Indian tribes.

Effect

Reading Social Studies

A **cause** is an event or an action that makes something happen. An **effect** is what happens as a result of that event or action.

(Focus Skill) Cause and Effect

Copy and complete this graphic organizer to show that you understand the causes and effects of how the culture of California Indian tribes is being kept alive today. A copy of a graphic organizer appears on page 38 of the Homework and Practice Book.

California Indians Today

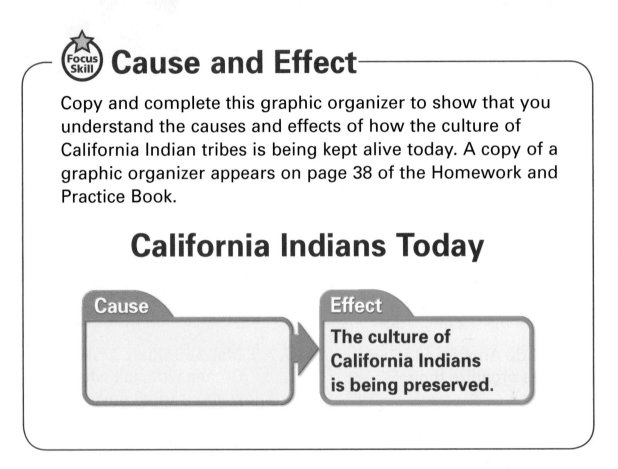

Cause	Effect
	The culture of California Indians is being preserved.

✏ California Writing Prompts

Write About Indian Reservations
Write a paragraph that explains why the United States decided to set up Indian reservations. Begin with a topic sentence, and include facts about reservations.

Write an Advertisement Write an advertisement about a powwow. Tell where and when the event will take place. Describe what visitors will see at the powwow and what the Indian tribes will be doing at the powwow.

Use Vocabulary

Write the word that correctly matches each definition.

reservation, p. 133
tradition, p. 144
constitution, p. 150

tribal council, p. 151
treaty, p. 152

1. a group of leaders elected by tribe members

2. an agreement between groups or countries

3. area of land reserved, or set aside, for the Indians

4. a way of doing something that is passed on to others

5. a written set of laws that tell how a government is to work

Apply Skills

Compare History Maps Use the maps on page 139 to answer the question.

6. **ANALYSIS SKILL** Which color is used to help you locate the Serrano tribal groups long ago and today?

Recall Facts

Answer these questions.

7. What kinds of companies operate today from California's reservations and rancherias?

8. What island has special meaning for the Wiyot Indians?

Write the letter of the best choice.

9. What group runs most reservations today?
   A the federal government
   B a tribal council
   C the state of California
   D a town near the reservation

10. Which branch of the federal government works with Indian tribes?
    A the BIA
    B the CIA
    C the FBI
    D the Congress

Think Critically

11. **ANALYSIS SKILL** What can people learn by visiting American Indian exhibits in California's museums?

INDIAN GRINDING ROCK

State Historic Park

Get Ready

Indian Grinding Rock State Historic Park is located in Pine Grove, California, in the foothills of the Sierra Nevada. The park is named for a rock formation where ancient Miwok women gathered to grind acorns and other seeds. Over time, their work wore 1,185 bowl-shaped depressions in the stone. Some of the holes for grinding—and the decorative carvings around them—may be as much as 3,000 years old!

Locate It
California

Indian Grinding Rock
State Historic Park

What to See

Visitors are asked to stay off the ancient rock to prevent it from wearing away.

Acorns are nutritious but taste terrible. Once acorns are ground into meal, the bitter tannin can be washed away.

The park is also home to the Chaw'se Regional Indian Museum, where visitors learn about the baskets, weapons, tools, clothing, and jewelry of the area's tribes.

Bark houses are part of a reconstructed Miwok village. There are also a ceremonial roundhouse and an Indian game field.

A Virtual Tour

Visit VIRTUAL TOURS at www.harcourtschool.com/hss

Unit 2

Review

THE BIG IDEA

California Indians Long ago, American Indians developed cultures in which they used the land to meet their needs. Indian groups differed in their languages and customs. Many of their traditions survive today.

Summary

American Indians

Indian tribes lived in California long before Europeans arrived. The tribes are divided into four groups based on where they lived. Each tribe used the natural resources found where it lived and showed a respect for Earth.

California tribes bartered with each other for things they did not have in their area. Tribes had different kinds of government and were often led by chiefs. They also had different customs and traditions.

Settlers changed the way California Indians lived. Today, some Indians live on reservations, on rancherias, and in cities. They are preserving their culture for the future.

Main Ideas and Vocabulary

Read the summary above. Then answer the questions that follow.

1. How are California Indians divided into tribal groups?
   A based on their chiefs
   B based on their constitutions
   C based on where they lived
   D based on their traditions

2. Why did Indian tribes barter?
   A to make a profit
   B to get things they could not find in their area
   C to meet other tribes
   D to gain more land

Recall Facts

Answer these questions.

3. What were the four main Indian groups in California?

4. What kinds of tools did Indians use for fishing?

5. What did Spanish newcomers want from the Indians?

6. What is D-Q University?

Write the letter of the best choice.

7. Who was a curing doctor found in many villages?
   A a shaman
   B the chief's oldest son
   C the chief
   D the chief's mother

8. What type of government is separate from the federal government?
   A state
   B national
   C sovereign
   D local

Think Critically

9. Many Indian tribes have their own government. How is a tribal government like a national government?

10. **ANALYSIS SKILL** Why did the Gabrielino Indians build boats and why did the Mojave not?

Apply Skills

Compare History Maps

ANALYSIS SKILL Use the two history maps below to answer the following questions.

11. Where would you have gone to visit the Wailaki long ago? Where would you go today?

12. Which tribal groups live in Elk Valley today?

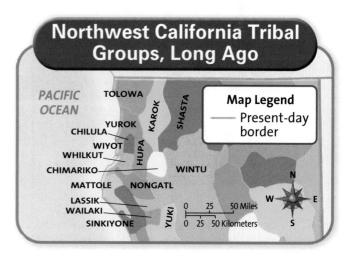

Northwest California Tribal Groups, Long Ago

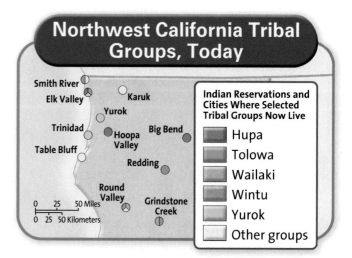

Northwest California Tribal Groups, Today

Read More

■ *The Chumash,* by Renee Skelton.

■ *Cheryl Seidner: Wiyot Leader,* by Belinda Hulin.

■ *American Indians: The Hopi, Iroquois, and Ojibway,* by Leslie Dickstein.

Unit Writing Activity

Write an Article Write a newspaper article about California Indians. Choose one of the following topics—how some California Indians used the land to meet their needs, how the four Indian groups differed, or how Indians are keeping their traditions alive today.

Unit Project

California Indian Cultures Fair Work with classmates to research a tribe of California Indians. Make a poster that illustrates the past and present lives of the tribe. Find maps and pictures of cultural objects. At the fair, have members of your group tell about the tribe you researched.

GO ONLINE Visit ACTIVITIES at
www.harcourtschool.com/hss

Community History

![bear icon] **Start with the Standards**

3.3 Students draw from historical and community resources to organize the sequence of local historical events and describe how each period of settlement left its mark on the land.

The Big Idea

History

California communities have a long history. They have changed greatly from the time of early explorers to today. Every community has its own story.

What to Know

✓ Who were the early explorers of California?

✓ Who started the early communities in California and what was life like in these communities?

✓ How did California grow and change during and after the Gold Rush?

✓ What are some ways to find out about your community's history?

Show What You Know

★ Unit 3 Test

✎ Writing: A Journal Entry

🖌 Unit Project: A Community History Scrapbook

Community History

Talk About

Community History

California Gazette

Transcontinental Railroad Is Completed!

On May 10, 1869 the Central Pacific and the Union Pacific Railroad met at Promontory, Utah. A solid gold spike was the last one laid to complete the track. A telegraph was sent to President Ulysses S. Grant that said, "The last rail is laid, the last spike is driven, the Pacific Railroad is completed." The railroad will connect California

" We make projects to show what we learn about the history of our community. "

"New discoveries caused changes in California."

"California's people are important to the history of our state and community."

Vocabulary

VIEW OF SAN FRANCISCO (FORMERLY YERBA BUENA) IN 1846-7
BEFORE THE DISCOVERY OF GOLD

explorer A person who goes somewhere new to find out about a place. (page 174)

settler One of the first people to live in a new place. (page 182)

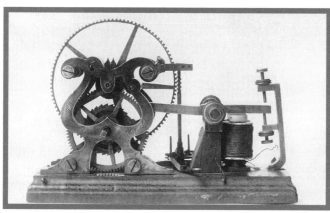

invention Something that has been made for the first time. (page 212)

technology The inventions that people use in everyday life. (page 220)

heritage A set of values and customs handed down to a group from those who have lived before them. (page 226)

GO ONLINE Visit INTERNET RESOURCES at **www.harcourtschool.com/hss** to view Internet Resources.

Reading Social Studies

Focus Skill

Sequence

Sequence is the order in which events happen.

Why It Matters

Noticing the sequence of events helps you understand what you read.

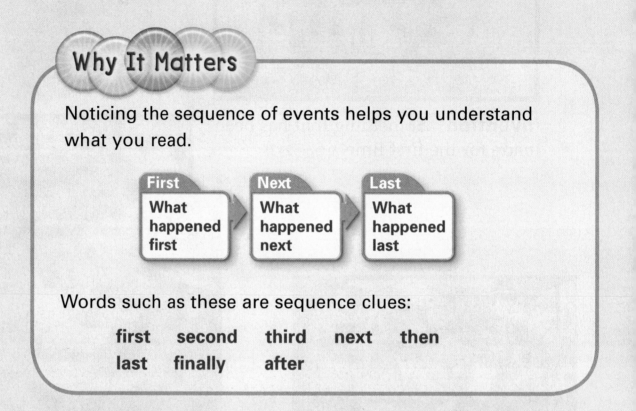

First
What happened first

Next
What happened next

Last
What happened last

Words such as these are sequence clues:

first	second	third	next	then
last	finally	after		

Practice the Skill

Read the paragraph. Look for sequence clues as you read.

Before California became a state, it was home to many different people. First, American Indians were the only people in the area. European explorers came next. Most of them did not stay for long. Finally, some people from Spain stayed. Some of them set up missions.

Read the paragraphs. Then answer the questions.

The Story of Simi Valley

The city of Simi Valley is in southwestern California. The city sits between mountains and the Simi Hills, near Los Angeles. Simi Valley was not always a city, though. It has a long history.

This place was first home to the Chumash Indians. They called it *Shimiji*. The Chumash built canoes to travel to islands in the ocean.

In 1795, the Spanish governor of that area gave away the village of Shimiji. He gave the land to Santiago Pico and Luis Peña. The two men and their families raised sheep and cattle.

Later, in the 1880s, Pico and Peña sold the land to settlers from the eastern United States. The settlers built houses.

Today, about 100,000 people live in Simi Valley. Many work in Los Angeles. Others work in small businesses in the city of Simi Valley.

(Focus Skill) Sequence

1. Who lived first in the Simi Valley?

2. Who owned the land in Simi Valley after the Chumash?

MAKE AN OUTLINE

An outline is a good way to record main ideas and details.

➤ **Topics in an outline are shown by Roman numerals.**

➤ **Main ideas about each topic are shown by capital letters.**

➤ **Details about each main idea are identified by numbers.**

How Communities Began

I. Exploring California
   A. Columbus explores
      1. Finds and explores North America
      2. Tells Europeans about North America
   B. Other European explorers come to North America
      1. They come for riches
      2.
      3.

Apply As You Read

As you read this chapter, remember to pay attention to the topics, main ideas, and details. Use that information to complete an outline of the chapter.

California History-Social Science Standards, Grade 3

3.3 Students draw from historical and community resources to organize the sequence of local historical events and describe how each period of settlement left its mark on the land.

How Communities Began

Mission San Juan Capistrano

STANDING at the Edge of the WORLD

by D. E. Bostian
illustrated by Ron Himler

From the 1500s to 1821, Spain ruled the lands that now make up California. Among the few settlers who lived in California in the early 1800s were the members of the Argüello (ar·GWAY·yoh) family. They lived in a presidio (pray·SEE·dee·oh), or fort, that had been built to protect Spain's claim to the land. Their settlement would later become part of the city of San Francisco.

María de la Concepción Marcela Argüello—Concha for short—was the sixth of the thirteen Argüello children. Born at the presidio, she would grow up to become famous in California. Concha's father, Don José Argüello, was the community's *comandante*, or commander. His job was an important one, and his responsibilities kept him away from home for months at a time. The family waited for his return in a small, rough cabin at the fort. In heavy rains, its grass roof leaked and its mud walls washed away. The packed dirt floor felt cold to Concha's bare feet, even in summer. The entire family slept in the same room, where Concha shared a bed with at least two little sisters.

From the cabin's window, Concha could look out into the square courtyard and see the cabins of the presidio soldiers and their families. Their homes were made of adobe with thatched grass roofs, as hers was, but theirs were even smaller. Each house backed up to the inside of the fort wall, with its doors and windows facing into the courtyard. There were also low buildings for storing food and supplies. The church, right next door to Concha's house, was the center of all of their lives.

Concha loved her life at the presidio. The fort was perched on a high cliff almost completely surrounded by the ocean. Concha sometimes felt as if she were standing at the edge of the world. She loved the sight and sound and smell of the sea. More than anything, though, Concha loved the animals. For hours she would watch the playful sea lions dive for fish and sun themselves on the rocks. They seemed to bark nonstop!

Concha's favorites were the swallows—the swooping, diving, elegant swallows. Like many presidio birds, they lived in California through the warmer months and then flew far south for the winter. When spring came, the swallows were always the first of the birds to come back. They seemed to Concha like friends coming home from a long trip, swooping and circling in the air to celebrate their return. She tried to imagine the sights the birds must have seen, flying to and from their winter homes as far away as Argentina. Concha liked to watch them gather mud and grass for their cup-shaped nests. The birds nested under roof edges or even in the high corners of homes. It was said to be good luck to have swallows nearby, so they were always welcome.

One day, when Concha had grown up, an unexpected ship arrived at the presidio. The romance between Concha and the ship's Russian captain is a story still told in California. Born in the time of Spanish rule, Concha lived in California through Mexican independence and the first years of statehood. When she died, there were few Californians who could not remember some kindness she had shown them.

Response Corner

1 What job did Concha's father have?

2 Why were the swallows Concha's favorite birds?

Exploring California

What to Know
Who were the early explorers of California?

- ✔ Explorers from Spain, England, and Russia came to California.

- ✔ Explorers came to California for different reasons, including trade, treasure, land, and religion.

Vocabulary
explorer p. 174
voyage p. 175
claim p. 175
strait p. 175
harbor p. 178

Focus Skill Sequence

California Standards
HSS 3.2.4, 3.3, 3.3.1

Long ago, only American Indians lived in North America. Then, in 1492, an Italian explorer named Christopher Columbus sailed from Spain. An **explorer** is a person who goes to find out about a place. Columbus thought he could sail west around the world to the part of Asia that Europeans called the Indies. Instead, he reached a continent that people in Europe did not know about. Before long, other explorers came. In time, they reached the area that is now California.

❯ Christopher Columbus came to the Americas with three sailing ships. Pictured here are replicas, or copies, of those ships.

Rulers Send Explorers

European kings and queens sent explorers on **voyages**, or journeys by water, for different reasons. One reason was to find treasure. Other reasons were to spread their religion or to claim land. To **claim** something is to say that it belongs to you.

Europeans also wanted to buy silk and spices from Asia. Carrying these goods over land was slow and expensive. European explorers hoped there was a way to sail through North America to Asia. English explorers called this route the Northwest Passage. Spanish explorers called it the Strait of Anián (ahn•YAHN). A **strait** is a narrow water passage that connects two bodies of water.

▶ Explorers found their way with tools like this compass, from about 1750.

Reading Check ⚙ **Sequence**
What happened after Columbus reached the Americas?

Spanish Explorers Arrive

In the 1500s, the Spanish explorer Hernando Cortés (er•NAHN•doh kawr•TES) sailed from New Spain, which is now the country of Mexico. He was looking for the Strait of Anián. In 1535, Cortés landed in *Baja*, or "lower," California. The land north of Baja California was called *Alta*, or "upper," California. Cortés did not find a shorter way to Asia, but he claimed the land of Baja California for Spain. Today, Baja California is part of Mexico. Alta California is the state of California in the United States.

❱ Early explorers and mapmakers thought California was an island.

⚡Fast Fact

A Spanish novel written in the 1500s used the name *California*. It was a make-believe island filled with natural treasures. Cabrillo thought he had landed on an island, and he used the name *California* to describe it in his journals.

In 1542, Juan Rodríguez Cabrillo (HWAN rohd•REE•ges kah•BREE•yoh) sailed north from Mexico. He reached the area that is now San Diego Bay and became the first explorer to land in Alta California. As he sailed farther north, he also claimed Catalina Island and San Miguel Island for Spain.

"We saw an Indian town on the land next to the sea with large houses built much like those of New Spain,"* Cabrillo wrote in his journal in 1542. He and his crew met the Chumash Indians. From the Indians, they learned much about central California and its people. But Cabrillo did not find treasure or a shortcut to Asia. Not until the mid-1700s did explorers learn that the Strait of Anián did not exist.

Cabrillo died on San Miguel Island. Many years passed before any other Spanish explorers came to California.

Reading Check ŎSequence
Who was the first explorer to reach Alta California?

*From the journal of Juan Rodríguez Cabrillo, 1542.

▶ **The Cabrillo National Monument at San Diego Bay was completed in 1913.**

An English Explorer Arrives

► Francis Drake

In 1579, Francis Drake, an explorer from England, landed in California. His ship, called the *Golden Hind*, needed repairs. Drake stopped at a bay near what is now San Francisco, where he found a good harbor. A **harbor** is a place with deep water that lets ships sail close to the shore. Drake claimed the area for England.

In 1602, the Spanish returned to California. Sebastián Vizcaíno (vees•kah•EE•noh) followed Cabrillo's route. Along the way, he gave San Diego its name and discovered Monterey Bay. He also drew maps of the coast that travelers used for nearly 200 years!

Reading Check 🐚 **Sequence**
Who came to California first, Francis Drake or Sebastián Vizcaíno?

ANALYSIS SKILL **Analyze Paintings**

This painting is of Francis Drake's ship the *Golden Hind*.

❓ Do you think it would be easy or hard to sail a ship like this one?

Russian Fur Traders Come to California

During the 1700s, fur traders from Russia explored the California coastline. Many of them came south from places in Alaska, where they hunted and traded furs. In California, the Russians hunted seals and sea otters along the coast. The pelts, or furs, of these animals were very valuable for trade. People in China, Russia, and other places used them to make warm clothing.

Reading Check **Summarize**

Why did Russian fur traders explore California?

Summary Early explorers looked for a way through North America to Asia. They did not find it, but some did come to California's coast. There they looked for riches and land to claim.

▶ Russian fur traders built Fort Ross in what is today Sonoma County. The fort's chapel is pictured here.

Review

1. 💡 Who were the early explorers of California?

2. **Vocabulary** Write a sentence to tell how the words **explorer**, **voyage**, and **claim** are related.

3. **Your Community** Do research to find out which explorers came to your community or nearby.

Critical Thinking

4. **Make It Relevant** How might your life be different today if explorers had not come to California?

5. **ANALYSIS SKILL** What contributions did explorers make to what is now the state of California?

6. 🖌 **Make a Chart** Make a chart about explorers. Include each explorer's name, country, dates and places he explored, and the reason he came to California.

7. **Focus Skill** **Sequence** Copy and complete the graphic organizer.

First	Next	Last
Cabrillo explores		

Follow Routes on a Map

▶ Why It Matters

Learning to read a map that shows routes can help you understand how travelers got to a place and what they may have seen on the way. A **route** is the path or direction a person takes to get somewhere.

During the 1500s and 1600s, many European explorers traveled on the ocean. By looking at maps that show routes, you can follow their journeys. Maps showing routes are an important resource for people who want to travel to the same place or learn about it.

▶ What You Need to Know

On the map on page 181, the routes that explorers took are marked with different colors. The color red is used for Cabrillo's route, green for Drake's, blue for Vizcaíno's, and purple for Cortés's.

▶ Practice the Skill

Use the map to answer these questions.

1 Which explorers left from Mexico?

2 Which explorers traveled on land as well as on water?

3 Which explorer traveled the longest distance?

▶ Apply What You Learned

ANALYSIS SKILL **Make It Relevant** Make a map showing routes from your home to a store or school in your community. Draw at least two ways to get there, using a different color for each route. Label all the important places, and include a map legend and a title.

 Practice your map and globe skills with the **GeoSkills CD-ROM**.

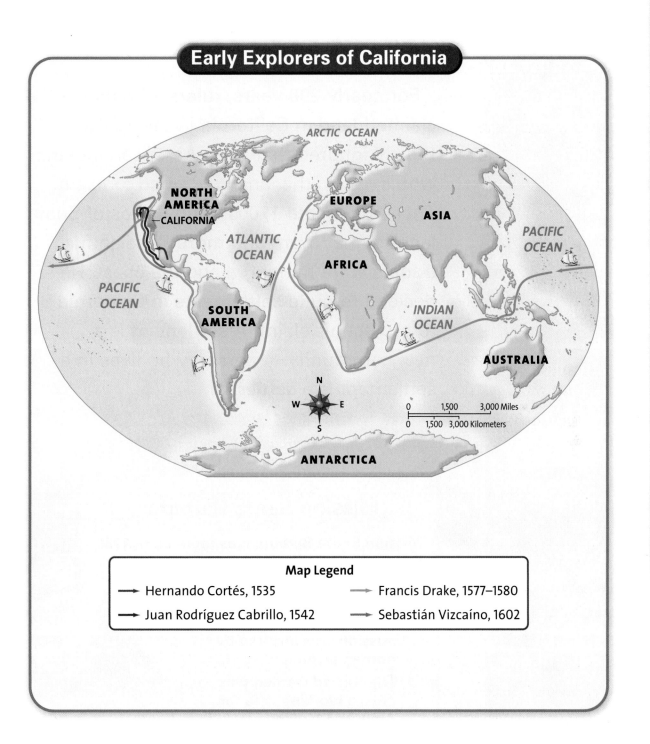

Early Explorers of California

ARCTIC OCEAN

NORTH AMERICA
—CALIFORNIA

EUROPE

ASIA

PACIFIC OCEAN

ATLANTIC OCEAN

AFRICA

PACIFIC OCEAN

SOUTH AMERICA

INDIAN OCEAN

AUSTRALIA

N
W E
S

0   1,500   3,000 Miles
0   1,500   3,000 Kilometers

ANTARCTICA

Map Legend

→ Hernando Cortés, 1535   → Francis Drake, 1577–1580

→ Juan Rodríguez Cabrillo, 1542   → Sebastián Vizcaíno, 1602

Early Communities

What to Know

Who started the early communities in California?

✔ Missions, presidios, and pueblos were some of the early settlements in California.

✔ Locations of settlements were chosen to meet the needs of the settlers.

Vocabulary

settlement p. 182
settler p. 182
presidio p. 185
pueblo p. 186

Focus Skill Sequence

California Standards
HSS 3.2.4, 3.3, 3.3.1

For nearly 200 years, rulers who had claimed land in California in the 1500s mostly ignored that land. American Indians who lived on the land continued to use it. Then, in the late 1700s, King Carlos of Spain learned that more and more Russian fur traders were hunting along the coast. He decided to build settlements in California to protect his claim. A **settlement** is a new community. A person who lives in a settlement is a **settler**.

A Closer Look

Mission Santa Barbara

Mission Santa Barbara was founded in 1786. It is the only California mission to be used continuously since it was founded.

❶ The facade, or front, of the mission was inspired by Roman architecture.

❷ The Sacred Garden was once a working area for American Indians.

❸ Workshops and living spaces were located in surrounding buildings.

❖ What does the Santa Barbara mission show you about what life was like for people in an early California community?

entrance

The Spanish Build Missions

In 1769, King Carlos sent Gaspar de Portolá (pawr•toh•LAH), a government leader, and Father Junípero Serra (hoo•NEE•pay•roh SAIR•rah), a priest, to Alta California. The king told them to find places to build settlements or missions.

A mission was a small religious community with a church, a few workshops, and rooms in which people lived. People at a mission grew crops and raised sheep and cattle.

The Spanish built a total of 21 missions in California. Each was located near the coast. The missions were built in a line, or chain, that stretched 650 miles from San Diego to Sonoma. Each mission was about a day's walk from the next.

Reading Check 🅾 **Sequence**
What happened after King Carlos sent Portolá and Serra to Alta California?

mission church

First Mission at San Diego

▶ Father Junípero Serra

Portolá and Serra built the first mission at San Diego in 1769. It was called San Diego de Alcalá (ahl•kah•LAH). Spanish priests led the mission communities. They taught the Christian religion and other Spanish ways to the Indians. Indians did most of the work on the missions. They grew wheat and corn and raised animals.

Some Indians adapted to life on the missions and stayed by choice. Others were forced to stay and give up their religion, language, and culture. Many Indians died of starvation and bad treatment. Others died from the new diseases the Spanish brought with them.

Reading Check ⚙ **Sequence**
Which of the Spanish missions was the first in California?

▶ Mission San Diego is also known as the Mother of the Missions.

▶ Each year, more than five million people visit the Presidio of San Francisco.

Locate It

CALIFORNIA

San Francisco

Presidios Protect the Missions

In addition to the missions, the Spanish built four presidios (pray•SEE•dee•ohs). A **presidio** was a fort built to protect missions from enemy attacks. The presidios were evenly spaced between the missions. They were located close to the best harbors. The first presidio was built at San Diego in 1769. Others were built at San Francisco, Santa Barbara, and Monterey.

Presidios were government buildings. Most of the people who lived in them were Spanish soldiers and their families. Some lived in log huts. Others lived in adobe (uh•DOH•bee), or mud-brick, houses. A large square wall was built around each presidio.

Reading Check ⚙ **Sequence**
Where was the first presidio built?

Pueblos Built in Alta California

Missions and presidios were two kinds of communities built in California. A third kind of community was a **pueblo** (PWEH•bloh), or village. Pueblos were not started by priests or soldiers. They were started by American Indians and by people from Spain, Mexico, and Africa.

Pueblos usually had adobe houses, churches, and public buildings. People in the pueblos helped supply missions and presidios with food and other goods. The first pueblo was built in 1777, near the present city of San Francisco. It became the town of San Jose. In 1781, settlers built a pueblo near the Los Angeles River. That pueblo grew to become Los Angeles.

Reading Check **Compare and Contrast**
How were pueblos different from missions and presidios?

Cultural Heritage

Olvera Street

In Los Angeles, you can go to Olvera Street and find Mexican food, goods, music, and dancing. Located in one of the oldest parts of the city, Olvera Street has historic buildings, a traditional Mexican-style plaza, and shops that sell Mexican crafts. Some of the buildings along Olvera Street were built when Los Angeles was a pueblo.

Missions, Pueblos, and Presidios

Analyze Maps

◆ **Location Why do you think the missions, presidios, and pueblos were located near the coast?**

Map legend:
- Mission
- Presidio
- Pueblo

Summary Spain built early communities to help keep control of the land it had claimed in California. The three kinds of communities were missions, presidios, and pueblos.

Review

1. Who started the early communities in California?

2. **Vocabulary** How are a mission, a **presidio**, and a **pueblo** related?

3. **Your Community** Do research to find out about the mission, presidio, or pueblo nearest your community. Share your findings.

Critical Thinking

4. **Make It Relevant** Which of California's missions, pueblos, or presidios have you visited?

5. **SKILL** Why do you think American Indians helped people from Spain, Mexico, and Africa start pueblos?

6. **Write a Statement** Write a sentence about each of the three types of early California communities.

7. **Focus Skill** **Sequence** Copy and complete the graphic organizer below.

First → Next → Last
first pueblo built

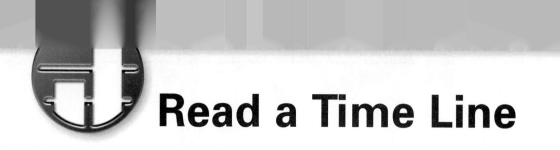

Read a Time Line

❱ Why It Matters

When you learn about the history of a community, you need to be able to follow the events in order. A time line can help you. A **time line** is a drawing that shows when and in what order events took place.

❱ What You Need to Know

You read a horizontal time line from left to right. The events at the left happened first. The events to the right happened later.

As you move from left to right, you follow the events in sequence, or time order.

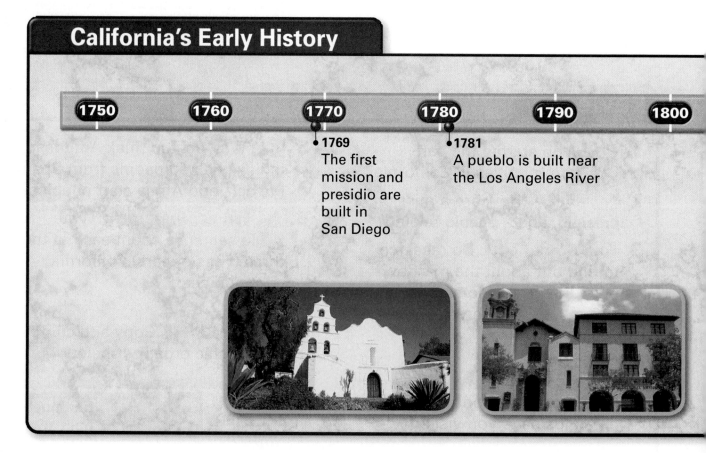

California's Early History

| 1750 | 1760 | 1770 | 1780 | 1790 | 1800 |

1769
The first mission and presidio are built in San Diego

1781
A pueblo is built near the Los Angeles River

❱ Practice the Skill

Use the time line to help you answer these questions.

1 When were the first mission and presidio built?

2 Was a pueblo built near the Los Angeles River before or after Fort Ross was built?

3 How many years passed between the discovery of gold and the time California became a state?

❱ Apply What You Learned

ANALYSIS SKILL Make It Relevant Gather information and dates that tell about your community. Make a time line of important events that happened in your community. Show in what order the events happened.

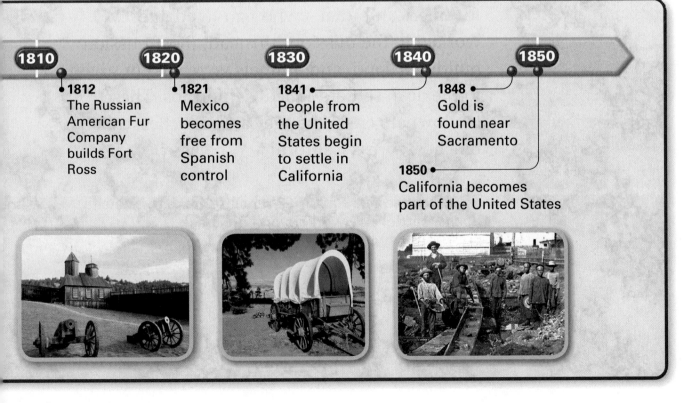

1810

1812
The Russian American Fur Company builds Fort Ross

1820

1821
Mexico becomes free from Spanish control

1830

1841
People from the United States begin to settle in California

1840

1848
Gold is found near Sacramento

1850
California becomes part of the United States

1850

Chart and Graph Skills

Communities Change

What to Know

What was life like in the early communities of California?

✔ Many people lived on ranchos in the early 1800s.

✔ Many pioneers from the United States settled communities in California.

Vocabulary
ranchero p. 191
pioneer p. 192

Focus Skill Sequence

California Standards
HSS 3.2.4, 3.3, 3.3.1

In the early 1800s, people in Mexico declared that they should be free from Spanish control. Their fight for freedom lasted until 1821. California was so far from the rest of Mexico that when independence came, most Californians did not hear the news for another year!

Mexican Ranchos

After Mexico became independent, Mexican leaders decided to close the Spanish missions. Much of the property was supposed to go to American Indians who had lived and worked at the missions. Instead, most mission buildings, land, and animals were sold or given to Mexican settlers called Californios. These landowners created huge cattle ranches, called ranchos, across California.

▶ **This scene of a California rancho shows the rancho house, cattle, and workers on horseback.**

▶ Ranchero Antonio Coronel (center) celebrates on his rancho.

Each rancho was owned by one person or a family. A man who owned a rancho was called a **ranchero**. Rancheros traded cowhides and tallow for goods from the United States. The hides were used to make leather saddles, shoes, and other products. Tallow, which came from cow fat, was used to make soap and candles.

American Indians did most of the work on ranchos. They received food, clothing, and a place to live, but no money. Indian women cooked and cleaned. Indian men farmed and worked as cowhands, or vaqueros (vah•KAY•rohs).

Reading Check ☼ **Sequence**
Which came first, the closing of the missions or Mexico's independence from Spain?

New Arrivals

People in the United States became interested in California. In 1826, Jedediah Strong Smith led a group of men into California. Smith helped open the way for other pioneers to follow. A **pioneer** is a person who helps settle a new land.

Explorer John C. Frémont drew maps of the Oregon Trail in an area north of California. This trail became an important route for pioneers. Frémont also played a role in the 1846 war between Mexico and the United States. In the end, Mexico gave up more than half of its land, including California.

Routes to California

Pacific Ocean

San Francisco

Monterey

Sierra Nevada

Los Angeles

San Diego

N W E S

Map Legend
——— Jedediah Strong Smith's first expedition
– – – Jedediah Strong Smith's second expedition
········ John C. Frémont's early expeditions

ANALYSIS SKILL **Analyze Maps**
⊘ Human-Environment Interactions Why do you think California pioneers chose the routes they did?

In 1848, a worker named James Marshall found gold near what is today Sacramento. Many people rushed to California, hoping to get rich. Some sailed from the eastern United States all the way around South America. Others traveled in covered wagons along the Oregon Trail and other land routes. Many died of disease or starvation on the 2,000-mile trip.

Gold seekers came from other places, too, including Mexico, Chile, Peru, China, France, and Hawaii. Boomtowns—towns that grew very fast—sprang up wherever there was gold nearby. Some disappeared as soon as the gold ran out. Others, including Sacramento and Stockton, kept growing. San Francisco was the biggest boomtown of all. From 1848 to 1849, its population grew from 800 to 25,000 people!

Reading Check **Summarize**
Why did people come from around the world to California in 1848 and 1849?

❱ People traveled to California and other western states in wagon trains.

Statehood for California

The gold rush brought so many changes that California needed new laws and a new kind of government. The United States was too far away to control California.

California leaders met at Monterey in 1849 and wrote their own state constitution. They drew California's official eastern boundary line. On September 9, 1850, President Millard Fillmore signed the bill that made California the thirty-first state. September 9 is still celebrated as Admission Day in California.

Reading Check **Summarize**
What happened to California on September 9, 1850?

Children in History

Pioneer Children

Life on the trail was hard for young pioneers. Many children could not wear shoes because their feet were swollen from walking so much. However, pioneer children found simple ways to have fun. They chased butterflies and grasshoppers. They went swimming. Games included I-spy, hide-and-seek, leapfrog, and jump rope. Pioneer children also read books at night by the light of a lantern.

Sweets were not very common. Eight-year-old Kate McDaniel wrote in her diary about cookies, "We would take a bite and nibble like mice. We would try to make them last as long as possible."

▶ **Californians celebrated becoming a state at gatherings like this one in San Francisco in 1850.**

Summary In the 1800s, communities in California began to grow when Mexico began giving away or selling land and cattle for ranchos. After gold was discovered in California in 1848, more people moved there. In 1850, California became a state.

Review

1. What was life like in the early communities of California?

2. **Vocabulary** What is the difference between a **pioneer** and a **ranchero**?

3. **Your Community** What sources in your community can help you do research about ranchos near you?

Critical Thinking

4. **Make It Relevant** Why did your family come to California?

5. **ANALYSIS SKILL** Which do you think would have been better—life as a ranchero or life as a pioneer?

6. **Write a Paragraph** Do research to write a paragraph describing one cultural tradition that newcomers to California brought with them.

7. **Focus Skill Sequence** Copy and complete the graphic organizer below.

First → Next → Last became a state

Use a Line Graph

❯ Why It Matters

Using a **line graph** can help you see patterns in information over time. You can use a line graph to see how population changes as time passes.

❯ What You Need to Know

To make a line graph, mark points on a grid. Then connect the points with lines. The diagram below shows the basic parts of a line graph.

How to Read a Line Graph

A horizontal direction (across)

B vertical direction (up and down)

C dots that mark the points for the information

D lines that show the change from one dot to the next

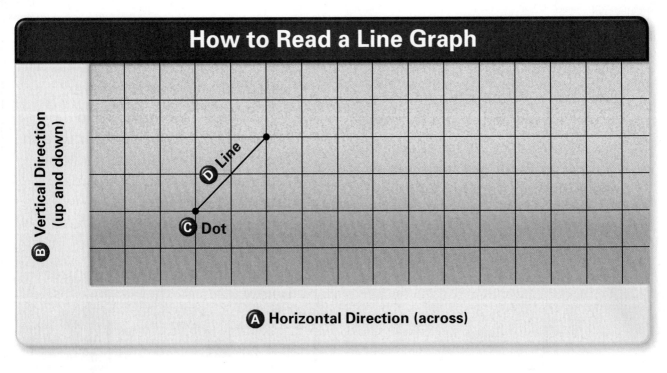

How to Read a Line Graph

B Vertical Direction (up and down)

D Line

C Dot

A Horizontal Direction (across)

❱ Practice the Skill

The line graph below shows how San Francisco's population changed from 1850 to 1900. Use the line graph to answer these questions.

1 What information is shown in the vertical direction?

2 What information is shown in the horizontal direction?

3 Between what years was the biggest change in population?

❱ Apply What You Learned

Make It Relevant Work in a small group to create a line graph that shows the number of students at your school over the past five years. Show the number of students who went to your school one year ago, two years ago, three years ago, and so on.

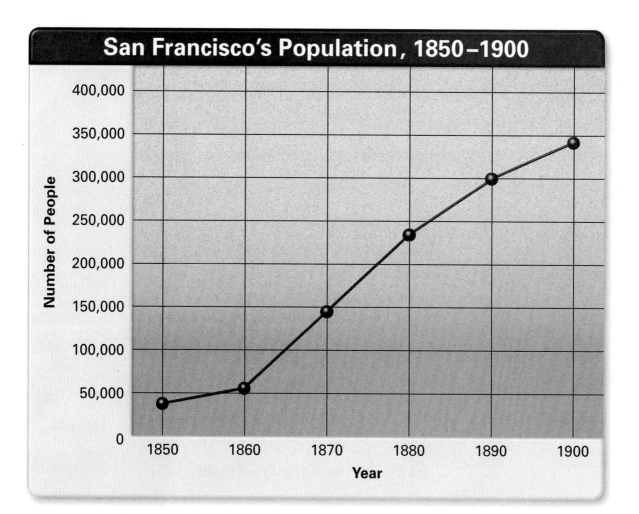

San Francisco's Population, 1850–1900

Chart and Graph Skills

Trustworthiness
Respect
Responsibility
Fairness
Caring
Patriotism

Julia Morgan

"My buildings will speak for themselves."*

Why Character Counts

❓ **How did Julia Morgan design buildings in a responsible way?**

When Julia Morgan was born in 1872, women did not become architects. Most did not even graduate from high school. None of that stopped Julia Morgan. She attended the University of California at Berkeley and studied civil engineering. She learned how to build roads and bridges. This knowledge helped her design good buildings.

During her senior year at the university, she began to study with a local architect. He told Morgan about a great school of architecture in France. He said the school might soon allow women to study there. Morgan decided to go to the school.

After Morgan graduated and became an architect, she moved back to California. Soon, Morgan opened her own architecture office.

Julia Morgan as a young woman

* Julia Morgan. *Artnews 80 magazine*, January 1981.

William Randolph Hearst and Julia Morgan in 1926.

Hearst Castle

She helped rebuild a famous hotel called the Fairmont. It had been damaged in the 1906 San Francisco earthquake. Morgan's civil engineering training helped. She knew how to design strong buildings.

In all her work, Morgan was responsible. She designed buildings that fit the needs of the people who would use the buildings. She wanted her buildings to look as if they belonged on the land where they were built.

Morgan's biggest job was for William Randolph Hearst. He was a rich newspaper publisher who wanted a castle. Morgan designed Hearst Castle with 115 rooms. People can tour Hearst Castle today.

Morgan designed many other houses and buildings. People knew she was responsible and took her job seriously.

A medal awarded to Morgan while she was a student

GO ONLINE Visit MULTIMEDIA BIOGRAPHIES at www.harcourtschool.com/hss

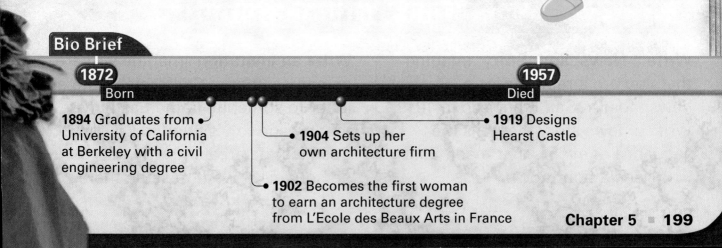

Bio Brief

1872 Born

1957 Died

1894 Graduates from University of California at Berkeley with a civil engineering degree

1904 Sets up her own architecture firm

1919 Designs Hearst Castle

1902 Becomes the first woman to earn an architecture degree from L'Ecole des Beaux Arts in France

Reading Social Studies

Sequence is the order in which events happen.

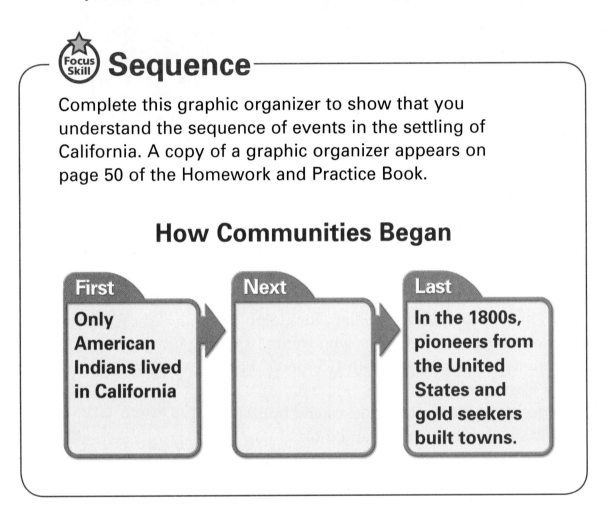

Sequence

Focus Skill

Complete this graphic organizer to show that you understand the sequence of events in the settling of California. A copy of a graphic organizer appears on page 50 of the Homework and Practice Book.

How Communities Began

First

Only American Indians lived in California

Next

Last

In the 1800s, pioneers from the United States and gold seekers built towns.

✏ California Writing Prompts

Write a Newspaper Story Imagine that you are a reporter for a newspaper in San Francisco in 1849. Write a news story that tells the sequence of events that made San Francisco a boomtown.

Write an Invitation Imagine you are an early settler in California. Write a letter to someone in the East. Invite that person to visit you in California. Describe the area and why the person might want to settle there.

Use Vocabulary

Write the word that correctly matches each definition.

1. a journey by water

   explorer, p. 174   **voyage,** p. 175

2. a narrow water passage that connects two bodies of water

   strait, p. 175   **harbor,** p. 178

3. a fort built to protect the missions from enemy attacks

   settlement, p. 182   **presidio,** p. 185

4. a village started by American Indians and people from Mexico, Spain, and Africa

   settlement, p. 182   **pueblo,** p. 186

5. a man who owned a huge cattle ranch in California

   ranchero, p. 191   **pioneer,** p. 192

Apply Skills

Follow Routes on a Map Use the map on page 181 to answer the question.

6. **ANALYSIS SKILL** Choose one of the routes taken by an explorer. Explain how it is different from the routes of the other explorers.

Recall Facts

Answer the questions.

7. What are three reasons European kings and queens sent explorers on voyages?

8. Who came to California in the 1700s to find places to hunt animals for their fur?

Write the letter of the best choice.

9. Which explorer was the first to land in Alta California?
   A Hernando Cortés
   B Francis Drake
   C Juan Rodríguez Cabrillo
   D Sebastián Vizcaíno

10. How long did it take to walk from one of California's missions to another?
    A about a month
    B about a week
    C about an hour
    D about a day

Think Critically

11. If you had lived in the United States in 1849, would you have come to California in search of gold? Why or why not?

Study Skills

WRITE TO LEARN

Writing about what you read can help you understand and remember information.

▶ **Many students write about their reading in learning logs. The writing in a learning log can be both creative and personal.**

▶ **Writing about the text leads you to think about it.**

▶ **Writing your reactions to the text makes it more meaningful to you.**

Building Communities

What I Learned	My Response
Many people came to California and made money from something other than gold. People developed new ways to travel and communicate.	This probably caused existing communities to grow. New communities also began.

Apply As You Read

As you read the chapter, pay attention to new and important information. Keep track of the information by completing a learning log for each lesson.

California History-Social Science Standards, Grade 3

3.3 Students draw from historical and community resources to organize the sequence of local historical events and describe how each period of settlement left its mark on the land.

Building Communities

Plaza Park in San Jose, California

Rachel's Journal

by Marissa Moss

In this story, set in 1850, ten-year-old Rachel and her family pack up their belongings and head west. They travel in a covered wagon going from Illinois to California. Read now what Rachel writes in her journal about their travels.

March 10, 1850

I have never had my own book to write in, but I have one now, and my own pen, too. Grandfather gave them to me. He says it is my task to <u>chronicle</u> our long journey and write letters back to the States.

chronicle
record

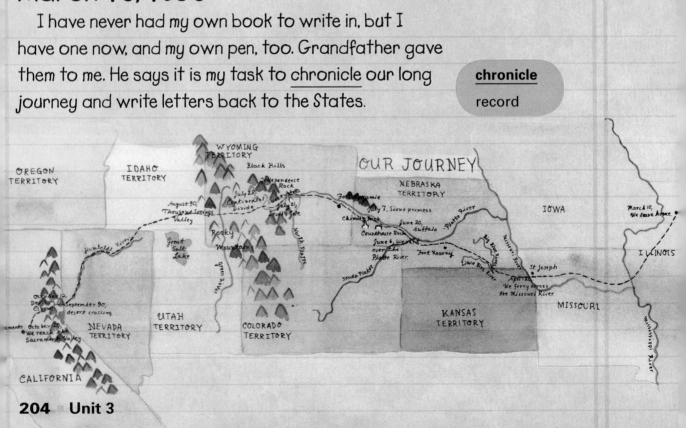

Grandmother and Grandfather were crying buckets. Pa joked that you would think we were going to the ends of the earth instead of to California. Mother said we are going so far from our home in Illinois, it may as well be to the ends of the earth. I wonder what is at the edge. Pa insists it is good earth, rich farmland and heaps of it, all for the taking, so long as we settle. Uncle Pete has written us so many letters about California, where the turnips grow as big as pumpkins and potatoes are the size of melons. I cannot wait to see for myself.

Pa had this picture taken before we left. Ben is 15 here, Will is 12, and I, Rachel, just turned 10.

I am holding my cat, Biscuit, but Pa said I could not take her with us, so I left her with my close friend, Millie Fremont. We will need a good mouser in California, but Pa said no.

our provisions

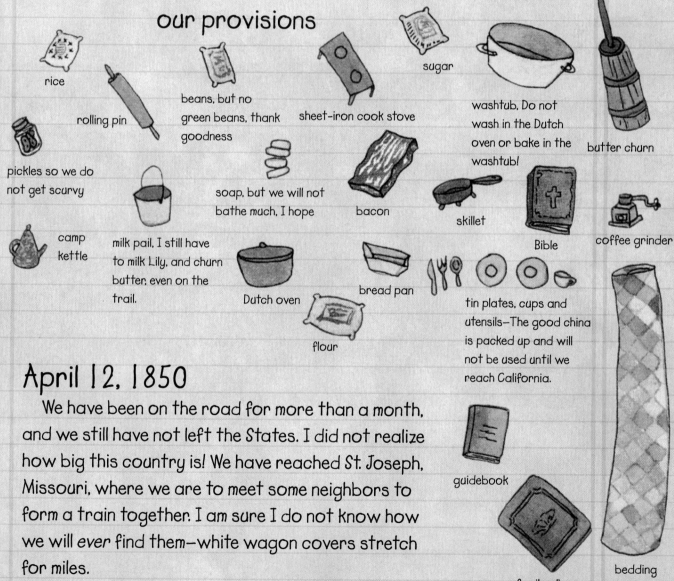

rice

rolling pin

beans, but no green beans, thank goodness

sheet-iron cook stove

sugar

washtub, Do not wash in the Dutch oven or bake in the washtub!

butter churn

pickles so we do not get scurvy

soap, but we will not bathe much, I hope

bacon

skillet

Bible

coffee grinder

camp kettle

milk pail, I still have to milk Lily, and churn butter, even on the trail.

Dutch oven

bread pan

tin plates, cups and utensils—The good china is packed up and will not be used until we reach California.

flour

guidebook

bedding

family album

April 12, 1850

We have been on the road for more than a month, and we still have not left the States. I did not realize how big this country is! We have reached St. Joseph, Missouri, where we are to meet some neighbors to form a train together. I am sure I do not know how we will *ever* find them—white wagon covers stretch for miles.

May 10, 1850

Pa says we are taking the Oregon Trail until it splits and we veer south for California. Now we are following the Platte River. The sight of the broad river and the bluffs is restful, but the dust kicked up by all the <u>stock</u> is not. But I found a way to escape the heat and dirt of the main road. All along the trail there are narrow cut-off paths. These cut-offs run diagonally to the road and are often by shady creeks so they are pleasant to walk along. I take the younger children with me, and we have great fun, picking berries and wildflowers and wading in the creeks.

These berries were a little sour.

stock
oxen, cattle, horses

These berries were sour if you ate them when they were red, but delicious if you ate them when they were black.

August 25, 1850

We passed where the Oregon Trail splits, Pa says. The right fork leads to Oregon, the left to California. We took the left, and it has been rocky ever since.

September 7, 1850

We follow the Humboldt River now and can see in the distance the tops of the Sierra Nevada Mountains, white with snow already, to our dismay. The oxen are thin and tired and our <u>provisions</u> low. We have passed small trading posts, but the prices are too high for us. Anyway, we will soon be in California. Only a little farther to go.

provisions
supplies

My thank-you to Vigor and Valor for getting all the wagons down—I gave them a handful of precious salt. They surely earned it.

October 3, 1850

We topped the next rise and were at the <u>summit</u>!
Before us lay the Sacramento Valley. We are in
California now. The worst is over. Unless it snows.

<u>summit</u>
top

I cannot recall how it feels to be inside a house anymore.
We passed a schoolhouse—oh, dear, we are back in civilization.

California,
the United
States of
America

October 23, 1850

This morning we woke up early. The
guidebook showed that there were only a
dozen or so miles ahead, and no one wanted
to sleep. We descended the last stretch of
8 miles. The road is smooth and level, dotted
with farms and homesteads. We are finally,
safely here!

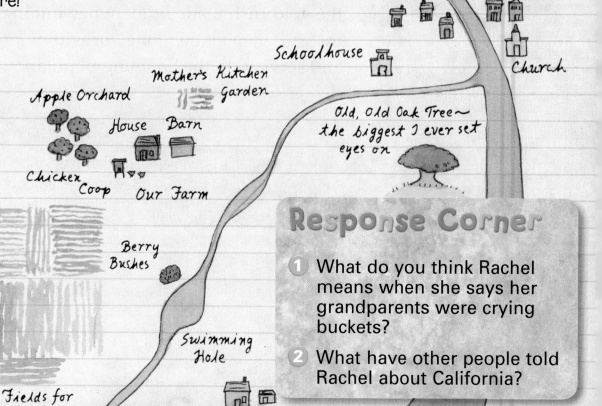

Mr. Bridger's
House

Sacramento

Schoolhouse

Mother's Kitchen
Garden

Apple Orchard

Old, Old Oak Tree—
the biggest I ever set
eyes on

House   Barn

Church

Chicken
Coop   Our Farm

Berry
Bushes

Swimming
Hole

Fields for
Crops

The Elias Farm

Response Corner

1. What do you think Rachel
   means when she says her
   grandparents were crying
   buckets?

2. What have other people told
   Rachel about California?

① Communities Grow

How did California change during and after the gold rush?

✔ Many people came to California and made money from something other than gold.

✔ People developed new ways to travel and communicate.

Vocabulary
entrepreneur p. 209
communication p. 210
transcontinental
   p. 210
immigrant p. 211
invention p. 212
port p. 213

 Focus Skill Sequence

🐻 California Standards
HSS 3.3, 3.3.1, 3.3.2

During the gold rush, many thousands of people poured into California. Most of them saw little gold, if any at all. Instead, new Californians found new ways to earn a living. New ways of traveling and sharing information soon followed.

Growing with the Gold Rush

Many people who came to California with the gold rush made little money mining gold. Instead, they made money providing products and services to the booming population.

⚡ *Fast Fact*

The camp at Auburn Ravine was a good "jumping off" spot for miners. It was centrally located and just a wagon ride from Sacramento.

▶ A gold rush miner at Auburn Ravine, 1852

In 1850, Levi Strauss came to San Francisco to sell goods to miners. Strauss had special pants made, first out of canvas tent cloth, then out of strong denim. He sold the pants, called waist overalls, to gold miners. Levi Strauss was an entrepreneur (ahn•truh•pruh•NER). An **entrepreneur** is someone who starts and runs a business. People still wear these pants today. They are called blue jeans.

Domingo Ghirardelli was another gold rush entrepreneur. He tried to start many businesses before he finally turned to the business he learned from his father, the making of chocolate candy. Ghirardelli chocolate is still a success today.

❯ Levi Strauss

Reading Check ❂Sequence
What did many people do after they found they could not make money mining gold?

❯ After the gold rush, people continued to move to San Francisco. The city offered jobs and new ways to make money.

The Railroad

The distance between California and the rest of the United States often made communication difficult. **Communication** is the sharing of information. In 1861, telegraph wires connected California with the East. Telegraph lines improved communication with California, but Californians still needed a way to move people and goods into and out of the state.

Theodore Judah, an engineer and entrepreneur, had an idea. He wanted to build a transcontinental railroad. The word **transcontinental** describes something that goes across the continent.

> ❯ **Railroad ticket from Omaha, Nebraska, to San Francisco**

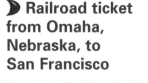

> ❯ **Chinese laborers at work on the transcontinental railroad near Sacramento**

▶ Theodore Judah

Judah got support from four Sacramento men who had made money during the gold rush. These men became known as the "Big Four." They helped Judah start the Central Pacific Railroad Company.

Work on the project began near Sacramento in 1863. Immigrants came to California from many places, especially China, to build the railroad. An **immigrant** is someone who comes to live in a country from somewhere else in the world.

Central Pacific workers laid tracks heading east. At the same time, Union Pacific workers laid tracks heading west. The tracks met in Utah in 1869.

The railroad brought many changes to California. People flooded into the state. Businesses grew quickly. Cities like Sacramento and Stockton became big transportation centers. Other communities grew near railroad lines. Thousands of the Chinese who helped build the railroad stayed in California and started businesses.

▶ Chinese railroad workers started businesses, like this grocery in San Francisco.

Reading Check **Main Idea and Details**
How did the railroad change California's economy?

Los Angeles Grows

By 1870, trains brought people and goods into Sacramento. From there, goods went to San Francisco in boats along the Sacramento River. In 1876, a railroad connected San Francisco and Los Angeles. Another soon linked Los Angeles directly with the Middle West. Railroad tickets from the Middle West to Los Angeles sold for as little as one dollar.

People came to California by the trainload to buy cheap land. Many used the land to grow citrus fruits, such as oranges and lemons. These crops were shipped by train to be sold in the East. This was possible because in the late 1800s, an invention made it possible to use ice to chill, or refrigerate, railroad cars. An **invention** is something that has been made for the first time. Refrigerated railroad cars made it possible for farmers to send oranges and other fresh fruits and vegetables to the East.

❯ Citrus workers in Orange, California, pack fruit for shipping.

As Los Angeles grew, leaders decided their city needed a bigger port. A **port** is a place for ships to dock and pick up goods or passengers. Work on the new port began in 1899. The town of San Pedro became part of Los Angeles. At the old San Pedro port, waterways were made deeper and wider for bigger ships. New docks were added. The Port of Los Angeles soon became the busiest on the West coast.

Reading Check **Cause and Effect**
How did building the Port of Los Angeles affect Los Angeles?

▶ **Port of Los Angeles, 1916**

Summary The gold rush and the years that followed brought many changes to California. Those changes included new people, new businesses, and new ways to travel and communicate.

Review

1. How did California change during and after the gold rush?

2. **Vocabulary** How did **entrepreneurs** change life in California?

3. **Your Community** What has made your community grow?

Critical Thinking

4. **Make It Relevant** Have you ever traveled outside California? How did you get there?

5. **SKILL** Why do you think people took risks to build the railroad?

6. **Make a Map** Make a map of California that shows towns that grew because of the gold rush or the railroads.

7. **Sequence** Copy and complete the graphic organizer below.

First
gold rush → Next → Last

Read a Population Map

❱ Why It Matters

As communities change and grow, populations change and grow. People are not spread out evenly on Earth. Many people live in large cities. Others live in small communities. A population map can show you where people live.

❱ What You Need to Know

Different areas have different population densities (DEN•suh•teez). **Population density** is the number of people living in an area of a certain size, usually 1 square mile. A square mile is a square piece of land that is 1 mile wide and 1 mile long.

Population density affects the way people live. In places where 10 people live on each square mile of land, the population density is 10 people per square mile. Where 100 people live on each square mile, the population density is 100 people per square mile. The land there is more crowded.

❱ Practice the Skill

The map on page 215 shows population density in California today. Use it to answer these questions.

1 The map legend shows four population densities. What color is used to show the lowest population density?

2 Find Sacramento. It has a population density of more than 500 people per square mile. How do you think this affects people living there?

3 Why do you think the population density along the state's eastern border is low?

❱ Apply What You Learned

ANALYSIS SKILL Look in an almanac to find a population map of a state that borders California. Where is the population density highest in that state? Where is it the lowest?

 Practice your map and globe skills with the **GeoSkills CD-ROM**.

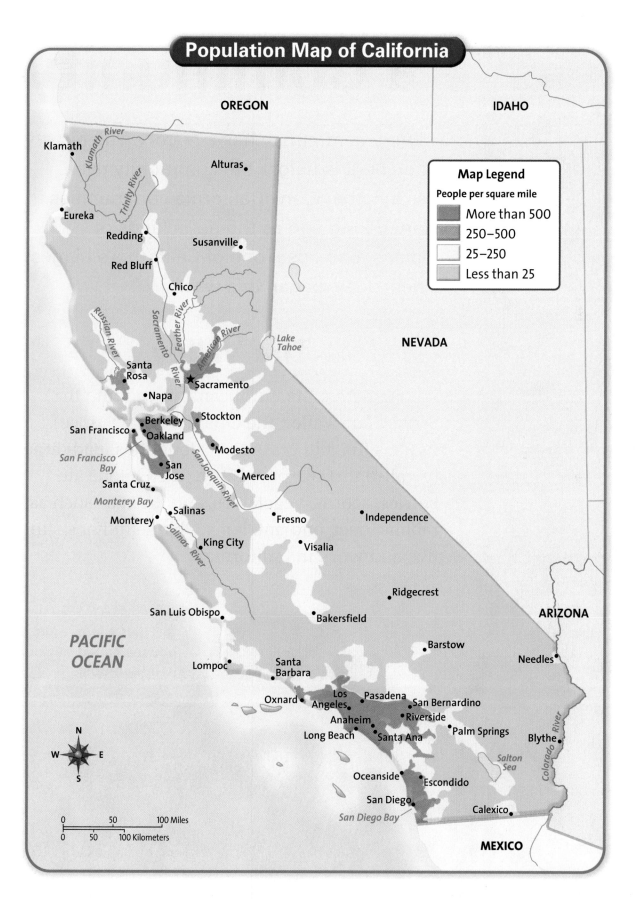

Population Map of California

OREGON

IDAHO

Klamath

Alturas

Eureka

Redding

Susanville

Red Bluff

Chico

Santa Rosa

Sacramento

Napa

Berkeley

Stockton

San Francisco

Oakland

Modesto

San Francisco Bay

San Jose

Merced

Santa Cruz

Monterey Bay

Salinas

Monterey

Fresno

Independence

King City

Visalia

San Luis Obispo

Ridgecrest

Bakersfield

PACIFIC OCEAN

Barstow

Lompoc

Santa Barbara

Needles

Oxnard

Los Angeles

Pasadena

San Bernardino

Anaheim

Riverside

Long Beach

Santa Ana

Palm Springs

Blythe

Oceanside

Escondido

San Diego

Calexico

San Diego Bay

Salton Sea

ARIZONA

NEVADA

Lake Tahoe

Klamath River

Trinity River

Russian River

Sacramento River

Feather River

American River

San Joaquin River

Salinas River

Colorado River

Map Legend

People per square mile

- More than 500
- 250–500
- 25–250
- Less than 25

N W E S

0 50 100 Miles

0 50 100 Kilometers

MEXICO

The Story of a Community

What to Know

How has San Jose grown and changed?

✔ The Pueblo de San Jose de Guadalupe was started in the Santa Clara Valley.

✔ Fruit processing became an important industry to San Jose.

✔ Today, the area around San Jose is known as Silicon Valley.

Vocabulary

public property p. 217
private property p. 217
industry p. 219
technology p. 220

 Sequence

California Standards
HSS 3.3, 3.3.1, 3.3.2, 3.3.3

Every community has a history. The history often begins before the community even has a name. Many California communities started long ago as the homelands of Indians. San Jose, one of California's biggest cities today, began this way.

The Valley

Long before the Europeans moved into the Santa Clara Valley, the Ohlone (oh•LOH•nee) Indians lived in grass huts along the Guadalupe (gwah•dah•LOO•pay) River. The Ohlone ate berries, acorns, vegetables, and animals such as rabbits, deer, and antelope. Ohlone Indians still live and work in California.

▶ The Ohlone built houses called wickiups (wih•kee•ups).

The Peralta Adobe is the last remaining building of the Pueblo de San Jose.

In the 1700s, the Spanish came to the Santa Clara Valley. They found that the land was good for farming and for grazing cattle. In 1777, Jose Joaquin Moraga started a farming community along the Guadalupe River called the Pueblo de San Jose de Guadalupe. Moraga's settlement provided wheat, vegetables, and cattle to nearby presidios.

Much of daily life took place in the pueblo's central plaza. It was surrounded by the council house, church, storerooms, and other public property. **Public property** is property used by all the people and not just by a small group or family. People of the pueblo lived in houses made of adobe or wood. Their homes were **private property**, or property that belongs to one person, family, or group of people. Businesses and farms are other examples of private property.

Reading Check ᔕ **Sequence**
Who lived in San Jose first?

Original map of the Pueblo de San Jose

The City of San Jose

▶ The train depot in San Jose, California

Between 1846 and 1849, the population in the Santa Clara Valley boomed. During this time, gold was discovered in the Sierra Nevada. Thousands of people came to California looking for gold. Few found it, but many stayed in the Santa Clara Valley to do business and later to farm.

By 1850, San Jose was a busy trading center. Its population had increased to 4,000. On March 27, 1850, San Jose became the first official city in California. For one year, it was the capital of California. San Jose saw many changes during the 1860s. Streets were improved, and a streetcar line was built. A courthouse and hotels were added. A railroad between San Jose and San Francisco was completed in 1864.

▶ This sign told about the products of the San Jose Fruit Packing Company in the late 1800s. By 1945, the fruit industry in San Jose was using machines to help speed the work.

The trade of farm products greatly increased when the railroad reached San Jose. Fruits, such as plums, grapes, and apricots, could then be shipped easily to San Francisco. The Santa Clara Valley soon became known as a fruit-growing region. By 1876, San Jose was the fruit-shipping capital of California. Many businesses in the area processed, or prepared, the fruit to ship and sell. The business of processing fruit grew into an **industry**—a type of business.

▶ At this packing plant, fruit is prepared for market.

Reading Check **Cause and Effect**
What happened to help the fruit-growing business?

Geography

Santa Clara Valley

The city of San Jose is the largest city within the Santa Clara Valley, located in west-central California. The Santa Clara Valley lies between the Santa Cruz Mountains on the west and the Diablo Range on the east. The area, with its rich soil, came to be known as "The Valley of Heart's Delight." This was because of the huge numbers of fruits and vegetables that were grown and processed here and the beauty of the valley and the fruit orchards.

The Silicon Valley

▶ Frederick Terman (right) helped start an industrial park that became the center of Silicon Valley.

Until the 1940s, most of San Jose's industries had something to do with fruit products. However, after World War II, a big change took place. More than 500,000 military people were brought into northern California during World War II. After the war, most stayed.

Large businesses moved into the area to build parts for spacecraft and computers. The area became a center for new technology. **Technology** is the inventions people use every day. So many computer companies moved into the area that it was nicknamed Silicon Valley. Silicon is a material used to build computer parts. By 1980, San Jose's population had grown to more than 600,000 people.

Today, San Jose is the third-largest city in California. Computer chip, software, and equipment companies occupy the land that used to be covered with orchards of fruit trees.

▶ This same area after 1973 was home to computer companies.

▶ Leonard family orchards in Cupertino, around 1935

Silicon Valley companies brought new groups of people from around the world to become part of the San Jose community. Immigrants from Vietnam, India, Taiwan, and many other places continue to come to San Jose to work in Silicon Valley. San Jose is one of the fastest-growing cities in the United States. Its population is now almost 1 million people.

Reading Check ö**Sequence**
What industries were started in San Jose after the fruit-processing industry?

Summary San Jose grew from a small farming community to one of the largest cities in the state of California. The area that was once home to many fruit orchards is now home to many technology companies.

❱ **Overhead view of downtown San Jose**

Review

1. 💡 How has San Jose grown and changed?

2. **Vocabulary** Explain the difference between **public property** and **private property**.

3. **Your Community** What industry or industries are most important to the area in which you live?

Critical Thinking

4. **Make It Relevant** How far is San Jose from where you live? If you wanted to visit San Jose, about how long would it take to get there?

5. **ANALYSIS SKILL** Why do you think so many people have moved to San Jose?

6. ✏ **Make a Travel Brochure** Make a travel brochure about your community. Your brochure should tell its history and why it would be a good place to visit.

7. (Focus Skill) **Sequence** On a separate sheet of paper, copy and complete the graphic organizer below.

First
The Ohlone

Next

Last

A History Museum

Imagine that you have been asked to write the history of your community. How should you begin? First, think of yourself as a historian. José Pantoja has a special interest in history. He uses primary sources in museums to form a picture of what life was like long ago.

Primary Source

Primary sources are records made by people who saw or took part in an event. Perhaps the people told their story in a newspaper or wrote it in their journals. They may have taken a photograph or painted a picture.

This document from San Jose is a primary source.

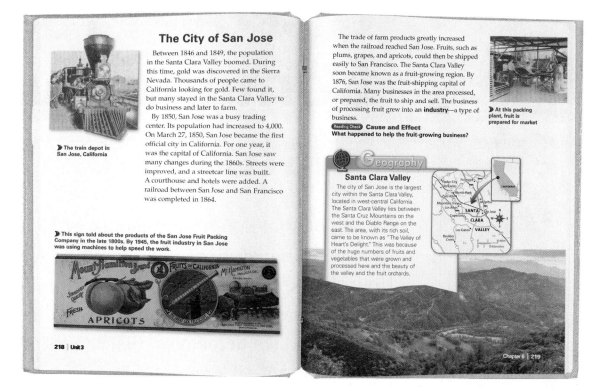

> This textbook is a secondary source.

Secondary Source

Pantoja also uses information from primary sources to write reports. His reports then become a secondary source. A **secondary source** is written by someone who was not there when an event took place.

ANALYSIS SKILL Analyze the Primary Source

1. Why do you think historians are interested in both pictures and writings from the past?

2. How can primary and secondary sources be combined to describe the history of a place?

GO ONLINE Visit PRIMARY SOURCES at www.harcourtschool.com/hss

3

Discover Your Community's History

What to Know

What are some ways to find out about a community's history?

✓ Discover how talking to people and visiting special places can help you find out about your community's history.

Vocabulary

reference works p. 225
heritage p. 226
ancestor p. 226
historic site p. 228
historical society p. 230

Focus Skill **Sequence**

California Standards
HSS 3.3, 3.3.3

Imagine that you have been asked to discover the history of your community. How should you begin? First, think of yourself as a historian. Historians are history detectives. Like detectives, historians look for facts about all kinds of things, from the biggest events to the smallest details. Historians make notes about each discovery. Then they put all the information together to form a picture of what life was like in a community.

❯ Students study old community photographs.

◗ The library has many resources that you can use to do your research.

Become a Historian

As you explore your community's history, you will study the people, places, and events that have shaped life there. You will learn what life was like when American Indians lived in or near what is now your community. You will also learn when the first Europeans settled the area and how people lived during different times in California's history.

To discover the history of your community, start at your local library. The library has many **reference works**, or sources of facts. Ask a librarian to help you find what you need. Take notes when you find something useful at the library.

Reading Check ☼ **Sequence**
Where is the first place to start exploring your community's history?

Interview Someone in Your Community

Asking people questions, or interviewing, is a good way to learn about the history of your community. There are many people you can interview. For example, if you want to know what life was like long ago, you can interview one of your grandparents or an older member of your community. An older person can also teach you about your heritage. **Heritage** is a set of values and customs handed down from people who lived in the past. A grandparent may also be able to tell you about your ancestors. An **ancestor** is someone in a person's family who lived a long time ago. Some people have family members that have lived in their community for generations.

▶ **These students are interviewing a person from their community, San Diego, California.**

Plan the Interview

- Write to or call the person to ask for an interview. Tell the person who you are and why you would like to interview him or her.
- Ask the person to set a time and place to meet.

Before the Interview

- Find out as much as you can about your topic and the person you will be interviewing.
- Make a list of questions to ask.

During the Interview

- Listen carefully. Do not interrupt the person.
- Take notes as you talk with the person. Write down some of his or her exact words.
- If you want to use a tape recorder or a video camera, first ask the person if you may do so.

After the Interview

- Before you leave, thank the person.
- Follow up by writing a thank-you note.

Reading Check ☼ **Sequence**
What should you do after you interview someone?

Find Photographs and Maps of Your Community

Looking at photographs and maps from different years can help you see changes in your community. You can find photographs and maps at libraries, museums, and historic sites. A **historic site** is a place that is important in history. Here are two photographs of a community in California. What changes do you see in the community?

▶ Powell Street in San Francisco in 1866

Long Ago

Today

▶ Powell Street in San Francisco today

These maps show a community in California that has grown. What things on the two maps have changed? What things have stayed the same?

Reading Check Ŏ**Sequence**
What can you learn from studying maps and photographs of your community?

▶ San Francisco today

Today

Welcome to *San Francisco*

▶ San Francisco around 1900

Long Ago

THE CITY OF SAN FRANCISCO.
BIRDS EYE VIEW FROM THE BAY LOOKING SOUTH-WEST.

Write to or Visit Special Places

To get more information about the history of your community, you can write to or visit historic sites, museums, and historical societies. A **historical society** is an organization of people who are interested in the history of their community. Historical societies and museums usually have old photographs, books, maps, diaries, newspapers, and artifacts that give information about the past.

How to Write for Information

You can write a letter to ask for information about the history of your community. When you write, be sure to do these things.

- Write neatly or use a computer.
- Tell who you are and why you are writing.
- Tell exactly what you want to know.

▶ California Historical Society in San Francisco

How to Ask Questions During a Visit

If you have a chance to visit a museum, historical society, or historic site, be sure to do these things.

- Take along a list of questions you want to ask.
- Tell who you are and why you are visiting.
- Listen carefully, and take notes.
- Take any folders or booklets of information that the place has for visitors.
- Before you leave, thank anyone who has helped you.

Reading Check ꙮ **Sequence**
What is the first thing you should write in a letter asking for information about your community?

> You may write letters to ask for information about your community's history.

Summary Every community has a history. You can learn about your community by gathering information from people in your community and from special places there.

Review

1. 💡 What are some ways to find out about a community's history?

2. **Vocabulary** What might you find out from a **historical society**?

3. **Your Community** Whom can you ask about the history of your community? What places can you visit?

Critical Thinking

4. **Make It Relevant** What do you know about the history of your community that you could share with another person?

5. **ANALYSIS SKILL** How is your community the same as it was in the past? How is it different?

6. 🖌 **Make a Web Page** Make a web page to show major events and changes that have taken place in your community.

7. **Focus Skill** **Sequence**
On a separate sheet of paper, copy and complete the graphic organizer below.

First: Visit a library. → Next: → Last:

California's Great Wall

People in the United States have always worked to make their communities better. In Los Angeles, some people made their neighborhood better by painting a wall.

The wall along one Los Angeles street was gray and bare. It did not stay that way. During five summers, more than 400 young people came together to paint a story on the wall.

An artist named Judy Baca got the community together. She helped plan the huge mural, or wall painting. The mural would tell the story of the working people who helped make California what it is today.

The young people set to work painting their history. Painting the mural made the young people proud. They were also proud of their history, painted on the wall.

Judy Baca and volunteers

Like these people, people all over the United States work to make communities better. They fix up houses. They work to clean neighborhoods. They build playgrounds and parks. All these are ways people can make their communities better places to live, work, and play.

People painting the Great Wall of Los Angeles

Did You Know?

The Great Wall of Los Angeles is the longest mural in the world. It is one-half mile long. Today, Judy Baca and people in the neighborhood are working to take care of the mural and to make it even longer so that they can tell more of California's story.

Think About It!

Make It Relevant
How could you and your neighbors work to make your community a better place to live?

FOREBEARERS OF CIVIL RIGHTS

Reading Social Studies

Sequence is the order in which events happen.

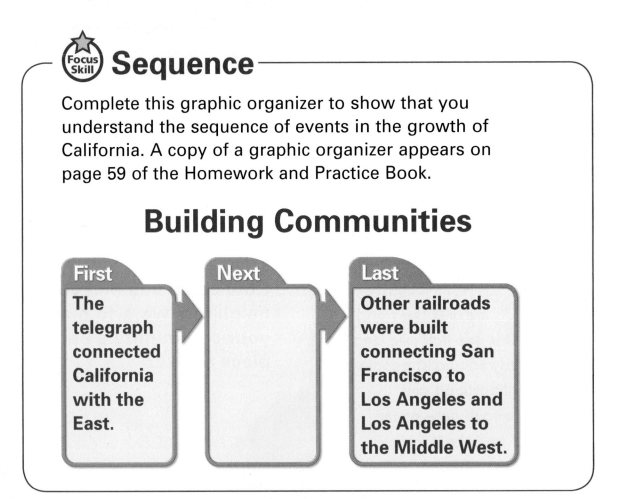

Focus Skill Sequence

Complete this graphic organizer to show that you understand the sequence of events in the growth of California. A copy of a graphic organizer appears on page 59 of the Homework and Practice Book.

Building Communities

First
The telegraph connected California with the East.

Next

Last
Other railroads were built connecting San Francisco to Los Angeles and Los Angeles to the Middle West.

California Writing Prompts

Write a Speech Imagine you are the mayor of a California town in 1861. Telegraph wires have just connected your town to others. Write a speech describing how this invention may affect your town.

Write a Folktale Think about folktales you have heard. Make up a folktale character. Write a tale about how the character may have helped build California into the place it is today.

Use Vocabulary

Write the word or words that complete each sentence.

entrepreneur, p. 209
transcontinental, p. 210
port, p. 213
public property, p. 217
industry, p. 219

1. Kayla's father works in the computer ___.

2. The ___ opened a new toy business.

3. The ___ railroad connected the Pacific coast with the rest of the United States.

4. The state park is ___. Everyone can enjoy it.

5. The ship docked at the ___ to pick up goods and passengers.

Apply Skills

Read a Population Map Use the population map on page 215 to answer the question.

6. **ANALYSIS SKILL** What is the population density of San Diego?

Recall Facts

Answer the questions.

7. Who began selling blue jeans to gold miners?

8. What was the first big industry in San Jose?

Write the letter of the best choice.

9. What enabled people and goods to move easily between California and the rest of the United States in the 1800s?
   A the telegraph
   B telephones
   C trains
   D cars

10. How can you learn about the history of your community?
   A interview a person
   B look at photographs and maps from different years
   C visit a historical society
   D all of the above

Think Critically

11. **ANALYSIS SKILL** Why do you think many companies began doing business in the San Jose area after World War II?

OLD SACRAMENTO

Get Ready

Historic Old Sacramento, overlooking the Sacramento River, gives visitors an exciting look at life in California during the Old West days. The busy district is home to the Discovery Museum of Sacramento's history, the California Military Museum, and the California State Railroad Museum. Take time to visit the monuments, attractions, and variety of shops and restaurants in the historic buildings.

Locate It
California

Sacramento

What to See

The riverboat *Delta King* once carried people and goods between Sacramento and San Francisco. Today, it houses a floating hotel, theater, and a popular restaurant.

Old Sacramento showcases California transportation history, including horse-drawn carriages and the California state Railroad Museum.

SACRAMENTO RAILROAD SOUTHERN

A monument pays tribute to the young riders of the Pony Express.

Rows of wooden desks line Old Sacramento's one-room schoolhouse.

A Virtual Tour

GO ONLINE

Visit VIRTUAL TOURS at www.harcourtschool.com/hss

Review

THE BIG IDEA

History California communities have a long history and have changed greatly over time. From early explorers and settlers to today's workers, every community has a unique story.

Summary   Community History

European explorers came to California's coast in search of riches and to claim land. Spain built missions.

When gold was discovered in 1848, many people came to California, hoping to get rich. Pioneers came to California in search of land. Entrepreneurs began businesses in California. California's history is part of the story of your own community's history.

Main Ideas and Vocabulary

Read the summary above. Then answer the questions that follow.

1. Which country built missions in California?
   A Russia
   B Spain
   C England
   D United States

2. What did entrepreneurs do in California?
   A began businesses
   B opened missions
   C explored California's coast
   D invented the telegraph

3. What did most explorers, gold miners, and pioneers want in California?
   A to have peace and quiet
   B to see the Pacific Ocean
   C to build big churches
   D to get land and riches

Recall Facts

Answer these questions.

4. What explorer claimed the San Francisco area for England?

5. Who did King Carlos send to Alta California?

6. Who started pueblo communities in California?

7. Why did many immigrants come to California?

8. Who started the Pueblo de San Jose?

Write the letter of the best choice.

9. What was the land north of Baja California called?
   A American California
   B Mexican California
   C Spanish California
   D Alta California

10. How many missions did the Spanish build in California?
    A 21
    B 200
    C 2
    D 2,000

11. What do you call someone who studies the past?
    A a pioneer
    B a detective
    C a historian
    D a settler

Think Critically

12. **ANALYSIS SKILL** How might California's history have been different without the transcontinental railroad?

13. **ANALYSIS SKILL** What kinds of primary sources might tell us how California towns got their Spanish names?

Apply Skills

Read a Population Map

ANALYSIS SKILL Use the map below to answer the following questions.

14. What color shows the highest population density?

15. Which city is more densely populated—Oxnard or Riverside?

Population of Los Angeles Area

Map Legend
People per square mile
More than 500
250–500
25–250
Less than 25

PACIFIC OCEAN

Read More

■ *Pioneer Living*, by Susan Ring.

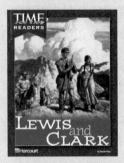

■ *Lewis and Clark*, by Susan Ring.

■ *Cities Yesterday, Today, and Tomorrow*, by Susan Ring.

Show What You Know

Unit Writing Activity

Write a Journal Entry Imagine that you are the explorer Juan Rodríguez Cabrillo. Write a journal entry to describe how Alta California looks when you land there in 1542.

Unit Project

Community History Scrapbook Work with classmates to make a scrapbook of your community's history. Assign each group a place in the community, such as the town hall, the school, or the library. Then collect old and new pictures, and write a report about the history of the place. Compile all the pages to complete the scrapbook.

GO ONLINE Visit ACTIVITIES at www.harcourtschool.com/hss

Government and Citizenship

4

Start with the Standards

3.4 Students understand the role of rules and laws in our daily lives and the basic structure of the U.S. government.

The Big Idea

Government

Communities and nations need laws and leaders to help protect citizens and keep order. Our governments rely on participation from citizens.

What to Know

✓ What rules and laws do people follow in a community?

✓ How is the government of the United States organized and why is a constitution important?

✓ What does local government do for its citizens?

✓ What are the rules and qualities of a good citizen?

Show What You Know

★ Unit 4 Test

✎ Writing: A Letter

✏ Unit Project: A Government Handbook

Government and Citizenship

" People in our
country vote for
their leaders. "

" Good citizens follow
rules and laws."

" Good citizens like to
help other people."

law A rule that people in a community must follow. (page 253)

citizen A person who lives in and belongs to a community. (page 254)

elect   To vote for, or choose, a leader. (page 254)

governor   The elected leader of a state's government. (page 272)

volunteer   A person who chooses to work without being paid. (page 297)

Visit INTERNET RESOURCES at **www.harcourtschool.com/hss** to view Internet Resources.

Reading Social Studies

Main Idea and Details

The **main idea** is the most important idea of a paragraph or passage. Supporting **details** give more information about the main idea.

Why It Matters

Finding the main idea can help you quickly identify the topic of a selection. In a paragraph, the main idea is often in the first sentence.

Main Idea

The most important idea

Details

| Facts about the main idea | Facts about the main idea | Facts about the main idea |

Practice the Skill

Read the paragraph. Find the main idea. Then find the supporting details.

Main Idea

Detail

The office of state governor can be a step toward becoming President of the United States. George W. Bush was governor of Texas before he became President. Bill Clinton was governor of Arkansas. Ronald Reagan was governor of California. Jimmy Carter was governor of Georgia.

Read the paragraphs. Then answer the questions.

One President's Background

On January 20, 1981, Ronald Reagan became the fortieth President of the United States. His background helped prepare him for this important job.

After college, Ronald Reagan worked as a radio sports announcer. His radio job gave him practice in speaking to large audiences.

In 1937, Reagan became a Hollywood actor. Acting taught him how to express himself in front of cameras. It taught him skills that would help him earn the nickname "the Great Communicator."

In 1966, Reagan was elected governor of California. He served as governor for two terms. During those years, he learned how to run a state. All of these experiences would help prepare him to run a country.

Focus Skill — Main Idea and Details

1. Which paragraph states the main idea of this selection?

2. How many paragraphs give supporting details about the main idea?

• Study Skills

UNDERSTAND VOCABULARY

Using a dictionary can help you learn new words as you read.

▶ **A dictionary shows all the meanings of a word and describes where the word came from.**

▶ **You can use a chart to list and organize unfamiliar words that you can look up in a dictionary.**

elect (i-ˈlekt) *vb* 1: to select by vote for an office, position, or membership (She was elected her class president.) 2: to make a selection of (He elected to go on the field trip.) 3: to choose

Word	Definition
elect	To select by vote

Apply As You Read

As you read this chapter, look up vocabulary words and other words that you do not know. Add them to a chart like the one above.

California History-Social Science Standards, Grade 3

3.4 Students understand the role of rules and laws in our daily lives and the basic structure of the U.S. government.

City Hall in
Pasadena, California

CAPITAL!
Washington D.C. from A to Z

by Laura Krauss Melmed
illustrated by Frané Lessac

Capitol

The House and Senate make their home
Beneath the Capitol's great dome.
The bills they vote upon each day
May soon be laws we must obey.

The bronze Statue of Freedom is a woman
in flowing robes. In her left hand she holds a
victory wreath and the shield of the United
States with thirteen stripes representing
the thirteen colonies. Her right hand
rests on the sheathed sword.

The dome is made of cast iron and
weighs almost 9 *million* pounds!

The Capitol has about 540 rooms,
658 windows, and 850 doorways.

THE SENATE

A member of the Senate is called a senator. Senators are elected every six years. There are two senators for each state.

Visitors may sit in the *gallery* in both the House of Representatives and the Senate, to see and hear Congress at work.

Each senator has a desk. One desk is called the candy desk, and each new senator who uses it keeps the drawer filled with mints, hard candies, and chocolates.

THE HOUSE OF REPRESENTATIVES

A member of the House of Representatives is called a representative, a congressman, or a congresswoman. Representatives are elected every two years. The number of representatives from each state depends on the state's population.

The head of the House of Representatives is called the *Speaker*.

In the House Chamber, members may sit in any seat. But Democrats usually sit to the right of the Speaker and Republicans to the left.

Supreme Court

Nine judges on this highest court
Hear cases of supreme import,
Oath-bound to reach a resolution
Upholding our Constitution.

Before the justices sit down the marshal chants:
"The Honorable, the Chief Justice and the Associate
Justices of the Supreme Court of the United States.
Oyez! Oyez! Oyez! All persons having business
before the Honorable, the Supreme Court of the
United States, are admonished to draw near and
give their attention, for the Court is now sitting. God
save the United States and this Honorable Court!"

The Constitution says the United States Supreme
Court is the highest court in the land. The justices
are appointed by the President and must be
approved by the Senate. They are appointed for life.

President's Bedroom | Study

State Dining Room | Red Room | Blue Room | Green Room | East Room

Map Room | Diplomatic Reception Room | China Room | Vermeil Room

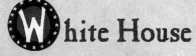hite House

A symbol of democracy,
This house belongs to you and me,
And each new U.S. President
May take a turn as resident.

The White House has six floors, 132 rooms, over 30 bathrooms, 147 windows, and 3 elevators. It is called the White House because of the whitewash paint used to protect the sandstone blocks that form the walls.

The private living quarters of the President and his family make up only a small portion of the total space. Some federal employees have offices in the White House.

During the War of 1812, British troops marched on the White House to torch it. The building was badly burned and would have been destroyed if not for a sudden thunderstorm quenching the flames.

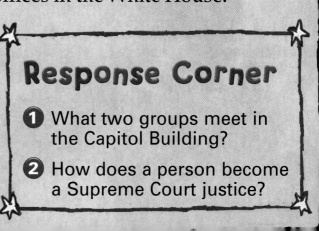

Response Corner

1 What two groups meet in the Capitol Building?

2 How does a person become a Supreme Court justice?

①

Rules and Laws

What to Know
What rules and laws do people follow in a community?

✓ Rules and laws help people get along and help keep people safe.

✓ Members of the community government make laws.

Vocabulary
cooperate p. 252
law p. 253
consequence p. 253
mayor p. 254
elect p. 254
citizen p. 254
court p. 255
judge p. 255

Main Idea and Details

California Standards
HSS 3.4, 3.4.1, 3.4.4

Most of the time, people in a community get along with one another, but there are times when they do not. People need to **cooperate** (koh•AH•puh•rayt), or work together, to keep their community a safe and peaceful place to live.

▶ The students and the bus driver are obeying traffic laws.

Community Laws

To keep people safe, communities have rules. These rules are called **laws**. Traffic laws help people travel safely on the streets of a community. Without traffic laws, many people might be hurt in accidents.

People who break laws face consequences. A **consequence** (KAHN•suh•kwens) is what happens because of what a person does. One consequence is being hurt in an accident. A person who breaks a law may have to go to jail.

Reading Check 👁 **Main Idea and Details**
What are some consequences of breaking a law?

❱ Paying a fine is one consequence of breaking a traffic law.

Community Government

► Edward Cortez is Pomona's mayor.

Each community has a way to make laws and to see that they are followed. In most communities, members of the government make the laws. The government members meet to talk about problems and decide how to solve them.

In some communities, the government leader is called a **mayor**. The mayor's job is to see that the community's problems are solved. The citizens of a community **elect** a mayor, or choose him or her by voting. A **citizen** is a person who lives in and belongs to a community.

► The mayor and other city officials work at Pomona City Hall.

Locate It

CALIFORNIA

Pomona

Courts are another part of a community's government. A **court** is a place where a judge makes decisions about a law. **Judges** are people from the community who are chosen to work as leaders in the courts. Judges decide whether a person has broken a law. They also decide the consequences for those who have broken a law. Judges must be fair, or treat everyone in the same way.

Reading Check ⏀ **Main Idea and Details**
What are some responsibilities of a community government?

Summary We have laws to help keep us safe and to help us get along with one another. The members of the community government make laws.

▶ **Judges decide consequences for people who break laws.**

Review

1. 💡 What rules and laws do people follow in a community?

2. **Vocabulary** What might a **consequence** be for someone who breaks a law?

3. **Your Community** Who is the mayor or leader of your community government?

Critical Thinking

4. **Make It Relevant** How do you follow your community's laws?

5. **ANALYSIS SKILL** What is the benefit of following rules and laws?

6. ✏️ **Write a List** Write a list of laws you have seen people follow in your community.

7. (**Focus Skill**) **Main Idea and Details** On a separate sheet of paper, copy and complete the graphic organizer below.

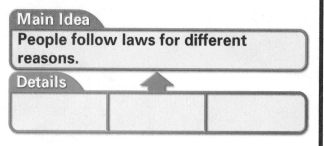

Main Idea
People follow laws for different reasons.

Details

Resolve Conflict

❯ Why It Matters

One job of the government is to help citizens resolve, or settle, **conflicts**. Most of the time, though, people can settle disagreements on their own. Knowing how to resolve conflicts can help you get along with others.

❯ What You Need to Know

You can use these steps when you have a conflict with someone. The same steps may not work every time. You may need to try more than one step.

Walk Away Let time pass. After a while, both people may feel less strongly about the conflict.

Smile About It Make things less serious. People who can smile together are more likely to work out their problem.

Compromise In a **compromise** (KAHM·pruh·myz), each person gives up some of what he or she wants.

Ask for Help A **mediator** (MEE·dee·ay·ter) is a person who helps other people settle a disagreement. The mediator may show them a new way to look at the problem.

Conflict

Resolution

❯ Practice the Skill

Imagine that there is a conflict between two people in your class. Role-play what happens when they try the steps. Write what each classmate says and does.

1 What happens when one person walks away?

2 What happens when one person offers a compromise?

3 What happens when one person asks a mediator to help resolve the conflict?

❯ Apply What You Learned

Make It Relevant Describe some ways people at your school resolve conflicts. Talk with a teacher or a family member about how those ways compare with the steps in this lesson.

2 The U.S. Constitution

What to Know
Why is a constitution important?

✔ The Constitution of the United States describes how our national government works.

✔ The Bill of Rights describes rights and freedoms.

Vocabulary
rights p. 260
amendment p. 261
Bill of Rights p. 261
representative p. 262
majority rule p. 263
minority rights p. 263

Focus Skill Main Idea and Details

California Standards
HSS 3.4, 3.4.1, 3.4.3, 3.4.4

The government of the United States of America is our national, or federal, government. It is located in Washington, D.C., our nation's capital. The national government is made up of three branches. The Constitution of the United States describes each branch. A constitution is a set of laws for a government.

❯ **This painting shows the signing of the Constitution of the United States on September 17, 1787.**

A New Government

Americans fought the Revolutionary War because they felt that the laws Britain made for them were unfair. For their new nation, they wanted a government that would make fair laws. The leaders of the states got together and wrote a plan of government. This plan is called the Constitution of the United States.

The states approved the Constitution in 1789. When Americans voted to elect their first President, they chose General George Washington. Washington became President on April 30, 1789, in New York City, which was the capital at that time.

Reading Check ☼ **Main Idea and Details**
Why did Americans fight the Revolutionary War?

▶ The Constitution of the United States

The Bill of Rights

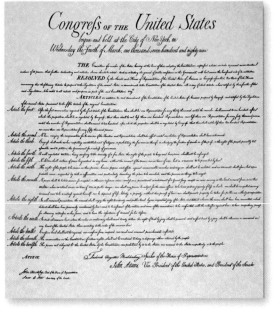

▶ The Bill of Rights

Finally, the new government had a Constitution, but something was missing. George Mason, from Virginia, was one person who felt strongly about what was *not* in the Constitution. "There is no declaration of rights,"* he wrote. Nowhere in the Constitution was there a list of the people's **rights**, or freedoms.

After the Constitution was written, the states of the new country had to agree to it. Some states said they would not agree unless the rights of the people were clearly stated in the Constitution.

*George Mason. *George Mason and the Bill of Rights.* Gary Williams, ed.
The Freeman: Ideas on Liberty. 1992.

▶ The Bill of Rights guarantees that citizens have the freedom to speak out against government decisions.

Freedom of the press is the right of United States citizens to write, read, and speak freely. Today, the press includes not only newspapers and magazines but also films, television, and the Internet.

George Mason had written the Virginia Declaration of Rights, which listed the rights of people living in that state. James Madison used that as a guide for writing ten **amendments**, or changes, to the Constitution. These ten amendments are called the **Bill of Rights**. This Bill of Rights lists freedoms and rights that the people of the United States will always have. Two of the freedoms listed are freedom of speech and freedom of religion. This means that people can say what they wish and worship in any way they choose.

Since the Bill of Rights was added, other amendments have been made to the Constitution. The Constitution is a document that can be changed when needed, but this does not happen very often.

Reading Check **Summarize**
Why was the Bill of Rights added to the Constitution?

▶ **This California worker is checking votes for accuracy.**

▶ **These San Diego citizens choose their leaders by voting.**

A Plan of Government

Our Constitution is a plan for running the national government of the United States. It is a short document because it gives only the basic rules. All the other laws in our country are based on the Constitution.

The writers of the Constitution decided to create a government with three parts, or branches. The writers added another important idea to the Constitution. They made sure each branch would keep an eye on the other two branches. So, no one part of the government has all the power.

The people of our country are the power behind the Constitution. The people elect representatives. A **representative** is a person chosen by a group of people to act or speak for them. In the United States, we do not work for our leaders. They work for us!

The Constitution works by **majority rule**. This means that if more than half the people vote for the same thing or person, they get what they want. However, the Constitution also states the importance of minority rights. **Minority rights** means that the smaller group, the one that did not vote for the same thing or person that the larger group voted for, still gets to keep its rights.

▶ **Citizens have the right to vote in private.**

Reading Check ☝ **Main Idea and Details**
Why do the branches of the government keep an eye on each other?

Summary The U.S. Constitution sets out the basic rules of our government. The Bill of Rights tells what rights the people have.

Review

1. ☀ Why is a constitution important?

2. **Vocabulary** How is the **Bill of Rights** related to the word **amendment**?

3. **Your Community** How do people use the right of freedom of speech in your community?

Critical Thinking

4. **Make It Relevant** How might your life change without the Bill of Rights?

5. **ANALYSIS SKILL** Why has the U.S. Constitution not had many amendments?

6. ✎ **Write a Classroom Constitution** Write a constitution for your classroom based on the U.S. Constitution.

7. **Focus Skill** **Main Idea and Details** On a separate sheet of paper, copy and complete the graphic organizer below.

Main Idea
The United States Constitution is an important document.

Details

The Constitution Question

Forming a new government was not easy. The delegates to the Constitutional Convention had many different ideas. Some delegates were not sure the Constitution was as good as it could be. Others thought the document was perfect. Many new Americans were afraid it would lead to a return of rule by a king.

In Their Own Words

George Washington, president of the Convention

"I wish the Constitution, which is offered, had been made more perfect, but I sincerely believe it is the best that could be obtained at this time."

— from a letter to Patrick Henry, Sept. 24, 1787.

Mount Vernon, Washington's home

George Washington

Patrick Henry, Convention delegate

" This Constitution is said to have beautiful features; but when I come to examine these features, Sir, they appear to me horribly frightful.... Your President may easily become King. **"**

— from a speech, on June 7, 1788.

Patrick Henry

Views from Today

Gerald Ford, past President

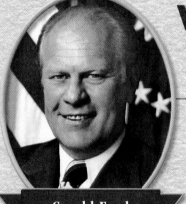

Gerald Ford

" Our Constitution works. Our great republic is a government of laws, not of men. **"**

— from a speech, on August 9, 1974.

Sandra Day O'Connor, U.S. Supreme Court Justice

" We have a written Constitution. It contains, now, a Bill of Rights ... I think the American people understand that fundamental concept and treasure it, and that's what's made it special in this country. **"**

— from an interview by Judy Woodruff, CNN, 2003.

It's Your Turn

ANALYSIS SKILL **Analyze Points of View** Explain the points of view of those for and against the Constitution.

Sandra Day O'Connor

3 Three Levels of Government

All over the United States, citizens work with their governments to keep their communities safe and peaceful. In some small communities, everyone takes part in the government by going to town meetings. In larger towns and cities, problems are discussed and solved by people who have been selected by citizens or by government leaders.

▶ At this community meeting in Los Angeles, citizens discuss ways to keep their urban garden open.

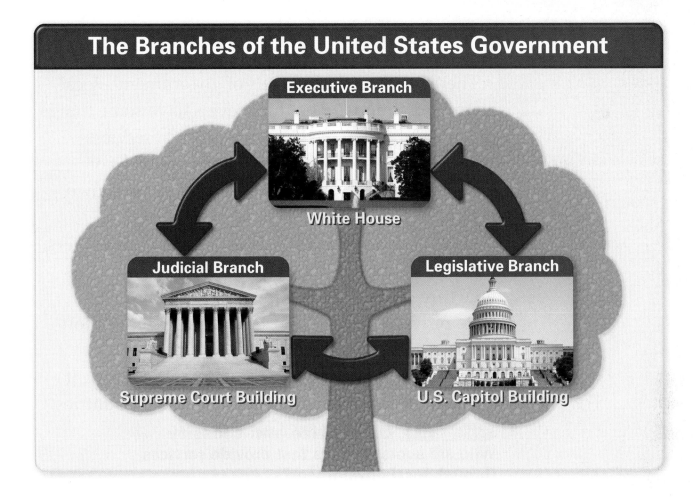

The Branches of the United States Government

Executive Branch

White House

Judicial Branch

Supreme Court Building

Legislative Branch

U.S. Capitol Building

Analyze Illustrations This drawing shows how the branches of government are connected.

❖ **Which photograph represents the legislative branch?**

The Branches of Government

The government of the United States is made up of three branches, or parts. Like the branches of a tree, they are separate but connected.

One part is called the **legislative** branch. This branch makes laws. Another part is called the **executive** branch. This branch sees that laws are obeyed. The third part is called the **judicial** branch. This branch decides whether laws are fair. It also decides whether laws have been carried out fairly.

Reading Check **Ŏ Main Idea and Details**
What are the three branches of the United States government?

Levels of Government

There are three main levels of government—local, state, and national. The three levels have some things in common. All make laws and provide services that people need. However, like the branches of government, each level of government has its own job to do.

Local governments provide services by firefighters, city police, and trash collectors. State governments take care of state parks and state highways. Each state provides driver licenses and public education for its citizens.

The national government protects our country. It also works with the governments of other countries.

Reading Check **Categorize and Classify**
Who are some workers that provide services through local government?

> State governments take care of state parks.

Levels of Government

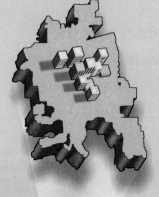

Local

Legislative
- Town Council or City Council

Executive
- Mayor or City Manager
- Departments such as Police and Parks

Judicial
- Courts

State

Legislative
- Senate
- House of Representatives or Assembly

Executive
- Governor
- Departments such as Health and Education

Judicial
- Supreme Court
- Local courts

National

Legislative
- Senate
- House of Representatives

Executive
- President

Judicial
- Supreme Court

Analyze Diagrams This diagram shows the different levels of government.

◆ What are the branches of state government?

The National Government

Congress is the legislative branch of the national government. Congress has two parts, the Senate and the House of Representatives.

Members of the Senate and the House work to solve national problems. Each of the 50 states has two members in the Senate. The more people a state has, the more members it can have in the House. California has more people than any other state, so it has the most members in the House.

Senators and representatives work in the United States Capitol building in Washington, D.C. They discuss problems and vote on how to solve them. They write new laws and decide how tax money should be used. Before a new law can pass, senators and representatives must agree on it. Then it goes to the President for approval.

▶ **United States senators from California, Dianne Feinstein and Barbara Boxer**

▶ **The United States Congress includes the Senate and House of Representatives.**

The United States Supreme Court justices are shown here. STANDING: Ruth Bader Ginsburg, David Hackett Souter, Clarence Thomas, and Stephen G. Breyer. SEATED: Antonin Scalia, John Paul Stephens, Chief Justice William H. Rehnquist, Sandra Day O'Connor, and Anthony M. Kennedy.

The **President** of the United States leads the executive branch of the national government, which suggests laws and makes sure the laws are obeyed. Some of the President's jobs include working with leaders of other nations and speaking to Congress.

The courts make up the judicial branch of the national government. The **Supreme Court** is the highest, or most important, court in the United States. Nine judges, called justices, serve on the Supreme Court. These justices of the Supreme Court study the laws. When cases are brought to the Supreme Court, the justices decide whether the laws have been used fairly.

Supreme Court justices are not elected. They are **appointed**, or chosen, by the President. To serve, they must be approved by the Senate.

The President of the United States George W. Bush

Reading Check Ŏ **Main Idea and Details**
How do representatives from California take part in the federal government?

State Government in California

California Lieutenant Governor Cruz Bustamante and Governor Arnold Schwarzenegger

In each state, voters elect a **governor**. In many ways, the governor's job is like the job of the President of the United States. The governor suggests laws that he or she thinks will be good for the state. The governor of California is the leader of the state's executive branch.

California has two groups of lawmakers. They are the senate and the assembly. The lawmakers meet in California's capital city in a building called the **capitol**. These lawmakers make up the legislative branch of California's government.

Geography

Sacramento

California's state government is based in Sacramento. In 1852, Vallejo, California, almost became the state capital, but it did not have a building for the lawmakers to meet in. A businessperson in Sacramento told the California lawmakers they could use the new courthouse for their meetings. They could also have a piece of land to build the capitol building. The lawmakers agreed. In 1854, Sacramento became the capital. The capitol building was built to look like the United States Capitol building in Washington, D.C. The governor's office is in the capitol building, along with offices for 80 state assembly members and 40 state senators.

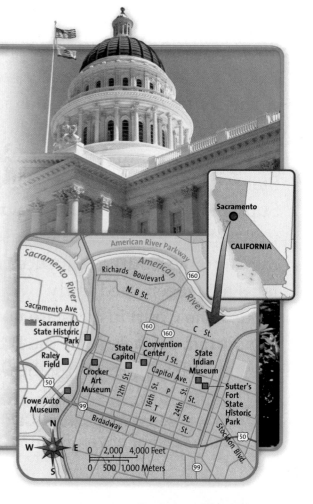

State governments also have judges who decide whether the state's laws are fair. In California, the highest court is the state supreme court. The courts and judges that hear and decide law cases in California make up the judicial branch of California's government.

▶ California state senators Gloria Romero and Jackie Speier

Reading Check **Categorize and Classify** What are the three branches of California's government?

Summary The government of the United States is made up of three branches—executive, legislative, and judicial. There are three main levels of government—local, state, and national.

Review

1. How is the government of the United States organized?

2. **Vocabulary** Use the words **President** and **executive** in a sentence.

3. **Your Community** What lawmakers represent your community in the state government? in the national government?

Critical Thinking

4. **Make It Relevant** How can the governor's decisions affect you?

5. **ANALYSIS SKILL** How does California take part in the federal government?

6. **Do Research** Find out who represents your community in the federal government. Research what this person has done for your community.

7. **Focus Skill** **Main Idea and Details** On a separate sheet of paper, copy and complete the graphic organizer below.

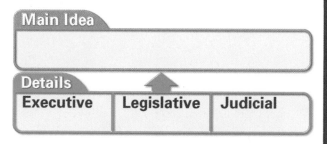

Main Idea

Details		
Executive	Legislative	Judicial

Read a Bar Graph

❱ Why It Matters

Graphs are used to compare the numbers of people in different categories, or groups. A **bar graph** is a kind of graph that uses bars to show amounts or numbers of things.

❱ What You Need to Know

Each state sends elected representatives to the United States Congress. The number of representatives that a state can send depends on the number of people living in the state. A state with a greater population has more representatives than a state with a smaller population. In 2000, there were 435 members of Congress.

The bar graph on the next page shows the number of members of Congress for some states. The title tells what the bar graph is about. The labels tell what the bars compare. You read a bar graph by looking at the bars. Follow these steps to read the bar graph.

Step 1 Read the title and the labels on the graph.

Step 2 To find how many representatives Florida has, locate the bar labeled *Florida*.

Step 3 Move your finger up the bar to where it ends. Look at the number on the left to find how many. Florida has 25 representatives.

▶ Practice the Skill

Use the bar graph below to answer these questions.

1 Which of these states has the most representatives? Which has the fewest?

2 Does California have more than 55 representatives or fewer than 55 representatives?

3 Which state has a larger population, California or Texas? How can you tell?

▶ Apply What You Learned

Make It Relevant Bar graphs can be used to compare numbers of things. Think of some numbers you want to compare. One example might be the number of baskets that each member of a team made during a basketball game. Collect the information, and use the numbers to create a bar graph. Share your bar graph with your family.

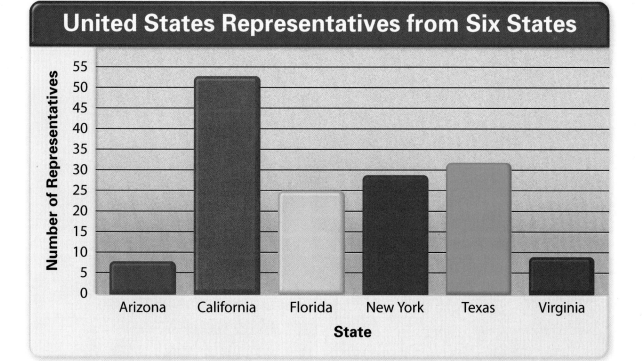

United States Representatives from Six States

Local Government in California

What to Know
What does local government do for its citizens?

✓ Local government performs many services for citizens.

✓ Community services are paid for mostly by taxes.

Vocabulary
council p. 278
government service p. 280
recreation p. 280
public works p. 281
tax p. 281
county p. 282
county seat p. 283

Main Idea and Details

California Standards
HSS 3.4, 3.4.4

There are two kinds of local government, county governments and city or town governments. Like the national government and state government, local governments make laws and provide services for citizens. These laws and services apply to the communities in which the local governments are located.

❱ **The Glenn County Courthouse in Willows, California**

▶ People look at the California Constitution at the California State Archives Museum in Sacramento.

History of Local Government

When California joined the United States in 1850, a system of government had to be set up for the new state. As more Americans came to California, they brought with them the values of their home states. These values included the idea of a constitution, or plan for a system of government.

A constitutional convention was held in 1849, resulting in the California Constitution of 1849. Though this constitution did mark the beginnings of a formal government, there were still problems to be solved. One of these was the need to create a standard process for forming cities and towns. Another was the need to decide on the proper roles of state and local governments. These issues were debated for 30 years, finally resulting in the California Constitution of 1879.

Reading Check ☼ **Main Idea and Details**
In what two years were state constitutions written for California?

City and Town Government

Cities and towns have their own governments. Cities have two different forms of government. Most cities in California have the council-manager form of government. A **council** is a group of people that makes laws.

In the council-manager form of government, voters elect a city council. The city council chooses one of its members as mayor and also hires a city manager to help run the city. In some cities, the mayor is elected directly by the people.

Analyze Diagrams

◆ **In the council-manager form of government, who elects the city council?**

▶ The city of Laguna Niguel has a council-manager form of government.

COUNCIL-MANAGER

People

elect

appoints   hires

Mayor ← City Council → City Manager

Fire   Police   Utilities   Others

▶ The city of Los Angeles has a mayor-council form of government.

MAYOR-COUNCIL

People

elect → Mayor

elect → City Council

Mayor → Fire | Police | Utilities | Others

Analyze Diagrams

❖ In the mayor-council form of government, who elects the mayor?

In the mayor-council form of government, voters in a city elect the mayor and the council members. The mayor and council work together to run the city. The mayor leads the executive branch. He or she makes sure city laws are carried out. The mayor also hires people to run city departments. A department is a part of government with a certain job to do, such as the police department or the fire department. The council is the legislative branch. It makes laws for the city and collects taxes. In California the mayor-council form is found in large cities such as Oakland, San Francisco, San Diego, and Los Angeles.

Reading Check ◔ **Main Idea and Details**

What form of government do most California cities have?

Local Governments Provide Services

More than three-fourths of Californians live in cities. City governments have the most direct effect on these citizens' lives. Local governments provide many services to their citizens. A **government service** is work that the government does for everyone in a city or town.

All cities and most towns have police and fire departments. Some communities have a health department. Many communities also have a parks department. Parks give people a place for recreation (reh•kree•AY•shuhn). **Recreation** is any activity, hobby, or game done just for fun.

❯ **Firefighters in San Diego**

▶ This family enjoys a picnic in a Los Angeles public park.

The **public works** department of a community government provides services to meet day-to-day needs. It sees that trash is collected and that streets are clean and in good repair. It makes sure that the community has clean water.

All these government services cost money. Equipment such as police cars and fire engines must be bought and kept in working order. Workers must also be paid. Most of the money for government services comes from taxes paid by citizens in the community. A **tax** is money that citizens pay to run the government and to provide services.

Reading Check ⚙ **Main Idea and Details**
What kinds of services do local governments provide?

▶ Brushes turn under this street sweeper to clean California roads.

County Government

County governments are the highest level of local government. A **county** is a section of a state. Each of California's 58 counties has its own government.

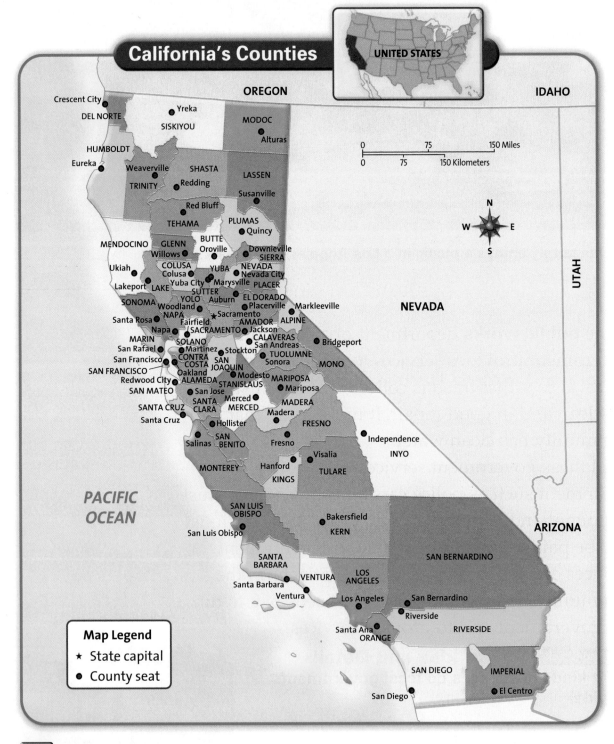

California's Counties

UNITED STATES

OREGON

IDAHO

Crescent City
DEL NORTE
Yreka
SISKIYOU
MODOC
Alturas

HUMBOLDT
Eureka
Weaverville
SHASTA
TRINITY
Redding
LASSEN
Susanville

Red Bluff
TEHAMA
PLUMAS
Quincy

MENDOCINO
GLENN
Willows
BUTTE
Oroville
Downieville
SIERRA

Ukiah
COLUSA
Colusa
YUBA
NEVADA
Nevada City
Lakeport
LAKE
Yuba City
Marysville
PLACER
SUTTER
Auburn
EL DORADO
SONOMA
YOLO
Woodland
Placerville
Markleeville
Santa Rosa
NAPA
Fairfield
Sacramento
NEVADA
Napa
SACRAMENTO
AMADOR
Jackson
ALPINE
MARIN
SOLANO
CALAVERAS
San Rafael
Martinez
Stockton
San Andreas
Bridgeport
San Francisco
CONTRA
COSTA
SAN
JOAQUIN
TUOLUMNE
Sonora
MONO
SAN FRANCISCO
Oakland
Redwood City
ALAMEDA
Modesto
MARIPOSA
SAN MATEO
San Jose
STANISLAUS
Mariposa
SANTA
CLARA
Merced
MADERA
SANTA CRUZ
MERCED
Madera
Santa Cruz
Hollister
FRESNO
SAN
BENITO
Fresno
Independence
Salinas
INYO
MONTEREY
Hanford
Visalia
KINGS
TULARE

PACIFIC
OCEAN

SAN LUIS
OBISPO
Bakersfield
San Luis Obispo
KERN
ARIZONA

SANTA
BARBARA
SAN BERNARDINO
VENTURA
LOS
ANGELES
Santa Barbara
Ventura
Los Angeles
San Bernardino
Santa Ana
Riverside
ORANGE
RIVERSIDE

SAN DIEGO
IMPERIAL
San Diego
El Centro

Map Legend
★ State capital
• County seat

NEVADA

UTAH

ANALYSIS SKILL Analyze Maps

◈ **Location** What is the county seat of Humboldt County in northern California?

A **county seat** is the city or town where the main government offices of the county are located. A county board of supervisors meets in the county seat. The board of supervisors is elected by citizens of the county. The board members discuss and solve problems that affect the county.

Reading Check 🅞 **Main Idea and Details** Where do county leaders meet?

Summary City and county governments help run communities. These governments provide many services. Money for the services comes from taxes paid by citizens.

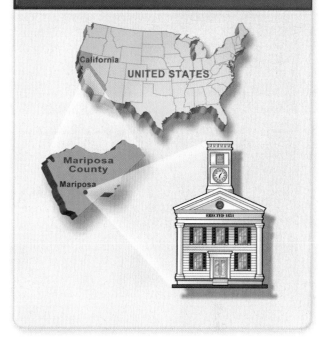

Local County Government

Analyze Diagrams
◈ **What is the county seat of Mariposa County?**

Review

1. What does local government do for its citizens?

2. **Vocabulary** What is an example of a **government service**?

3. **Your Community** What is your community's form of government?

Critical Thinking

4. **Make It Relevant** As you travel to and from school each day, what examples do you see of local government services?

5. **ANALYSIS SKILL** Why do you think communities have local governments?

6. 🖍 **Give a Speech** Imagine that you are running for mayor. Write and give a speech telling what you will do for your community if elected.

7. 🅕 **Main Idea and Details** On a separate sheet of paper, copy and complete the graphic organizer below.

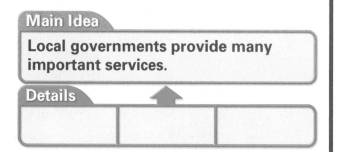

Main Idea

Local governments provide many important services.

Details

Trustworthiness

Respect

Responsibility

Fairness

Caring

Patriotism

Gloria Molina

"My involvement has always been to empower the community."*

Why Character Counts

❖ Why do you think Gloria Molina wants to help children in working-class families?

Gloria Molina, a Mexican American, is the oldest of ten children. Her father worked hard as a laborer. He could not give her many clothes or toys. However, he gave her something of greater value. He gave her words to live by. He told her that she could achieve anything with hard work and a dream.

When Molina grew up, she understood the problems of working people. She especially wanted to help children in working-class families.

Molina believed she could best help people by getting involved in government. So, she decided to run for office.

Gloria Molina

* Gloria Molina. "Power Broker: Gloria Molina's Political Hand Stretches from L.A. to D.C." by Ana Radelat. *Hispanic Magazine*, June 2001.

Molina in a parade

Molina is sworn into office.

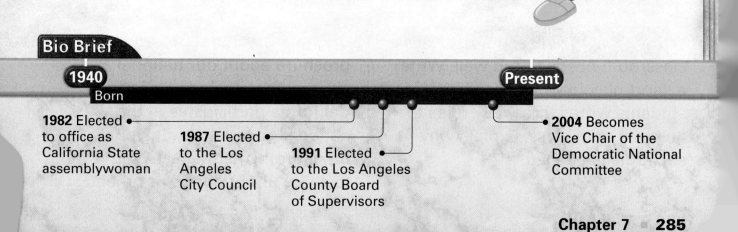

Gloria Molina,
her parents, and
supporters

Then Gloria Molina made history. In 1982, she became the first Hispanic woman to be elected to the California State Assembly. Five years later, she was elected as Los Angeles's first Hispanic city councilwoman. Then, in 1991, she made history once again as the first Hispanic on the Los Angeles County Board of Supervisors.

Gloria Molina was chosen because voters saw that she understood them and cared about them. Molina has used her power as an elected official to help many people. She has introduced laws that help protect children. She has started programs that provide more nurses for sick people. Molina has also worked to clean up communities and parks so that they are safe for families.

GO ONLINE Visit MULTIMEDIA BIOGRAPHIES at www.harcourtschool.com/hss

Bio Brief

1940 — Present

Born

1982 Elected to office as California State assemblywoman

1987 Elected to the Los Angeles City Council

1991 Elected to the Los Angeles County Board of Supervisors

2004 Becomes Vice Chair of the Democratic National Committee

Reading Social Studies

The **main idea** is the most important idea of a passage. **Details** are facts, reasons, or examples that support the main idea.

Main Idea and Details

(Focus Skill)

Complete this graphic organizer to show that you understand important ideas and details about each part of our government. A copy of a graphic organizer appears on page 68 of the Homework and Practice Book.

The United States Government

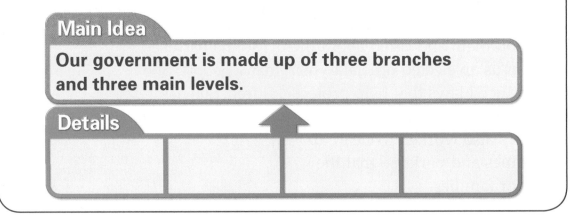

Main Idea

Our government is made up of three branches and three main levels.

Details

California Writing Prompts

Write a Play Think about the rules a classroom needs to run well. Write a short play in which a group of students writes three new rules to help run your class. Explain why each rule is needed.

Create a Brochure Design a brochure about our national government. Include the ways California participates in the national government. In your brochure, write the facts you want to share about our government.

Use Vocabulary

Write the word that best fills each blank.

law, p. 253   **Congress,** p. 270
mayor, p. 254   **governor,** p. 272
rights, p. 260   **county,** p. 282

1. A ____ is a person who leads a community government.

2. A rule that a community makes is a ____.

3. A ____ is the leader of a state's government.

4. People's freedoms are their ____.

5. A part of a state is called a ____.

6. ____ is the legislative branch of the national government.

Apply Skills

Read a Bar Graph Use the bar graph on page 275 to answer the question.

7. Which state has 32 representatives?

Recall Facts

Answer these questions.

8. What is the U.S. Constitution?

9. How do states have a part in national government?

Write the letter of the best choice.

10. Which can be a consequence of breaking a law?
    A paying a fine
    B losing the Bill of Rights
    C having a town meeting
    D becoming a representative

11. Which job is part of our national government?
    A mayor
    B governor
    C President
    D Manager of Parks

Think Critically

12. Why are laws important to a community?

13. How are local, state, and national levels of government alike?

Study Skills

SKIM AND SCAN

Skimming and scanning are two ways to learn from what you read.

- **To skim, quickly read the lesson title and the section titles. Look at the pictures and read the captions. Use this information to identify the main topics.**

- **To scan, look quickly through the text for specific details, such as key words or facts.**

Skim	Scan
Lesson: Being a Good Citizen	**Key Words and Facts**
Main Idea: Good citizens are responsible.	• character trait • volunteers are important members of a community.
Titles/Headings: • What Is a Good Citizen? • _____	• _____ • _____

Apply As You Read

Before you read each lesson, skim the text to find the main idea of each section. Then look for key words. If you have questions about a topic, scan the text to find the answers.

California History-Social Science Standards, Grade 3

3.4 Students understand the role of rules and laws in our daily lives and the basic structure of the U.S. government.

Governor Arnold Schwarzenegger
at a rally in San Diego, California

WHO TOOK My CHAIR?

by Pleasant DeSpain
illustrated by John Hovell

"Who Took My Chair?" is written as a play, or a story to be acted out. The scene and setting describe where the action takes place. After each character's name are the lines which that character says. Words in italic (eye•TAL•ick), or slanted, letters describe the characters' actions.

Characters

Ms. Koto (KOH•toh)—Third-grade teacher
Mateo (mah•TAY•oh)—Student
Dakota—Student
Ziggy—Student
Keshawn (KEY•shawn)—Student

Scene

Time: Beginning of school day
Setting: Ms. Koto's third-grade classroom with desks, wooden chairs, chalkboard, and set of encyclopedias

Ms. Koto stands at the chalkboard, writing the name and country of the new student.

MS. KOTO: Good morning, everyone. We have a new student today. His name is Mateo, and he comes all the way from Ecuador in South America. Please tell us about your homeland, Mateo.

MATEO: (*He looks nervous. English is his second language and he wants to make a good impression.*) Buenos Días . . . I mean, good morning. I was born near Quito (KEE•toh), the biggest city in Ecuador. We lived in the mountains . . .

DAKOTA: (*She rushes in, late to class. Mateo is sitting at her desk, in her chair. She is angry, drops her books, and points her finger.*) Who took my chair? You can't sit there. It's my place.

MS. KOTO: Calm down, Dakota.

DAKOTA: But he's in my chair . . .

MS. KOTO: The chairs belong to all of us, Dakota. Mateo is now a member of our class.

DAKOTA: (*She pouts.*) But where will *I* sit? It isn't fair.

MS. KOTO: (*She points to her desk.*) Sit at my desk. I'll go find another chair. (*She speaks to the class.*) Dakota will be the teacher while I'm gone. I want Dakota and all of you to help make Mateo feel welcome. (*Ms. Koto exits. Dakota sits in Ms. Koto's chair.*)

ZIGGY: (*He grins big and waves his arm in the air.*) Teacher! Oh teacher?

DAKOTA: Yes, Ziggy?

ZIGGY: How are we going to make the new kid feel welcome?

DAKOTA: *(She thinks for a moment.)* I know. Mateo, please name three things you really like.

MATEO: Soccer . . . and dogs. And I like chairs.

ZIGGY: Chairs? That's silly.

DAKOTA: No, it isn't, Ziggy. I have a pink chair in my bedroom. I like it very much.

MATEO: My uncle made a chair just for me. Then he showed me how to paint it. It's red, yellow, and blue. Those are the colors in the flag of Ecuador.

DAKOTA: It sounds like a neat chair, Mateo.

ZIGGY: I would paint one red, white, and blue, the colors of our American flag.

KESHAWN: My grandmother was born in the Congo, in Africa. I wonder what colors are in her flag.

DAKOTA: Let's look in the encyclopedia. *(Keshawn and Dakota look up "Congo" in the encyclopedia. They see a picture of that country's flag.)*

KESHAWN: Here it is. Green, yellow, and red. It's beautiful. I want to paint a chair for my granny.

MATEO: I'll show you how to do it.

ZIGGY: What about me?

MATEO: I'll show everyone.

DAKOTA: We could choose the colors of the flags of all the countries represented by our class. We could even . . . (*The door opens. Ms. Koto arrives carrying a chair.*)

MS. KOTO: Here we are, class, a new chair.

KESHAWN: Can I have it?

MS. KOTO: What do you mean?

DAKOTA: I'll explain, Ms. Koto. We are helping Mateo feel at home. And he is making us feel at home.

ZIGGY: Can we have a show-and-tell tomorrow, Ms. Koto? Mateo has something special to bring to class.

KESHAWN: And can we ask the art teacher for some paint?

Response Corner

1 Why is Mateo's favorite chair painted red, yellow, and blue?

2 How does each character show that he or she is a good citizen of the classroom?

1

What are some qualities of a good citizen?

✔ Good citizens follow laws, pay taxes, and vote.

✔ Students can be good citizens if they follow rules, do their best work, and show good character traits.

✔ Americans honor people who have shown good character traits.

Vocabulary

responsibility p. 294
justice p. 294
character trait p. 295
volunteer p. 297
hero p. 299

Focus Skill

Main Idea and Details

California Standards
HSS 3.4.2

Being a Good Citizen

People who are good citizens have responsibilities. A **responsibility** is something a person should do because it is necessary and important. Responsibilities include participating, or taking part, in the classroom, community, and civic life.

What Is a Good Citizen?

Good citizens follow the laws of the nation, the state, and the community. They pay taxes and take part in the government by voting. Good citizens care about others. They believe that freedom and **justice**, or fairness, are important. They respect themselves and others.

❯ Cooperating with classmates is one way to be a good citizen.

Good citizens have some important character traits. A **character trait** is a quality that a person has, such as caring, fairness, responsibility, and respect.

Both adults and students are good citizens when they show these character traits. Students who are good citizens show caring, fairness, and respect for their fellow students and their teachers. They show that they are responsible by following rules. They do their best work in their classes and participate in classroom activities.

Reading Check ○**Main Idea and Details**
What are some character traits of good citizens?

❯ These adults show they are good citizens by working to help others.

Children in History

Lillie Hitchcock Coit and Engine Company No. 5

Lillie Hitchcock Coit became interested in San Francisco firefighters when she was 8 years old. In 1851, she and two friends were in a building that caught on fire. Knickerbocker Engine Company Number 5 rescued Lillie.

When Lillie was 15 years old, she saw the Engine Company Number 5 on the way to a large fire. There were not enough people to pull the truck carrying the water to the fire. She grabbed part of the rope and began pulling. Soon others came and helped pull the engine to the fire. Later, Lillie became an honorary member of the Knickerbocker Company.

Fairness
Franklin Delano Roosevelt (1882–1945)

When Franklin D. Roosevelt became President in 1933, the United States was having problems. Millions of people were out of work. People were hungry and scared.

Roosevelt felt that his job was to make sure that Americans had jobs and food. During his first talk to the American people, he told them to have courage. "The only thing we have to fear is fear itself,"* he said. He and Congress began programs that created jobs and got people working. He gave people hope that their lives would get better.

Reading Check Ŏ **Main Idea and Details**
How did Roosevelt help the country?

❱ President Roosevelt used crutches or a wheelchair. This statue is part of the FDR Memorial in Washington, D.C.

❱ Roosevelt was an admired President.

*Franklin Delano Roosevelt. "Franklin Delano Roosevelt: First Inaugural Address" in *The American Reader*. Diane Ravitch, ed. HarperCollins. 2000.

Responsibility
Larry Sly (1950–)

Even as a child, Larry Sly looked for solutions to problems. After finishing college, he decided to take on a big problem in California, where he lived. A lot of people in Contra Costa County were out of work. Their families were hungry. Sly noticed that grocery stores were throwing away bread each day.

Sly decided to work with volunteers in his community. A **volunteer** is someone who chooses to work without being paid. Sly started volunteering at a "food bank." He collected leftover food from stores and took it to people who needed it. Sly's efforts have helped many people.

Reading Check ⚙ **Main Idea and Details**
How did Larry Sly help his community?

❭ Larry Sly

❭ Volunteers of all ages work at the food bank.

Maya Angelou was honored with her own postage stamp.

Respect
Maya Angelou (1928–)

Maya Angelou (AN•juh•loh) has been a singer, an actor, and an editor. But she is best known as a writer of poetry and of books about her life.

Through her books, Maya Angelou tells about her difficult childhood and how she overcame it. Learning to respect herself and others helped her grow into the person she is today. Angelou travels all over the world, speaking to people. She still writes, telling her readers to believe in themselves.

Reading Check **Ŏ Main Idea and Details**
What is Maya Angelou best known for?

Maya Angelou was invited to write a poem for the 1993 inauguration of President Bill Clinton.

Caring
Community Heroes

Recently, wildfires burned on hills and across roads in California. To many people, the thousands of men and women who fought those fires are heroes. A **hero** is a brave person who sets an example. These heroes showed what brave citizens will do for their neighbors and their country.

▶ **Firefighters do dangerous work to help others.**

Reading Check ☼ **Main Idea and Details**
Why do people call the California firefighters heroes?

Summary Good citizens are caring. They treat people with fairness. They are responsible. They show respect for themselves and for others.

Review

1. 💡 What are some qualities of a good citizen?

2. **Vocabulary** Write one or two sentences to tell about the qualities of a **hero**.

3. **Your Community** Think of a good citizen in your community. What makes him or her a good citizen?

Critical Thinking

4. **Make It Relevant** How do you show caring, fairness, respect, and responsibility in the classroom?

5. 📊 **SKILL** Why is it important for people to care about others?

6. 📚 **Make a Bulletin Board** Cut out newspaper or magazine articles about people and how they show good character traits. Make a bulletin board titled "How Good Citizens Participate."

7. ⭐ **Focus Skill** **Main Idea and Details** On a separate sheet of paper, copy and complete this graphic organizer.

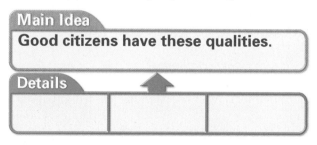

Main Idea
Good citizens have these qualities.

Details

Read a Flowchart

▶ Why It Matters

A **flowchart** shows how to do something or how something works. The flowchart shows the steps in order.

A flowchart uses words, pictures, and arrows. Follow the arrows to read the steps in the correct order.

▶ What You Need to Know

One way to become a United States citizen is simply by being born in the United States. Another way is through naturalization (na•chuh•ruh•luh•ZAY•shun)—the legal process by which someone can become a citizen.

To become a naturalized citizen, a person must be at least 18 years old and have lived in the United States for a certain number of years. In addition, the person needs to follow several steps.

▶ Practice the Skill

The flowchart on page 301 shows some steps that a person from another country must take to become a citizen of the United States. Use the flowchart's photographs and labels to answer these questions.

❶ What is the first step in becoming a naturalized United States citizen?

❷ What happens after the person fills out an application?

❸ What is the last step in becoming a naturalized citizen?

▶ Apply What You Learned

Make It Relevant Discuss events or items from the past that you could put into a flowchart. Perhaps you helped wash a pet, helped make a meal, or wrote a report. Then make a flowchart that tells a younger student how to do something.

How People Become Naturalized Citizens of the United States

1

Completing the application

2
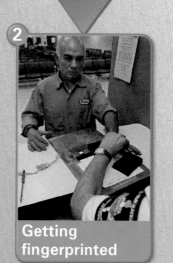
Getting fingerprinted

3

Being interviewed and taking tests

4

Taking the oath

5

Receiving Certificate of Naturalization

2 Roles of Citizens

Every day in our communities, people show good citizenship. They follow rules and laws, vote, and speak out about problems they want to fix.

Make Choices by Voting

One way good citizens get involved in civic life is by voting in elections. An **election** is the time set aside for voting. In the United States, citizens elect their leaders by voting. To vote in the United States, citizens must be at least 18 years old.

▶ Senior volunteers help with elections.

 What to Know

What is a citizen's role in the community?

✔ Voting is one responsibility of a good citizen.

✔ A citizen's role in the community includes paying taxes and serving on juries.

Vocabulary
election p. 302
ballot p. 303
jury p. 304

 Main Idea and Details

California Standards
HSS 3.4, 3.4.1, 3.4.2

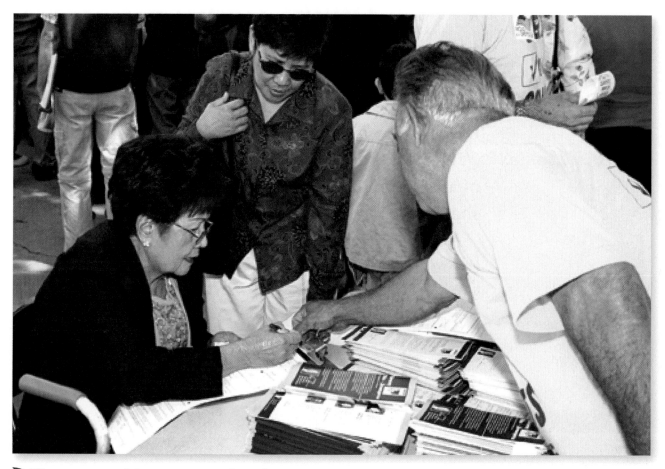

▶ These new citizens are registering to vote.

To vote, citizens mark on a ballot the name of the person they choose for each office. A **ballot** is the list of choices in an election. Sometimes, citizens use a machine to record their choices. Each person's vote is secret. People make their choices without anyone watching. After the voting time ends, the votes are counted. The person with the most votes wins.

Some people get involved in elections by speaking out about what they believe in. They may even run for election themselves.

Reading Check ⚙ **Main Idea and Details**
How do people in the United States choose their leaders?

Doing Their Part

Another way that people show good citizenship is by serving on a jury. A **jury** is a group of 6 to 12 citizens who decide if a person has broken a law. Juries are an important part of our government.

Jury members sit in a courtroom to hear the facts of a case. In this room, a judge is in charge. He or she tells the jury about the laws in the case.

After jury members have heard the facts, they leave the room and decide if the person is guilty. If they say that the person is guilty, the judge decides on the punishment.

Fast Fact

The oldest known use of the jury system was in Europe about 900 years ago. When people had arguments about something that had happened, the king would ask a group of 12 knights to decide what the truth was.

❱ Serving on a jury is one of the rights and responsibilities of adults in the United States.

Following laws that the government makes and paying taxes are other important responsibilities of citizens. Taxes pay for the services that people in communities all over the United States need and enjoy.

Reading Check **Summarize**
How can an adult be a good citizen?

Summary Citizens have an important role in the community. Good citizens follow laws, vote, pay taxes, and serve on juries.

▶ Using the public library is this girl's right. Returning books on time is her responsibility.

Review

1. What is a citizen's role in the community?

2. **Vocabulary** Use the words **ballot** and **election** in a sentence about voting.

3. **Your Community** Who are some people who have been elected to lead in your community?

Critical Thinking

4. **Make It Relevant** How are you a good citizen of your classroom?

5. **ANALYSIS SKILL** What are some ways people promote rules and laws?

6. **Write a Poem About Citizenship** Title your poem "I Am a Good Citizen." On a sheet of paper, write these starters: *I am _____, I follow _____, I serve _____. I am a good citizen.* Finish each sentence to make a poem.

7. **Focus Skill** **Main Idea and Details** On a separate sheet of paper, copy and complete the graphic organizer.

Main Idea

Details		
Follow laws.	Vote.	Pay taxes.

Make a Choice by Voting

❯ Why It Matters

The United States has a form of government called a **democracy** (dih•MAH•kruh•see). In any democracy, every adult citizen has the right to vote for the country's leaders, who pass laws. In this way, everyone can take part in running the country.

Citizens vote for community, state, and national leaders. After the votes are counted, the candidate with the most votes is the winner. A **candidate** is a person who wants to be elected as a leader.

❯ What You Need to Know

Before you vote for someone or something, find out as much as you can about the candidates or about the law that is being voted on. Read or listen to what the candidates say or what people say about the law. Ask questions about matters that are important to you.

Step 2

Step 1

Step 1 **Prepare the ballots.**

Step 2 **Vote in secret.**

Step 3 **Count the ballots.**

Step 4 **Announce the winner.**

❯ Practice the Skill

You may have belonged to clubs that have leaders who are elected. Being a club member gives you chances to practice voting.

Step 3

Look at the four steps on this page and discuss why it is important to follow the steps in order.

❯ Apply What You Learned

Make It Relevant Hold an election for a student to be president of your class for the day. Ask for volunteers to be candidates. Have each candidate make a speech about what he or she would do as president. Then follow the steps shown on these pages to hold an election.

Step 4

Citizens Who Serve

What to Know
What are some ways that citizens serve their community?

✓ People and organizations can work for the common good.

✓ A good leader believes in public service and is willing to work for the common good.

Vocabulary
public service p. 308
common good p. 309

Main Idea and Details

California Standards
HSS 3.4.2

People in **public service** work for the good of the community. They work to make life better for others. Public service includes many ways of helping in a community.

People Work Together

One way to help others is to do volunteer work. You probably know people who are volunteers. The coach of your sports team may be a volunteer. Your school may have parents who volunteer. When you pick up trash and throw it in a trash can, you are also a volunteer.

❯ In Santa Barbara, volunteers put together care packages for people in need.

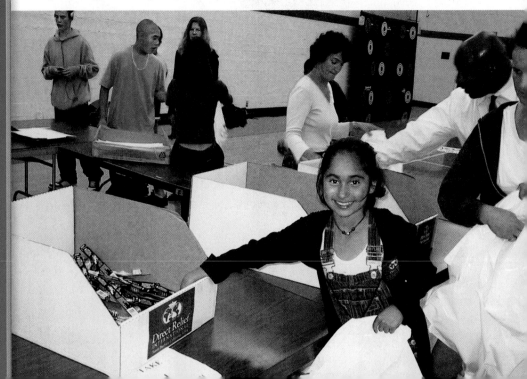

California Story Fund Project

Volunteering is a way to be a good citizen. The California Story Fund encourages people to collect and share stories about ways of life in California. In a project at the Lakeshore Elementary School in San Francisco, students interview older members of their families. Then they write poems based on the interviews. Later, the students will read their poems at schools and at libraries. The California Story Fund project helps people learn about the history and cultures of California.

Being a government leader is another kind of public service. Some government leaders, such as the mayor or judges, are elected. Others, such as the chief of the police department, are appointed, or chosen, to do certain jobs.

Every community has volunteers and government leaders who work for the **common good**—the good of everyone. Some work to get food and clothing to people who need it. Others help people stay safe or help keep neighborhoods and parks clean.

❱ Public service workers help a woman after a fire destroyed her Malibu home.

Reading Check ✿ **Main Idea and Details**
How do volunteers and government leaders help their communities?

309

Myldred Jones

▶ Myldred Jones

Myldred Jones is a person who believes in public service. In 1977, she sold her house in Los Alamitos, California. She used the money to set up a center where teenagers in trouble could go for help. Since then, the Casa Youth Shelter has helped more than 8,000 teenagers. At first, there was little money to run the shelter. Myldred Jones's vegetable garden provided many meals that first year.

Reading Check **Summarize**
What qualities does Myldred Jones have that make her a good community leader?

▶ Residents and volunteers at the Casa Youth Shelter in Los Alamitos

▶ Using dogs is often the best way to find people who have been trapped during disasters.

California Rescue Dogs

Some people work together as a group to provide public service. One such group is the California Rescue Dog Association.

For more than 20 years, this volunteer group has been training dogs and the people they work with to help find people who are lost or trapped. Members of this group have taken part in more than 2,000 searches.

The rescue dogs have found people who were trapped during earthquakes. They have found lost children, and they have searched for people after fires. The volunteers and the dogs are true community heroes!

Reading Check **Summarize**
Why are these volunteers community heroes?

Young People Can Help

Many young people help in their communities every day. One of those young people is Samuel Nassie, of Paradise, California. Nassie worried that the veterans in his community's cemetery would be forgotten.

He made a map of the grave markers in the cemetery. Then Nassie researched each veteran.

When he had finished his research, he presented the information to local veterans' groups and community groups. "The reason I continue to do this project is to provide a way for us to never forget our community's heroes,"* said Nassie.

Reading Check **Summarize**
What did Samuel Nassie do to help his community?

▶ Samuel Nassie won an award for the work he did for his community.

*Samuel Nassie. From the Prudential Spirit of Community Awards Speech. 2004.

How to Help

Reading about ways in which some people help may make you want to do more. You can help by sharing with others the skills you have. If you enjoy reading, you could read to a younger child. You can help by sharing your time with others. Perhaps you can help a friend or a family member care for a pet.

Reading Check **Summarize**
What are two ways to help?

Summary Many people in public service do work for the common good of the community. Some of these people are volunteers, and some are government leaders.

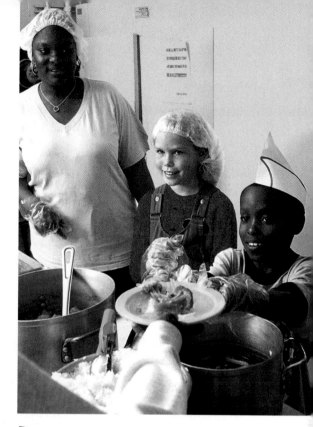

▶ **These volunteers serve food to others.**

Review

1. What are some ways that citizens serve their community?

2. **Vocabulary** Write a sentence or two to explain **public service**.

3. **Your Community** How do people in your community help each other?

Critical Thinking

4. **Make It Relevant** How could you volunteer in your community?

5. **ANALYSIS SKILL** What effect do you think volunteers have on your community?

6. **Write an Advertisement** Think of a volunteer group you know. Write an advertisement asking listeners to join.

7. **Focus Skill** **Main Idea and Details** On a sheet of paper, copy the graphic organizer. Fill it in to tell how volunteers can make their community better.

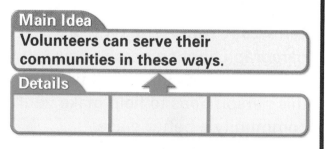

Main Idea
Volunteers can serve their communities in these ways.

Details

Reading Social Studies

The **main idea** is the most important idea of the passage. **Details** are the facts, reasons, or examples that support the main idea.

(Focus Skill) Main Idea and Details

Complete this graphic organizer to show that you understand important ideas and details about being a good citizen. A copy of a graphic organizer appears on page 77 of the Homework and Practice Book.

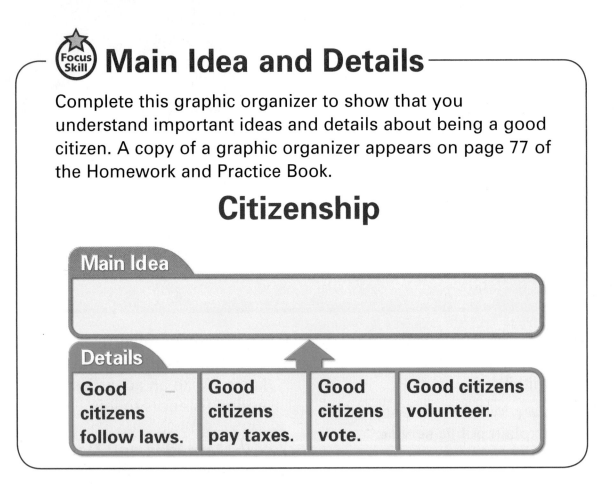

Citizenship

Main Idea

Details

| Good citizens follow laws. | Good citizens pay taxes. | Good citizens vote. | Good citizens volunteer. |

✏️ California Writing Prompts

Tell About Your Hero Write a paragraph about a person you think is a good citizen. Tell what this person does to help make your community a better place.

Write a Commercial Imagine you write television commercials. Think about how you can convince people to vote in the next election. Explain why it is important to vote.

Use Vocabulary

Write the word that correctly matches each definition.

justice, p. 294

volunteer, p. 297

election, p. 302

jury, p. 304

public service, p. 308

common good, p. 309

1. working for the good of the community

2. fairness

3. the time set aside for voting

4. someone who chooses to work without being paid

5. the good of everyone

6. a group of 6 to 12 citizens who decide if a person has broken a law

Recall Facts

Answer these questions.

8. What are two ways citizens can get involved in elections?

9. What character traits do good citizens have?

Write the letter of the best choice.

10. How does Larry Sly help people?
    A He volunteers at a food bank.
    B He fights forest fires.
    C He became President.
    D He writes about freedom.

11. Which of these do you need to be in order to vote?
    A on a jury
    B 18 years old
    C elected to office
    D a person who volunteers

Apply Skills

Read a Flowchart Use the flowchart on page 301 to answer the question.

7. What happens after a person is interviewed?

Think Critically

12. What are some ways you could help your community?

13. How does a citizen help choose who will be mayor? Explain.

Young Active Citizens

Get Ready

Across the United States, young citizens are helping in their communities. Some help build homes or write and print useful health-care information. Others write letters and help with fund-raising. While their activities may be different, they all want to make their community a better place to live.

Locate It

California

Menlo Park

Fresno   Hemet

What to See

Tim is a volunteer in his community of Hemet. He helps build homes for low-income families. He volunteers with the Habitat for Humanity organization. This organization believes that everyone should have a simple, decent place to live. Tim and other volunteers work to make a difference in the lives of families in their community.

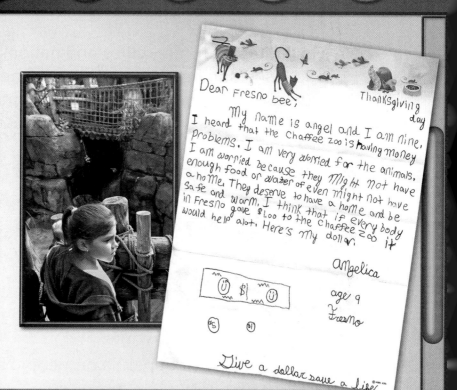

Angelica heard that Fresno's Chaffee Zoo was having money problems. So she wrote a letter to the local newspaper about this and included a dollar. In Angelica's letter, she suggested that everyone give a dollar to the zoo to help the animals. Her one-dollar donation encouraged others to give money, and soon about $200,000 had been collected. This money will help the zoo pay for many of its projects.

Dear Fresno bee,
Thanksgiving day

My name is angel and I am nine, I heard that the Chaffee zoo is having money problems. I am very worried for the animals, I am worried because they might not have enough food or water or even might not have a home. They deserve to have a home and be safe and warm. I think that if everybody in Fresno gave $1.00 to the chaffee zoo it would help alot. Here's my dollar.

Angelica
age 9
Fresno

Give a dollar save a life

Ariane learned that Spanish-speaking people in Menlo Park were having difficulty finding information about health care. So she did research about the medical services and programs available. Ariane put together this research in a Spanish-language brochure and gave it out to the people in her community.

Guía-Médica

Una Referencia para
Servicios Médicos
gratis o económicos

SALUD

El Condado Sud de San Mateo
Ciudades de Redwood City, Menlo Park,
y East Palo Alto, y también Palo Alto

© 2000 Ariane
Proyecto de Servicio para la Comunidad
Con estímulo de Corporación Prudential, Corporación Raychem,
y el Club de Rotary en Menlo Park

A Virtual Tour

GO
ONLINE
Visit VIRTUAL TOURS at
www.harcourtschool.com/hss

Unit 4 Review

🔆 **THE BIG IDEA**

Government Communities and nations need laws and leaders to help protect citizens and keep order. Our governments rely on participation from citizens.

Summary ## Government and Citizenship

In the United States, we elect leaders to make the laws. Local leaders in government make laws for our community. State leaders pass laws for the whole state. Our national government makes laws for the whole country. The United States Constitution tells how our government works.

Our government depends on people being good citizens. A good citizen votes in elections. A good citizen serves on a jury when asked. Citizens may make their communities better by doing <u>public service</u>.

Main Ideas and Vocabulary

Read the summary above. Then answer the questions that follow.

1. On what does our government depend on people being?
   - **A** local leaders
   - **B** lawmakers
   - **C** good citizens
   - **D** election workers

2. Who chooses the country's leaders?
   - **A** a jury
   - **B** the people
   - **C** state laws
   - **D** the Constitution

3. What is <u>public service</u>?
   - **A** homework
   - **B** work you must do
   - **C** paying bills for what you buy
   - **D** work done for the good of the community

Answer these questions.

4. What is the Bill of Rights?

5. Which branch of government makes sure that laws are obeyed?

6. What does a jury do?

Write the letter of the best choice.

7. How many branches of government are there?
   A one
   B two
   C three
   D four

8. Which is a responsibility of every citizen?
   A paying taxes
   B making laws
   C paying to vote
   D becoming a judge

9. What are the three main levels of government?
   A teachers, police, nurses
   B local, state, national
   C parks, courts, schools
   D council, manager, mayor

10. **ANALYSIS SKILL** How does the United States Constitution affect you?

11. Why does a state need a government?

Read a Bar Graph

Use the bar graph below to answer the following questions.

12. What does this bar graph explain?

13. Which county has the greatest number of post offices?

14. Which county has fewer post offices—Sacramento or San Diego?

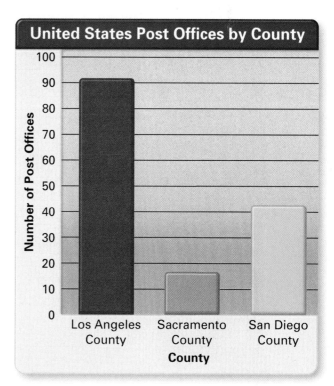

United States Post Offices by County

Read More

■ *New England Town Meeting,* by Dan Ahearn.

■ *Community Helpers,* by Bill Doyle.

■ *A Day in the Life of Washington, D.C.,* by Julie Seyfert Lillis.

Show What You Know

Unit Writing Activity

Write a Letter Think about a government job that you would like to know more about. Find out who has that job. Write a letter to that person, and ask how he or she got the job and what the duties of the job are.

Unit Project

Government Handbook Work with classmates to make a government handbook. Find out about the people and the jobs in your state and local government. Make a section for each level of government, and describe the job of each level. Display your government handbook in the classroom.

GO ONLINE Visit ACTIVITIES at www.harcourtschool.com/hss

Standing United

Start with the Standards

3.4 Students understand the role of rules and laws in our daily lives and the basic structure of the U.S. government.

The Big Idea

Symbols

Our country's government was established as a democracy. The principles we share are found in our documents, landmarks, symbols, and long-standing beliefs.

What to Know

✔ What do the symbols of our country and state mean?

✔ What kinds of special landmarks celebrate our history?

✔ Why are songs and documents important to our country and to California?

✔ Who has fought for freedom and justice in our country?

Show What You Know

★ Unit 5 Test

✎ Writing: A Brochure

✐ Unit Project: A Patriotic Show

Unit 5

Standing United

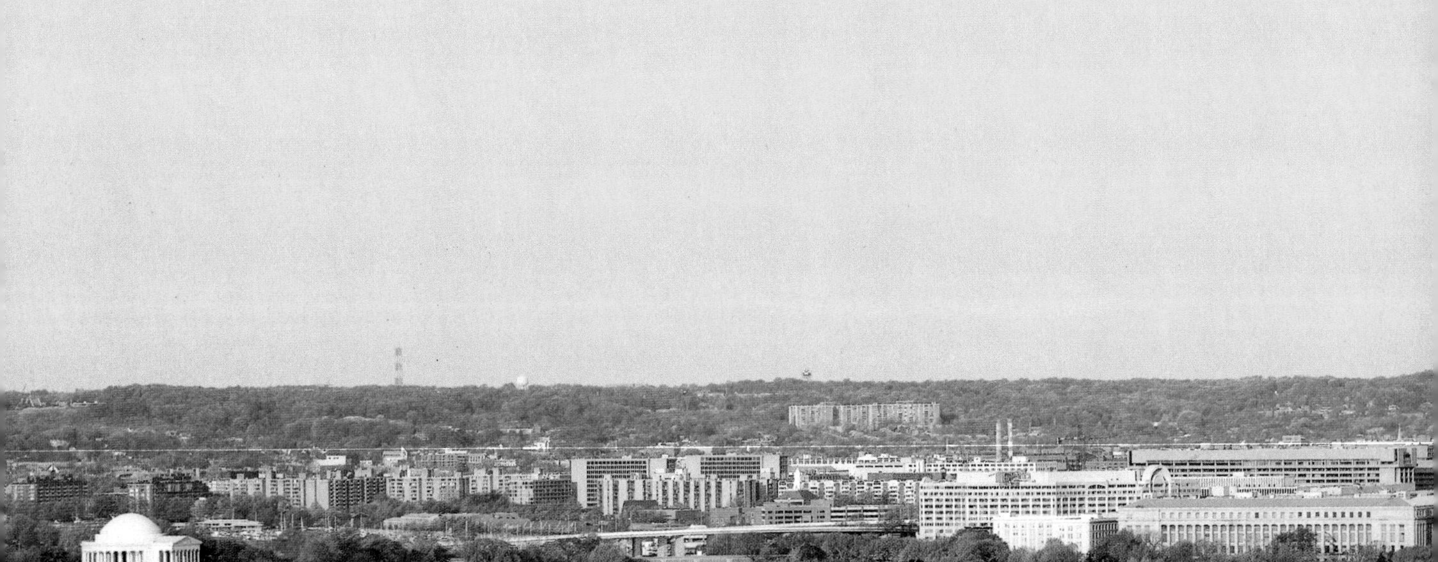

Talk About

Important People and Symbols

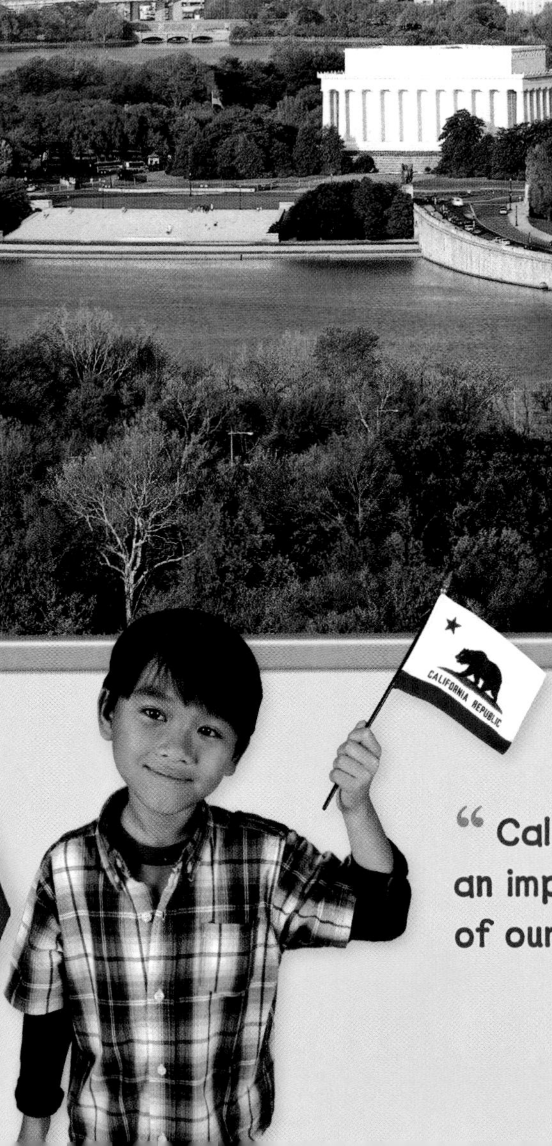

“California's flag is an important symbol of our state.”

"We remember the people who worked for our freedoms."

"Our nation's laws are written in an important document called the Constitution."

Vocabulary

liberty The power to be free and to make choices. (page 372)

patriotism A feeling of pride that people have for their country. (page 332)

equality Being treated the same as everyone else. (page 386)

holiday A special day for remembering a person or an event. (page 387)

monument Something built to honor and remember a person or an event. (page 342)

Visit INTERNET RESOURCES at **www.harcourtschool.com/hss** to view Internet Resources.

Reading Social Studies

Summarize

When you **summarize**, you retell the main events and ideas of a passage in your own words.

Why It Matters

Summarizing is one of the most important skills you can learn. When you summarize, you say in a few sentences what is most important.

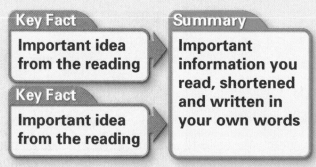

Key Fact	Summary
Important idea from the reading	Important information you read, shortened and written in your own words
Key Fact	
Important idea from the reading	

A summary includes only the main idea and the most important details. You can summarize a paragraph or a whole selection.

Practice the Skill

Read the paragraph. Find the most important information. Then summarize the paragraph in one sentence.

Fact   California's state capitol has a dome, as do some other state capitol buildings. The United States Capitol has a dome, too. Its dome is a symbol of **Summary** America. Many capitol buildings have domes.

Read the paragraphs. Then answer the questions.

California's Capitols

Sacramento has not always been the home of California's capitol. Four other cities were once California's capitol city.

Colton Hall in Monterey is considered the first capitol building. It was in Colton Hall that the first California constitutional convention was held in 1849.

California's legislators knew that a real home for the state government was needed. First they tried the town of Pueblo de San Jose. By 1851, however, the legislators decided that a new capital was needed.

General Mariano Vallejo offered to build the capitol in his town, Vallejo. Unfortunately, the legislators were not happy with the capitol Vallejo built. In 1853, they moved to the city hall in Benicia.

Once again, however, the legislators were unhappy with their meeting rooms. Finally, a decision was made in 1854 to build the capitol in Sacramento.

(Focus Skill) Summarize

1. How could you summarize the selection?

2. What key facts helped you summarize the selection?

USE VISUALS

Visuals can help you better understand and remember what you read.

▶ **Photographs, illustrations, diagrams, charts, and maps are different kinds of visuals. Many visuals have titles, captions, or labels that help readers understand what is shown.**

▶ **Visuals often show information that appears in the text, but in a different way. They may also add new information that is not in the text.**

	Checklist for Visuals
✓	What kind of visual is shown? a photograph
✓	What does the visual show?
✓	What does the visual tell you about the topic?

Apply As You Read

As you read this chapter, look closely at the visuals and the text that goes with them. Answer the checklist questions to better understand how a visual can help as you read.

California History-Social Science Standards, Grade 3

3.4 Students understand the role of rules and laws in our daily lives and the basic structure of the U.S. government.

America's Cherished Ideals

Liberty Bell Center in Philadelphia, Pennsylvania

This Land Is Your Land

by Woody Guthrie
illustrated by Kathy Jakobsen

An American singer and songwriter named Woody Guthrie often wrote about the natural beauty of the United States. Guthrie lived in California in the 1930s. He wrote about his experiences in California in some of his songs. "This Land Is Your Land" is his most famous song.

As I was walking that ribbon of highway,
I saw above me that endless skyway;
I saw below me that golden valley;
This land was made for you and me.

This land is your land, this land is my land,
From California to the New York island;
From the redwood forest to the Gulf Stream waters,
This land was made for you and me.

I've roamed and rambled and I followed my
  footsteps
To the sparkling sands of her diamond deserts;
And all around me a voice was sounding:
This land was made for you and me.

This land is your land, this land is my land,
From California to the New York island;
From the redwood forest to the Gulf Stream waters,
This land was made for you and me.

When the sun came shining, and I was strolling,
And the wheat fields waving and the dust clouds
    rolling,
As the fog was lifting a voice was chanting:
This land was made for you and me.

This land is your land, this land is my land,
From California to the New York island;
From the redwood forest to the Gulf Stream waters,
This land was made for you and me.

Nobody living can ever stop me,
As I go walking that freedom highway;
Nobody living can ever make me turn back;
This land was made for you and me.

Response Corner

❶ Guthrie describes a highway as "a ribbon." What is another object that a highway might look like?

❷ What "New York island" do you think Guthrie is talking about?

National and Local Symbols

There are many kinds of flags. States and cities have flags. So do some businesses and sports teams. Each country also has a flag. A country's flag is a **patriotic symbol** that stands for the ideas the people believe in, such as freedom. The feeling of pride in one's country is called **patriotism**.

Our Country's Flag

The design of the United States flag has changed over time. On early flags, the numbers of both the stars and the stripes showed the number of states in the nation.

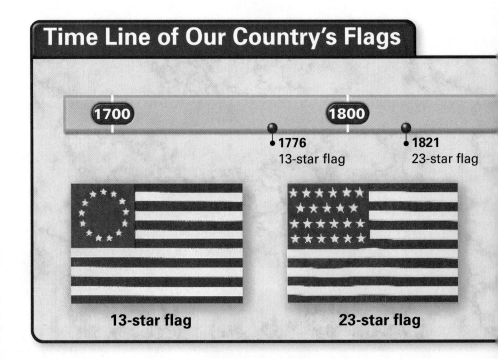

Time Line of Our Country's Flags

1700   1800

1776
13-star flag

1821
23-star flag

13-star flag   **23-star flag**

The nation of the United States of America grew, and soon there were too many states to show as stripes. Congress decided that only a star should be added to the flag when a new state joined the nation. The number of stripes stayed at 13, to stand for the first 13 states.

Congress did not say how the stars should be grouped, so flags had different designs. In 1912, the President said that stars must always be grouped in straight rows. The latest change to the nation's flag was made in 1960. In that year, the fiftieth star was added to stand for the state of Hawaii.

Reading Check ⏾ **Summarize**
What do the stars on the American flag stand for?

▶ A document called the Flag Code explains how the flag should be displayed and cared for. This is the current flag, which has 50 stars.

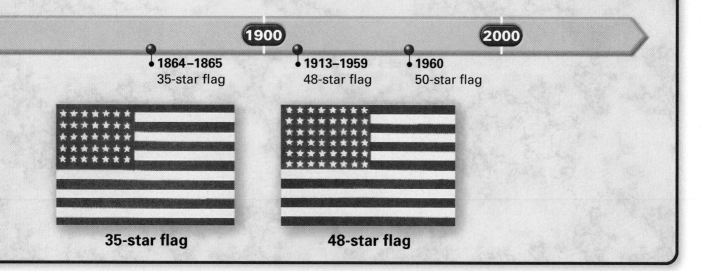

1864–1865
35-star flag

1913–1959
48-star flag

1960
50-star flag

1900

2000

35-star flag

48-star flag

The Bald Eagle

Since 1782, the American bald eagle has been the national bird of the United States. The bald eagle is a large and powerful bird. It lives in tall trees or on high cliffs and is a fierce and independent hunter. United States lawmakers felt that the bald eagle showed the strength, courage, and freedom of their new nation. They also liked the fact that the bald eagle lives nowhere else on Earth but in North America. More than 180 years after the bald eagle was made a national symbol, President John F. Kennedy said, "The fierce beauty and proud independence of this great bird aptly [very well] symbolizes the strength and freedom of America."*

❯ The bald eagle is a symbol of our nation's strength and freedom.

*John F. Kennedy. From a letter to Charles H. Callison, special assistant to the president of the National Audubon Society, 1961.

The bald eagle is used on many objects and documents, including the Great Seal of the United States. The Great Seal is an important symbol of our country. It can be seen on government papers and on government buildings in the nation's capital.

The design for the seal was begun after the Declaration of Independence was signed in 1776. Congress adopted the final design on June 20, 1782.

Reading Check **Sequence**
When did the American bald eagle become the national bird of the United States?

▶ The bald eagle is on the Great Seal of the United States.

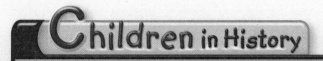

Children in History

Judy Bell and Smokey Bear

Fires have destroyed many forests in California and other states. After one forest fire in 1950 in New Mexico, a black bear cub was found without its mother. Its paws and legs had been burned. The bear cub was named Smokey after the bear pictured on fire prevention posters. Forest rangers used these posters to teach people about the danger of forest fires.

A forest worker named Ray Bell took the cub home, and his five-year-old daughter, Judy, helped take care of it.

When the bear started to get bigger, it went to live at the National Zoo in Washington, D.C. Smokey Bear has continued to be a symbol for fire prevention.

California's State Flag and Bird

The California state flag, which was adopted in 1911, has an interesting history. In 1846, California was under Mexican control. On June 14, 1846, a small group of settlers took as prisoner the leader of a Mexican government post in Sonoma. They said that California was a republic independent of Mexico.

The settlers put up a flag that had a grizzly bear, a star, a red bar, and the words "California Republic." This event became known as the Bear Flag Revolt. The flag flew only until July 9, 1846. It was replaced with the American flag when the settlers learned that Mexico and the United States were already at war.

The red of the star stands for courage. The star stands for sovereignty, or power.

The brown California grizzly bear is a symbol of great strength.

CALIFORNIA REPUBLIC

ANALYSIS SKILL **Analyze the Flag**

❓ **Why do you think California used the Bear Flag as the model for its state flag?**

In 1931, the California quail became California's state bird. It is also known as the valley quail. Though it is smaller than a pigeon, the California quail is plump and strong. The bird is blue-gray with a black plume on its head that curves downward. It also has a black bib with a white stripe under its beak. The California quail was an important food source for American Indians and settlers.

Reading Check ⏱**Summarize**
Why was the California quail important to Indians and settlers?

Summary Patriotic symbols stand for the ideas that the people of the United States believe in. They show our pride in our country. Symbols can also show things important to our state.

⚡**Fast Fact**

The California quail was one of the first birds in California to be given a scientific name.

Review

1. 💡 What do the symbols of our country and state mean?

2. **Vocabulary** What is one way to show **patriotism**?

3. **Your Community** What is a symbol of your community?

Critical Thinking

4. **Make It Relevant** What national symbols can you find around you?

5. **ANALYSIS SKILL** Why are state symbols used to help people identify with their state?

6. ✏ **Write a Speech** Write and give a short speech about one symbol of California. Tell what it means and why it is important.

7. **Focus Skill** **Summarize** On a separate sheet of paper, copy and complete the graphic organizer below.

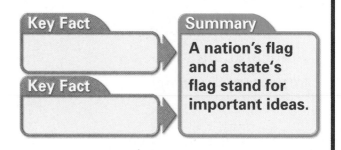

Key Fact		Summary
	→	A nation's flag and a state's flag stand for important ideas.
Key Fact	→	

The California State Seal

The Great Seal of California appears on state buildings, signs, and official documents. The symbols on the seal represent California's history, people, and resources. The seal was designed in 1849, before California became a state in 1850.

"Eureka," Greek for "I have found it," refers to the discovery of gold in California.

The miner is digging with a pick in search of gold.

The grizzly bear, California's official state animal, represents courage.

The group of stars at the top of the seal represents California as the 31st state.

A stained-glass version of the seal was placed in the ceiling of California's capitol building in 1907.

This four-foot bronze version of the seal is set in the walkway outside Colton Hall in Monterey.

The Sierra Nevada, a range of mountains, show the natural beauty of California's land.

Minerva, a Roman goddess, symbolizes wisdom and strength.

ANALYSIS SKILL Analyze Artifacts

1. In the seal, what items is the miner using?

2. How are the three seals shown on these pages the same? How are they different?

3. The original seal was designed in 1849. How do you think it would be different if it were designed today?

GO ONLINE Visit PRIMARY SOURCES at www.harcourtschool.com/hss

American Landmarks

 What to Know
What kinds of special landmarks celebrate our history?

✓ Americans are proud of their historical landmarks and monuments.

Vocabulary
landmark p. 340
monument p. 342
memorial p. 342

Focus Skill Summarize

California Standards
HSS 3.4.3

Long ago, most immigrants who arrived in the United States came by ship into New York Harbor. One of the first things they saw was the Statue of Liberty. To them, the statue was a symbol of a land where anything is possible.

The Statue of Liberty

A **landmark** is an important human or natural feature that helps people find their way. For many people, the Statue of Liberty has been an important landmark.

❱ Workers in Bartholdi's Paris studio built a full-sized model of the statue's left hand.

Frédéric-Auguste Bartholdi (fray•day•REEK aw•GOOST bar•TAHL•dee), the French artist who created the Statue of Liberty, wanted it to be large and amazing. In 1885, the statue arrived in the United States in 214 crates. The statue was a gift from France to the United States. Many Americans, including children, raised money to have the statue set up in New York Harbor.

▶ **Emma Lazarus**

On the base of the statue are lines from a poem by Emma Lazarus. The last line says, "I lift my lamp beside the golden door!" The "golden door" is the door of opportunity for those arriving in the United States. More than a century after it arrived, the Statue of Liberty still lights the way to freedom.

Reading Check ⏳ **Summarize**

Why is the Statue of Liberty a good symbol of our country?

▶ The tablet in the statue's left hand reads "July 4th, 1776," the date on which the Declaration of Independence was adopted.

Washington Monument

Lincoln Memorial

U.S. Capitol building

A City of Monuments

One way people honor their country is by building monuments. A **monument** is something built to honor or remember a person or an event in history. It may be a sculpture, a wall, a fountain, or some other lasting marker. Almost everywhere you look in our nation's capital, Washington, D.C., you see a monument or a memorial. A **memorial** is something that keeps a memory alive.

Some of the people honored by monuments and memorials include George Washington, Thomas Jefferson, and Abraham Lincoln.

▶ The National Mall (shown at the left) in Washington, D.C., has many monuments. The U.S. Capitol building is shown above.

Washington, D.C., is also known for the Capitol building, the White House, and other government buildings. The Capitol building is not only a landmark. It is also a place of history. The United States Congress meets in this building to make new laws that affect our daily lives. The Capitol is also a museum that displays important items from American history.

Today, citizens of the United States and people from around the world visit Washington, D.C. Our capital city is filled with symbols of our nation's history.

Reading Check **Make Inferences**
Why do people build memorials and monuments?

Landmarks Across the United States

In the Black Hills of South Dakota, a rocky cliff was carved into a huge sculpture designed by the artist Gutzon Borglum (GUHT•suhn BAWR•gluhm). Mount Rushmore National Memorial shows the faces of American Presidents George Washington, Thomas Jefferson, Theodore Roosevelt, and Abraham Lincoln. Mount Rushmore is one of many human-made landmarks found all across the United States.

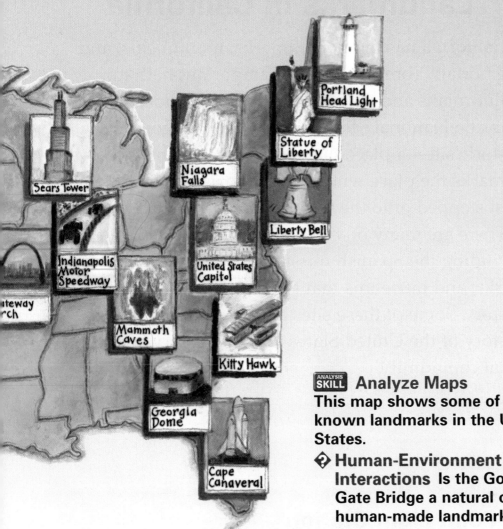

Labels on map: Sears Tower, Niagara Falls, Statue of Liberty, Portland Head Light, Liberty Bell, Indianapolis Motor Speedway, United States Capitol, ateway rch, Mammoth Caves, Kitty Hawk, Georgia Dome, Cape Canaveral

ANALYSIS SKILL Analyze Maps
This map shows some of the best-known landmarks in the United States.

❖ **Human-Environment Interactions** Is the Golden Gate Bridge a natural or a human-made landmark?

Some landmarks, such as the Grand Canyon, are formed by nature. Millions of years ago, the water of the Colorado River wore away its rocky bed to form the Grand Canyon. The canyon is more than one mile deep in some places. Another natural landmark is Niagara Falls, which is between New York and Canada. Old Faithful in Wyoming and Crater Lake in Oregon are also examples of landmarks formed by nature.

Reading Check **Compare and Contrast**
What is the difference between a human-made landmark and a natural landmark?

Landmarks in California

California has many landmarks, monuments, and memorials. Some of these are important both to Californians and to people all over the United States. Cabrillo National Monument, in San Diego, is a historic site—a place that is important in history. It marks the place where Juan Rodríguez Cabrillo first stepped onto the California coast in 1542.

There are many other historic sites in California, including the Spanish missions, gold-rush towns, parks, and museums that tell the story of the state's history. Some of these sites are also important to the history of the United States and the history of your local community.

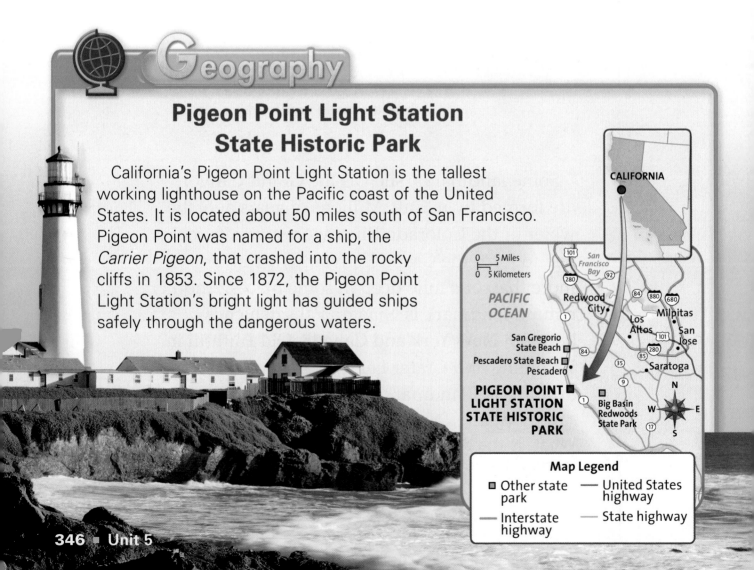

Geography

Pigeon Point Light Station State Historic Park

California's Pigeon Point Light Station is the tallest working lighthouse on the Pacific coast of the United States. It is located about 50 miles south of San Francisco. Pigeon Point was named for a ship, the *Carrier Pigeon*, that crashed into the rocky cliffs in 1853. Since 1872, the Pigeon Point Light Station's bright light has guided ships safely through the dangerous waters.

CALIFORNIA

0   5 Miles
0   5 Kilometers

PACIFIC OCEAN

101 San Francisco Bay 92
280
Redwood City 84 880 680
1 Milpitas
Los Altos 101 San Jose
San Gregorio State Beach 84 280 85
Pescadero State Beach 35 Saratoga
Pescadero 9
PIGEON POINT LIGHT STATION STATE HISTORIC PARK
1 Big Basin Redwoods State Park 17

N
W   E
S

Map Legend

■ Other state park
— United States highway
— Interstate highway
— State highway

California also has many state and national parks, including Yosemite (yoh•SEH•muh•tee), Joshua Tree, Death Valley, and Redwood National Parks. Many beautiful parks are also located along the California coastline. People come from all over California and the rest of the United States to see the natural beauty found in these parks.

Reading Check **Categorize and Classify**
Why does a place become a historic site?

Summary There are landmarks, monuments, memorials, and historic sites in California and all across the United States. They help us remember important events and people who have made our country great.

❱ **Visitors come from far away to see California's redwoods.**

Review

1. 💡 What kinds of special landmarks celebrate our history?

2. **Vocabulary** How are **monuments**, **landmarks**, historic sites, and **memorials** alike?

3. **Your Community** What monuments or memorials are found in your community?

Critical Thinking

4. **Make It Relevant** What landmarks have you visited?

5. **ANALYSIS SKILL** How can landmarks help us think about the past?

6. 🖌 **Make a Postcard** Make a postcard. Draw a landmark on one side. On the other side, write a note about the landmark.

7. **Focus Skill** **Summarize**
On a separate sheet of paper, copy and complete the graphic organizer below.

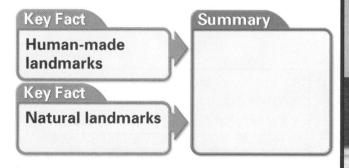

Key Fact		Summary
Human-made landmarks	➡	
Key Fact		
Natural landmarks	➡	

Identify State Capitals and Borders

❱ Why It Matters

The map of the United States on these pages shows the states and their capitals. You can use this map to find the location and shape of your state. You can also use it to identify your state's capital city.

❱ What You Need to Know

A star is the map symbol that tells you a city is a state capital. A star in a circle shows a national capital.

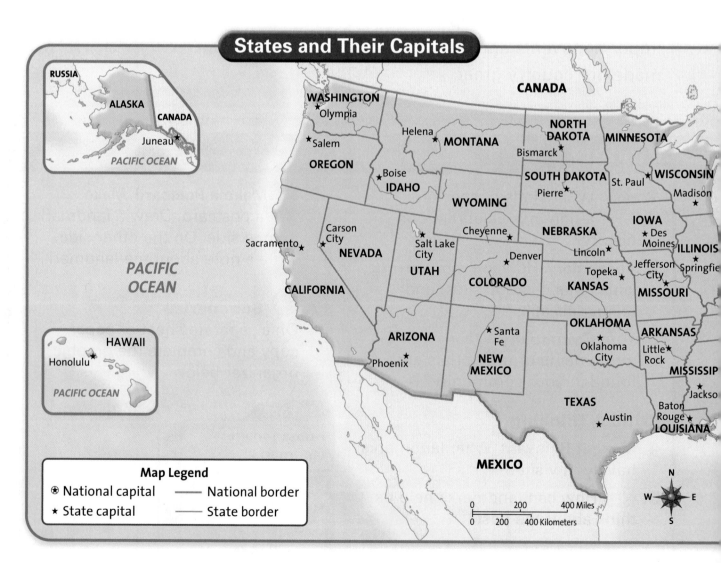

States and Their Capitals

RUSSIA

ALASKA
CANADA
Juneau ★
PACIFIC OCEAN

PACIFIC OCEAN

HAWAII
Honolulu ★
PACIFIC OCEAN

CANADA

WASHINGTON
★ Olympia

★ Salem
OREGON

Helena
★
MONTANA

★ Boise
IDAHO

WYOMING

Carson
City ★
NEVADA

Sacramento ★

★ Salt Lake
City
UTAH

CALIFORNIA

ARIZONA

★
Phoenix

Cheyenne ★

Denver
★

COLORADO

★ Santa
Fe
NEW
MEXICO

NORTH
DAKOTA
Bismarck ★

MINNESOTA

SOUTH DAKOTA   St. Paul
Pierre ★   ★

NEBRASKA

Lincoln ★

Topeka ★
KANSAS

WISCONSIN

Madison
★

IOWA
★ Des
Moines   ILLINOIS
Jefferson ★ Springfie
City
MISSOURI

OKLAHOMA
★
Oklahoma
City

ARKANSAS
Little ★
Rock

MISSISSIP

★
Jackso

TEXAS
★ Austin

Baton
Rouge ★
LOUISIANA

MEXICO

N
W   E
S

0   200   400 Miles
0   200   400 Kilometers

Map Legend
⊛ National capital   —— National border
★ State capital   —— State border

Find both symbols in the map legend. Then find them on the map.

The map shows state and national borders, too. A border is also called a **boundary**. Find the symbols for state and national borders in the map legend. Then find them on the map.

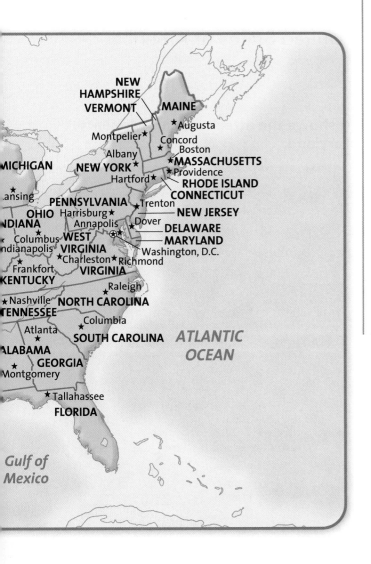

❭ Practice the Skill

Use the map and the map legend to answer these questions.

1. Where is California?

2. Where is California's capital city? What is its name?

3. What are the capital cities of the states that share borders with California?

4. What symbol stands for our state capital?

❭ Apply What You Learned

ANALYSIS SKILL **Make It Relevant** Find a map of your state that shows counties and county seats. Find your city or town. What county is it in? What is the name of your county seat? How many counties does California have?

 Practice your map and globe skills with the **GeoSkills CD-ROM**.

Map and Globe Skills

Songs and Words of Liberty

Many people have written about what the United States means to them. Some have written about important ideas, such as freedom. Others have written about the country's natural beauty. The words of some of these writers express what many people feel about the United States of America.

> ▶ **This painting shows the attack on Fort McHenry in Baltimore, Maryland.**

The Star-Spangled Banner

Francis Scott Key was a lawyer in Washington, D.C. During the War of 1812, he watched from a ship as the British attacked Fort McHenry, in Baltimore, Maryland. The battle went on into the night. When the fighting finally stopped, Key could not tell which side had won.

As the sun rose the next morning, Key could see the American flag still flying above the fort. He knew then that the United States had won. His feeling of patriotism was so strong that he wrote a poem. That poem, "The Star-Spangled Banner," later became our nation's **anthem**, or song of patriotism.

▶ **Francis Scott Key**

Reading Check Ŏ **Summarize**
What is the national anthem of the United States?

The Star-Spangled Banner
by Francis Scott Key

Oh, say can you see by the dawn's early light
What so proudly we hail'd at the twilight's last gleaming,
Whose broad stripes and bright stars through the perilous fight
O'er the ramparts we watch'd were so gallantly streaming?
And the rockets' red glare, the bombs bursting in air,
Gave proof through the night that our flag was still there.
Oh, say does that star-spangled banner yet wave
O'er the land of the free and the home of the brave?

Charters of Freedom

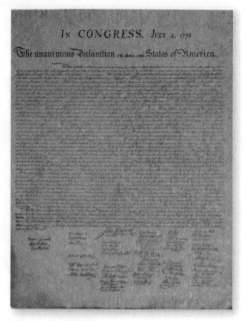

▶ **The Declaration of Independence**

The Declaration of Independence and the Constitution of the United States of America are two of the most important documents in our nation's history. They are often called the Charters of Freedom. *Charter* is another word for *document*. The Declaration stated that the United States was a free nation. The Constitution provided a plan of government for the new nation. Soon it also listed the rights of citizens.

In June 1776, the Second Continental Congress chose a group of five leaders to write the Declaration of Independence. Thomas Jefferson was asked to write down the group's ideas.

▶ **The murals on these pages were painted by Barry Faulkner in 1936. They are part of the Charters of Freedom display in the National Archives Building in Washington, D.C. The mural below shows Thomas Jefferson handing a draft of the Declaration of Independence to John Hancock.**

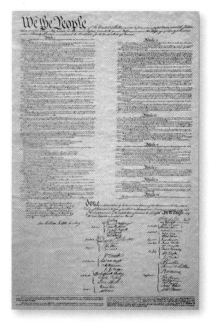

▶ The mural above shows James Madison (center) holding a draft of the Constitution.

Jefferson wanted to tell what was in the minds of most Americans. He wrote that all people are "created equal." He listed the reasons the colonists were angry with Britain. He wrote that the colonies had the right to form their own nation. The members of the Continental Congress liked what Jefferson wrote. On July 4, 1776, they made a few changes and then approved it.

The Constitution was based on the Virginia Plan, which had been written by James Madison. Because of his efforts in planning the Constitution and getting it approved, Madison is remembered as the Father of the Constitution. Madison himself said that the Constitution was "the work of many heads and many hands."*

▶ The Constitution of the United States was adopted in 1788.

Reading Check ŏ**Summarize**
What are two of the most important documents in our nation's history?

*James Madison. *Letters and Other Writings of James Madison, Volume 4.* J.B. Lippincott & Co., 1865.

▶ The California Constitution was written in Colton Hall in Monterey.

California in Words

The state of California also has a constitution. This constitution sets up the plan of government for the state. The preamble (PREE•am•buhl), or beginning, says, "We, the People of the State of California . . . do establish this Constitution."*

On September 1, 1849, representatives gathered in Monterey to write California's first constitution. They worked on it for six weeks. The California Constitution was signed on October 13, 1849. Like the United States Constitution, the California Constitution set up a government with three branches and included a declaration of rights.

▶ The California Constitution

*The California Constitution, adopted October 13, 1849.

Most states have a motto and a nickname. A motto tells what a state stands for. California's state motto is "Eureka!" It is a Greek word that means "I have found it!" The state motto refers to gold found during the 1849 gold rush. The motto has appeared on the state seal since 1849. It was made the official state motto in 1963.

California's nickname is "The Golden State." Lawmakers made that nickname official in 1968. The nickname refers to the gold once found in the hills of California as well as to the fields of golden poppies seen each spring throughout the state.

Reading Check ♂ Summarize
What is California's state motto and state nickname?

▶ This postcard shows California's nickname as well as other state symbols and landmarks.

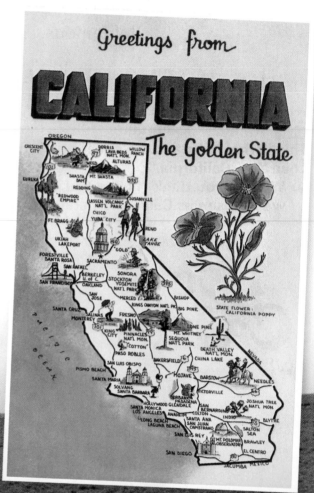

▶ The golden poppy is California's state flower.

California in Song

California has a state song called "I Love You, California." It was written by F. B. Silverwood, a merchant from Los Angeles. The words were later put to music by Alfred Frankenstein, who had been a conductor for the Los Angeles Symphony Orchestra. The song was played at expositions, or fairs, held in San Francisco and San Diego in 1915. It was first sung by famous Chicago opera singer Mary Garden.

ANALYSIS SKILL **Analyze Documents**

This is the cover and the sheet music for "I Love You, California."

◆ Why do you think "I Love You, California" was chosen as California's state song?

California's state legislature named it California's state song in 1951. Afterward, some people tried to make another song, "California, Here I Come," the state song. However, "I Love You, California" was made the state song by law in 1988.

Reading Check ☼**Summarize**
Where was the state song first played?

Summary Documents, mottoes, nicknames, and songs are important to Americans. They tell what is important to us and why we are proud of our country and our state.

❱ Chiura Obata's painting, *Evening Glow at Mono Lake, from Mono Mills*, shows California's natural beauty.

Review

1. 💡 Why are songs and documents important to our country and to California?

2. **Vocabulary** What is the **anthem** of the United States?

3. **Your Community** What is the song or motto of your community or school?

Critical Thinking

4. **Make It Relevant** What patriotic songs do you know? How did you learn them?

5. **ANALYSIS SKILL** Tell why the Declaration of Independence is important to Americans.

6. ✏ **Write a Song** Write a song that honors your community. Share your song with your classmates.

7. (Focus Skill) **Summarize**
On a separate sheet of paper, copy and complete the graphic organizer below.

Key Fact		Summary
	➤	Documents and songs are important to Californians.
Key Fact	➤	

Tell Fact from Fiction

❯ Why It Matters

Legends are tales that often begin as stories about real people and real events. As they are told again and again, more and more details are added. These details may not always be true.

Sometimes facts are mixed with fiction. When you are reading, it is important to be able to tell fact from fiction.

❯ What You Need to Know

Facts are statements that can be proved. Stories about real people, things, or events often have dates and names that can be checked.

In **fiction**, the story is made up. It may be based on a real person or event, but many of the details are imaginary, or made up.

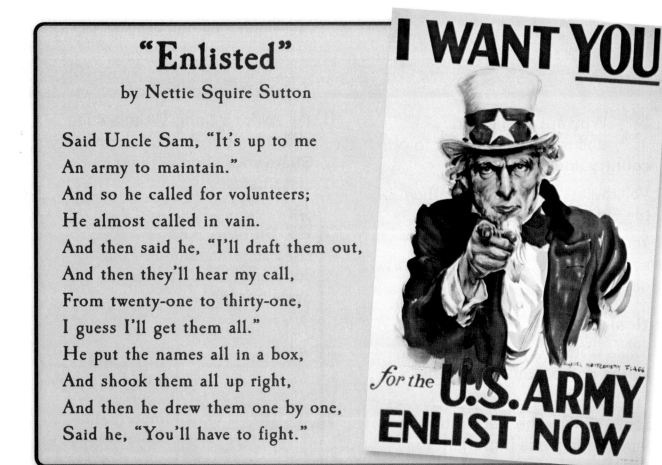

"Enlisted"
by Nettie Squire Sutton

Said Uncle Sam, "It's up to me
An army to maintain."
And so he called for volunteers;
He almost called in vain.
And then said he, "I'll draft them out,
And then they'll hear my call,
From twenty-one to thirty-one,
I guess I'll get them all."
He put the names all in a box,
And shook them all up right,
And then he drew them one by one,
Said he, "You'll have to fight."

I WANT YOU

for the U.S. ARMY ENLIST NOW

*From *A Book of Poems* by Nettie Squire Sutton, Messenger Press.

❱ Practice the Skill

On these pages are two selections about "Uncle Sam." One is a poem, and the other is an article. Use the selections to answer the following questions.

1 Which selection contains *facts*? How do you know?

2 Which selection is *fiction*? What details helped you decide?

❱ Apply What You Learned

ANALYSIS SKILL **Make It Relevant** To think about what you read, use what you have learned. As you read, ask yourself these questions.

• Is this fact or fiction?

• Can this be proved?

• How can it be proved?

• Which details are imaginary?

Samuel Wilson (1766–1854)

Samuel Wilson, who became known as "Uncle Sam," was born in Arlington, Massachusetts. In 1789, Wilson moved to Troy, New York. He and his brother owned a meatpacking business there. They supplied beef, pork, and salt to troops stationed near Troy. Wilson also worked as an Army inspector. He would stamp "US" on each barrel of food that was approved.

Workers joked that the "US" on the barrels stood for "Uncle Sam" instead of "United States." These workers later became soldiers. They continued to tell others that "US" stood for "Uncle Sam."

The story grew until Uncle Sam became a symbol for the United States. In 1961, Congress officially declared that Samuel Wilson was the person behind the nation's Uncle Sam symbol.

Reading Social Studies

When you **summarize,** you restate the key points, or most important ideas, in your own words.

 **Summarize**

Complete this graphic organizer to show what you have learned about our country's symbols. A copy of a graphic organizer appears on page 86 of the Homework and Practice Book.

America's Cherished Ideals

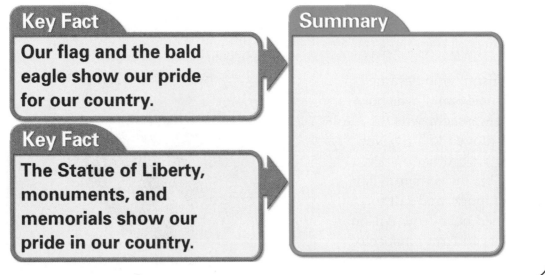

Key Fact

Our flag and the bald eagle show our pride for our country.

Key Fact

The Statue of Liberty, monuments, and memorials show our pride in our country.

Summary

California Writing Prompts

Write a Story Choose a symbol of the United States or of California that you learned about. Find out how it became a symbol. Then write the story to tell others about it.

Write a Poem Write a poem about the United States or about California. Tell why you are proud of your country or state. Share your new poem with the class.

Use Vocabulary

Choose the word or words that complete each sentence.

patriotic symbol, p. 332

memorial, p. 342

landmark, p. 340

anthem, p. 351

monument, p. 342

1. The Statue of Liberty is a ____ that helps people find their way.

2. Our flag is a ____ that shows how we feel about our country.

3. "The Star-Spangled Banner" is the ____ of the United States.

4. A ____ like the Lincoln Memorial is something that keeps a memory alive.

5. A ____ is built to honor a person or event in history.

Apply Skills

Identify State Capitals and Borders
Use the map on pages 348 and 349 to answer the question.

6. **ANALYSIS SKILL** What is the capital of Colorado?

Recall Facts

Answer these questions.

7. Why did Congress decide to stop adding stripes to the United States flag?

8. What is the national bird of the United States?

Write the letter of the best choice.

9. Which best describes Yosemite National Park?
   A landmark
   B memorial
   C monument
   D historical society

10. What are the Charters of Freedom?
   A monuments in Washington, D.C.
   B words to "The Star-Spangled Banner"
   C the Statue of Liberty and the Capitol building
   D the Constitution and the Declaration of Independence

Think Critically

11. Why would the people in a state want to have a state song?

Study Skills

POSE QUESTIONS

Asking questions as you read can help you understand what you are learning.

❯ **Form questions as you read. Think about why and how events happened and how events and ideas are related.**

❯ **Use the questions to guide your reading. Look for the answers as you read.**

Securing Our Freedoms	
Questions	Answers
Who were the colonists?	People living in the 13 English Colonies
What is independence?	
When was the Declaration of Independence approved?	

Apply As You Read

As you read, write down any questions you have about events, ideas, primary sources, people, or places discussed in the chapter. Then read on to look for the answers.

California History-Social Science Standards, Grade 3

3.4 Students understand the role of rules and laws in our daily lives and the basic structure of the U.S. government.

CHAPTER 10

Securing Our Freedoms

The *USS Ronald Reagan* enters the San Diego harbor.

Young Cesar E. Chavez

THE EARLY YEARS OF AN AMERICAN HERO

by Rebecca Valbuena
illustrated by Vilma Ortiz-Dillon

Many of the fruits and vegetables that we eat are harvested by migrant (MY•gruhnt) workers. A migrant worker is someone who works on a farm, picking the fruits and vegetables. Migrant workers move from place to place, harvesting the crops when they are ready to pick. There was a time when migrant farm workers were not treated fairly. They worked long hours and did not have good living conditions. This is the story of Cesar Chavez, who was a migrant farm worker as a child. He later worked for better conditions for migrant workers.

When Cesar Chavez was born in 1927, his family had been in the United States for almost 40 years. His grandfather, called Papa Chayo, had come to Arizona from Mexico in 1888. The growing family settled on 80 acres of farmland. Librado Chavez, Cesar's father, lived on the farm until he married Juana Estrada and became a businessman. When their second child was born on March 31, 1927, they named him Cesar Estrada Chavez.

Though Mrs. Chavez could neither read nor write, she gave good *consejos* (advice) to her four children and taught with *dichos* (proverbs). Her stories and sayings always had a moral lesson about honesty and obedience. She taught Cesar about nonviolence and told him he must always "turn the other cheek." She also taught him about sacrifice and giving to others. Cesar's father instilled in Cesar the belief that it is honorable to stand up for your rights and the rights of others. Through example, his father also taught Cesar to value responsibility and hard work. Later, Cesar said, "It came naturally to us to hope for the future and to want to make things better in the world."

In 1937, Cesar's father lost his land, and the family was forced to join the many thousands of men, women, and children who traveled throughout California in search of work. The Chavez family followed the crops as migrant farm workers, a hard life.

Work in the fields was extremely difficult. On one farm, Cesar and his family picked peas. Like picking lettuce, this was one of several jobs known as "stoop labor." Walking rows of peas while bent at the waist was a great strain on the back. The Chavez family spent hours harvesting peas, but when they carried their load to the end of the field for weighing, they were told that the grower wanted only "good peas." The family had to go back to the fields to pick more, and after three hours, the entire family earned only 20 cents!

The housing camps were dirty, cramped, rundown shacks, often with no running water, electricity, or bathrooms. Month after month, the Chavez family was on the move. They lived in crowded conditions and never had enough food. Cesar went to school when he could, but because the family traveled so much, he was never in one school for long. These were tough times for farm owners and farm workers, but *every* part of life was hard for migrant workers. They were cheated by many farm owners and treated without respect or human dignity. Cesar learned at a young age how the farm workers suffered unfair treatment and lived in poverty.

In 1942, when Cesar's father was hurt in a car accident, Cesar had to leave school to become the primary money earner for his family. He continued to witness the suffering and injustices in the lives of migrant farm workers.

His future experience in the United States Navy, followed by continued farm work and the eventual meeting of important individuals, caused this brave man to fight for change in farm working conditions. The qualities that Cesar E. Chavez had developed while growing up led him to become an internationally known leader in the struggle for justice for farm workers.

Response Corner

1. What lessons did young Cesar Chavez learn from his parents?

2. How old was Chavez when he left school to become the primary money earner for his family? How do you know?

Fighting for Our Freedoms

What to Know

Who fought for our freedoms?

✓ Long ago, people fought for our freedoms.

Vocabulary
freedom p. 370
colony p. 371
colonist p. 371
revolution p. 372
independence p. 372
liberty p. 372

Focus Skill **Summarize**

California Standards
HSS 3.4.3, 3.4.6

In the United States, we have many freedoms. **Freedom** is the right to make your own choices. It is one of the ideas on which our country was founded. In our country's early days, people had to fight for many freedoms.

▶ Important events in the growth of the new United States happened here, in Boston, Massachusetts.

The Thirteen Colonies

Long ago, most of the settlements along the eastern coast of North America were colonies of England. A **colony** is a settlement ruled by a country that is far away. The colonies had their own laws, but England made laws for them, too.

By the 1700s, there were 13 English colonies that reached from what is now Maine to Georgia. These colonies were the beginning of what is today the United States of America.

For a long time, the **colonists**, or people living in the 13 colonies, did not mind being ruled by England. Then lawmakers in England began passing new laws that the colonists felt were unfair. The colonists were angry that they had no part in making their own laws.

Reading Check ö **Summarize**
Where in North America were the colonies started?

The Thirteen Colonies

New Hampshire

Maine (part of Massachusetts)

New York

Massachusetts

Pennsylvania

Rhode Island

Connecticut

New Jersey

Delaware

Virginia

Maryland

Chesapeake Bay

North Carolina

Atlantic Ocean

South Carolina

Georgia

N
W   E
S

ANALYSIS SKILL Analyze Maps
◈ Regions **Why do you think the 13 colonies were all on the eastern coast of what became the United States?**

▶ Angry about taxes on tea, colonists dumped crates of tea into Boston Harbor in 1773. The event became known as the Boston Tea Party.

Freedom from England

The colonists began talking about starting their own country. In 1775, the Revolutionary War, or American Revolution, began. In a **revolution**, people are fighting for a change in government. The colonists fought against soldiers from England.

In 1776, John Adams, Benjamin Franklin, Thomas Jefferson, and other leaders wrote down the reasons that the colonies wanted independence. **Independence** is freedom from another country's control. The statement they wrote is called the Declaration of Independence.

It says that all people have the right to "Life, Liberty, and the pursuit of Happiness." **Liberty** is another word for *freedom*.

On July 4, 1776, the leaders of the 13 colonies voted to accept the Declaration of Independence. It told everyone that the colonies no longer belonged to England. They were now states in a new country, the United States of America.

Some of the signers of the Declaration of Independence, such as Benjamin Franklin, never fought in the war. Instead, they took risks by speaking out and writing about freedoms.

Thomas Jefferson also worked to make sure that Americans would have freedoms. The freedoms of speech, of the press, and of religion were important to him.

Reading Check **ŎSummarize**
What did the Declaration of Independence say?

▶ This painting shows Benjamin Franklin, John Adams, and Thomas Jefferson working on the Declaration of Independence. The final Declaration was approved in Independence Hall in Philadelphia, Pennsylvania, shown below.

Let Freedom Ring!

> Before he became President, General George Washington led American troops against the English.

The Revolutionary War began in 1775, a year before the Declaration of Independence was written. The Revolutionary War lasted for eight years. George Washington was chosen to lead the American troops against the English. Washington's army was made up of colonists who wanted to help. They were not trained or paid, and they had to get supplies from the towns for which they were fighting. The English soldiers, though, were well trained and were paid to fight. Their supplies were sent to them on ships from England.

ANALYSIS SKILL **Analyze Paintings**

This painting shows the Battle of Princeton, 1777.

What color were the uniforms of each side? How can you tell?

George Washington led the American soldiers in many battles. They won some, but they lost others badly. In 1783, after eight years, the Americans finally won the war and their independence from England. The United States is an independent country today because people were willing to fight for freedom.

Reading Check ☼**Summarize**
What did George Washington do to help the United States gain its freedom?

Summary The United States gained its freedom from England by fighting the Revolutionary War. Our early leaders worked to make sure Americans would have many freedoms.

▶ **Fireworks explode over the Golden Gate Bridge on the Fourth of July to celebrate our country's independence.**

Review

1. 💡 Who fought for our freedoms?

2. **Vocabulary** What **freedoms** are important to you?

3. **Your Community** Who are some of the everyday heroes in your community?

Critical Thinking

4. **Make It Relevant** How have you celebrated our nation's independence?

5. **ANALYSIS SKILL** What might be different today if people long ago had not fought for their freedoms?

6. ✎ **Write a Biography** Write a paragraph about a person who has fought for our freedoms.

7. (Focus Skill) **Summarize**
On a separate sheet of paper, copy and complete the graphic organizer below.

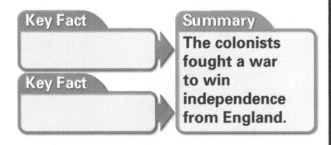

Key Fact		Summary
	➤	The colonists fought a war to win independence from England.
Key Fact		

Trustworthiness
Respect
Responsibility
Fairness
Caring
Patriotism

Franklin and Jefferson

"We hold these truths to be self-evident, that all men are created equal, that they are endowed by their Creator with certain unalienable Rights, that among these are Life, Liberty, and the pursuit of Happiness."*

–The Declaration of Independence

Why Character Counts

❓ **Why do you think the Congress chose Jefferson and Franklin to draft the Declaration of Independence?**

It was June 1776. The men of the Second Continental Congress had only one thing on their minds—drafting a Declaration of Independence.

To create the Declaration, the Congress had chosen two of the finest minds in the colonies. They had asked Thomas Jefferson to do the writing, with the help of Benjamin Franklin.

In some ways, Thomas Jefferson and Benjamin Franklin were very different. Jefferson was a rich landowner from Virginia. He had a college education.

Franklin, on the other hand, was from a working-class background. He went to school only two years and he had a job by age ten.

Benjamin Franklin

Thomas Jefferson

* Thomas Jefferson. "The Declaration of Independence." *The American Reader.* Diane Ravitch, ed. HarperCollins, 2000.

Painting called *Congress Voting the Declaration of Independence*

The first page of Thomas Jefferson's rough draft of the Declaration of Independence

Yet Jefferson and Franklin also were alike in many ways. They both were great writers and thinkers. Each loved science and new ideas. They loved the land of their birth. Both believed it could and should be a free and united country. They were willing to risk their lives for their country. Each was a true patriot.

Neither Benjamin Franklin nor Thomas Jefferson ever fought in a battle. Yet their gift to their country was just as great. They gave their ideas, their talents, and their understanding of government. They gave their dream of a country that was governed by its own people.

On July 4, 1776, the Second Continental Congress approved the Declaration that Jefferson and Franklin had worked so hard to write. With the help of these two great patriots, the United States of America began.

GO ONLINE Visit MULTIMEDIA BIOGRAPHIES at www.harcourtschool.com/hss

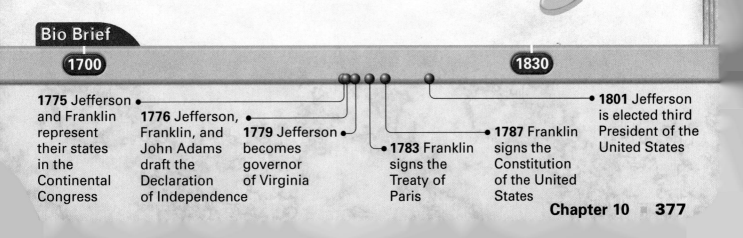

Bio Brief

1700

1830

1775 Jefferson and Franklin represent their states in the Continental Congress

1776 Jefferson, Franklin, and John Adams draft the Declaration of Independence

1779 Jefferson becomes governor of Virginia

1783 Franklin signs the Treaty of Paris

1787 Franklin signs the Constitution of the United States

1801 Jefferson is elected third President of the United States

2 Freedom of Religion

People in the United States follow many different religions. People who follow a religion share a belief in one god or several gods. Freedom of religion is one of our rights as citizens of the United States.

The Pilgrims and the Puritans

In 1620, a group of English settlers known today as Pilgrims arrived in North America. They settled the colony of Plymouth in what is now Massachusetts. They had left England so they could follow their own religion.

Locate It

MASSACHUSETTS

Plymouth Colony

❯ Visitors can tour a realistic 1627 Pilgrim village at the Plymouth Plantation Museum.

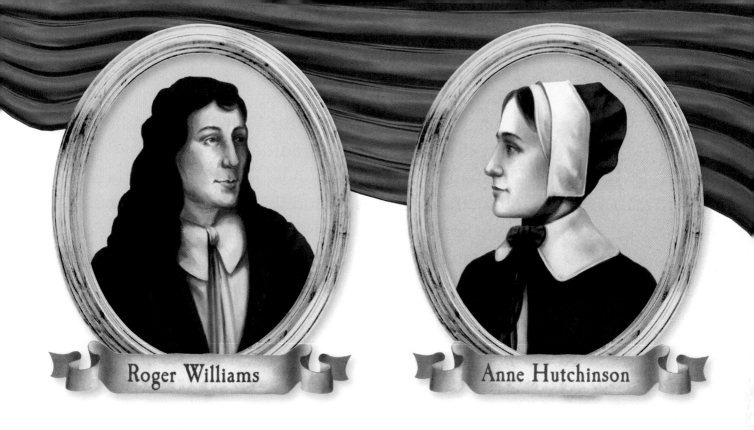

Roger Williams

Anne Hutchinson

Less than ten years later, a group called the Puritans also came. They started the Massachusetts Bay Colony. The lives of the Puritans centered on religion. The Puritans expected all newcomers to follow their beliefs or leave the colony.

Roger Williams taught that people should not be punished for having different beliefs. The Puritan leaders forced him to leave. Williams founded a settlement called Providence.

The leaders in Massachusetts also disliked the teachings of a woman named Anne Hutchinson. She, too, believed in freedom of religion and was told to leave Massachusetts. Hutchinson founded a settlement on an island near Providence. There people had the freedom to follow any religion. This settlement later joined the one founded by Williams. Together they became the Rhode Island Colony.

Reading Check **ŏSummarize**
What groups came to the American colonies for religious freedom?

Religion Today

Today, religion is an important part of the culture of many groups. People in the United States follow many different religious traditions. Some follow Christianity, and others follow Judaism. Still others follow the teachings of Buddhism, Hinduism, or Islam. Some people choose not to follow any religion. Freedom of religion is one of our rights as citizens of the United States.

Cultural Heritage

Places of Worship

People who follow Christianity go to services at a church or cathedral. Those who follow Judaism go to a synagogue (SIH•nuh•gahg), or temple, to pray. Followers of Islam pray in a masjid (MAHS•jid), or mosque (MAHSK). Buddhists visit temples to meditate. Churches, synagogues, temples, and mosques also serve as places where people can gather for celebrations or other events.

Buddhist Temple

Synagogue

Church

Mosque

Most people who follow a religion like to **worship**, or pray, together. For this reason, communities have special places where people can worship.

Reading Check ⏱️**Summarize**
What are some of the religions of the United States?

Summary Freedom of religion is an important right in our country. Many people in the past worked so that people in the United States today can worship according to their own beliefs.

Followers of Five Religions in the United States

Religion	Number of Followers
Buddhism	1,082,000
Christianity	159,030,000
Hinduism	766,000
Islam	1,104,000
Judaism	2,831,000

Analyze Tables This table shows how many people follow the five largest religions in the United States.
❖ Why do you think Christianity is the largest group?

Review

1. 💡 Who has fought for freedom of religion?

2. **Vocabulary** In what kinds of buildings do people **worship**?

3. **Your Community** What are some of the places where people in your community worship?

Critical Thinking

4. **Make It Relevant** In what ways do you—or people you know—show your freedom of religion?

5. **ANALYSIS SKILL** Why did people long ago think religious freedom was important?

6. 🖌️ **Make a Trading Card** Make a trading card about someone who has fought for an important freedom. On one side of the card, draw a picture of the person. On the other side, write a sentence or two describing what he or she did.

7. **(Focus Skill) Summarize** Copy and complete the graphic organizer below.

Key Fact		Summary
	→	Settlers left England to follow their own religion.
Key Fact	→	

"... and Justice for All"

The Pledge of Allegiance ends with the words "and justice for all." Many people have worked so that all Americans are treated equally and fairly.

The Civil War

Beginning in 1861, when Abraham Lincoln was President, Americans fought a terrible war known as the Civil War. People in the North fought people in the South. A **civil war** is a war in which the people of a country fight each other.

> **President Abraham Lincoln felt strongly that the nation should remain united.**

What to Know

Who has fought for equality and justice in our country?

✔ Many ethnic groups in our country fought for civil rights.

✔ Women fought for equal rights.

✔ People are still fighting today for human rights.

Vocabulary

civil war p. 382
slave p. 383
equality p. 386
civil rights p. 387
holiday p. 387
ethnic group p. 387
human rights p. 388

 Focus Skill Summarize

California Standards
HSS 3.4.6

One of the reasons for the war was that many people in the North thought that having slaves was wrong. A **slave** is someone who is forced to work for another person without pay.

One person who fought slavery was a slave named Harriet Tubman. In 1849, Tubman ran away from her owner's Maryland plantation, or large farm. She went to Philadelphia, Pennsylvania. Tubman then went back to Maryland to help other slaves escape to freedom. She risked her life many times to help more than 300 people escape from slavery.

> Harriet Tubman

Reading Check ŏ **Summarize**
Why did Harriet Tubman risk her life?

ANALYSIS SKILL **Analyze Maps**
During the Civil War, Southern states were called Confederate states and Northern states were called Union States.
◈ Regions Where were the Border states located?

Civil War States

MAP LEGEND
- Union state
- Border state
- Confederate state
- Territory

Frederick Douglass

Frederick Douglass was born in about 1817 into a family of enslaved Africans. He lived with his grandmother because his mother had to work on a farm miles away.

Young Frederick was given an opportunity few enslaved children had—the chance to learn to read and write. When he read about freedom, he knew that was what he wanted more than anything.

❭ In 1845 Frederick Douglass published this book. It tells the story of his life as a slave.

Frederick Douglass

NARRATIVE

OF THE

LIFE

OF

FREDERICK DOUGLASS,

AN

AMERICAN SLAVE.

WRITTEN BY HIMSELF.

> Beginning in 1847 in Rochester, New York, Douglass published *The North Star* newspaper.

While still a young man, Douglass escaped to the North, where he could be free. He continued his education and became a speaker for the Massachusetts Antislavery Society. He spoke out against slavery wherever he went. Soon he began publishing a newspaper called *The North Star*, in which he wrote about ending slavery.

In 1863, President Abraham Lincoln signed a document called the Emancipation Proclamation, which freed many slaves. In 1865 President Lincoln helped pass the Thirteenth Amendment to the Constitution of the United States. This amendment says that it is against the law to own slaves. Lincoln hoped the end of the Civil War in 1865 would bring the country together. Still, African Americans did not have the same freedoms as other citizens.

> Frederick Douglass spent most of his life speaking and writing about freedom.

Reading Check ⦿ **Summarize**

How did Douglass speak out against slavery?

Equal Rights for Women

In 1870, soon after the Civil War, the idea of **equality**, or equal rights, became law for the whole country. This new law gave all people born in the United States the right to be United States citizens. It also gave everyone the right to vote—except women.

Elizabeth Cady Stanton and Susan B. Anthony believed that women should be able to vote. They had worked hard for this right. They were unhappy when women did not get the right to vote in 1870. These women and others after them did not give up, though. They continued their work. Finally, in 1920, women won the right to vote.

Reading Check ŎSummarize
How did many women's lives change after 1920?

❱ These buttons and this postcard are about women's suffrage. *Suffrage* is the right to vote. The button at the left shows Susan B. Anthony.

Civil Rights

About 100 years after the Civil War, a man named Dr. Martin Luther King, Jr., fought for **civil rights**, or rights of personal freedom, for all people. He spoke against unfair laws. King's words made some people angry, but he told his followers to remain peaceful. King was given the Nobel Peace Prize for his work.

King's birthday is now a national holiday. A **holiday** is a day set aside for remembering a special person or event.

In the United States today, every person has the same rights, no matter what his or her religion or ethnic group. An **ethnic group** is a group of people who have the same language, culture, and way of life.

Reading Check ✎**Summarize**
What did Dr. Martin Luther King, Jr., do?

❯ Rosa Parks helped change laws that separated African Americans from others.

❯ Dr. Martin Luther King, Jr., after he received the 1964 Nobel Peace Prize

Human Rights

Human beings all over the world deserve other rights as well. These are called human rights. **Human rights** include the right to speak freely, to have a fair trial if accused of a crime, and to work. They also include the right to have food, clean water, and a safe place to live. People today, as in the past, work for human rights.

Cesar Chavez is one person who fought for human rights. Mexican American farmworkers were very poor. Chavez started an organization, called the National Farm Workers Association, to protect their rights. The organization worked to get the farmworkers better pay and living conditions. Today, March 31 is a holiday in California. It honors Cesar Chavez and the important work he did.

⚡Fast Fact

Mexican American Cesar Chavez started the National Farm Workers Association in 1962. Now called the United Farm Workers, the group won important rights for farmworkers in California and other states.

Eleanor Roosevelt, wife of President Franklin D. Roosevelt, also made a difference for people with poor living conditions. Eleanor Roosevelt visited California farmworkers, coal miners, and poor people in cities. She then wrote and spoke about what she saw.

Reading Check ⊙**Summarize**
How did Eleanor Roosevelt help people with poor living conditions?

Summary Many people have worked to make sure that all Americans are treated equally and fairly. Many also have worked for basic human rights for people all over the world.

▶ **Eleanor Roosevelt visiting children in Visalia, California, in 1940**

Review

1. 💡 Who has fought for equality and justice in our country?

2. **Vocabulary** Write a sentence about the importance of **equality**.

3. **Your Community** How has the work of people who fought for equal rights helped make your community a better place?

Critical Thinking

4. **Make It Relevant** How might your life be different if others had not worked for justice and equality?

5. **ANALYSIS SKILL** Why do you think some people worked so hard for equal rights?

6. ✏ **Make a Page for a Book** Make a page for a book about people who took risks to secure our freedoms. Choose one person and find or draw a picture of her or him. Explain why the person should be remembered.

7. (Focus Skill) **Summarize**
Copy and complete the graphic organizer below.

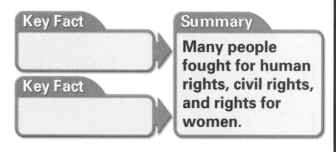

Key Fact

Key Fact

Summary
Many people fought for human rights, civil rights, and rights for women.

Understand Time Periods

▶ Why It Matters

As you read about people in the past, you learn about things that happened over long periods of time. It is helpful to know about the different periods into which time can be divided. Understanding time periods will give you a better idea of when things happened.

▶ What You Need to Know

Time lines can show events that happened during any period of time. For example, a time line might show events that happened during a day, a week, a month, a year, or any number of years.

All time lines are divided into smaller parts. These parts can stand for different time periods.

A part may stand for a **decade**, a period of 10 years. A part may also stand for a **century**, a period of 100 years. On the time line below, the space between two marks stands for one century.

Events in Our Country's History

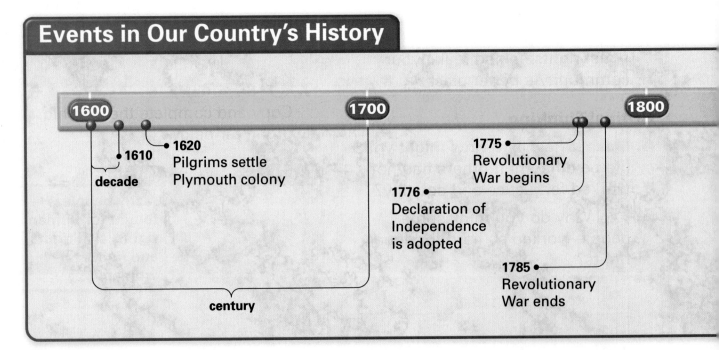

1600
1610
1620
Pilgrims settle Plymouth colony
decade
century
1700
1776 ●
Declaration of Independence is adopted
1775 ●
Revolutionary War begins
1785 ●
Revolutionary War ends
1800

The first part of the time line shows events that happened during the seventeenth century. The seventeenth century includes the years from 1601 to 1700.

❯ Practice the Skill

Use the time line on pages 390–391 to answer these questions.

❶ When did the Pilgrims arrive in North America?

❷ Was the Declaration of Independence adopted before or after the Revolutionary War began?

❸ What is the first event on the time line? In what century did that event happen?

❯ Apply What You Learned

ANALYSIS SKILL **Make It Relevant** Draw a time line with marks for the twentieth and twenty-first centuries. Use the time line to show events in your life from the past, present, and future. Label the year you were born. Mark the year you will go to middle school and some other important years for you in the past, present, and future. You can add drawings to your time line. Explain your time line to a classmate.

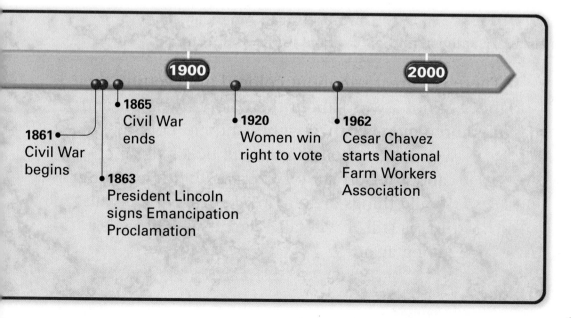

1861
Civil War begins

1863
President Lincoln signs Emancipation Proclamation

1865
Civil War ends

1900

1920
Women win right to vote

1962
Cesar Chavez starts National Farm Workers Association

2000

The Fight for Civil Rights

On January 1, 1863, President Abraham Lincoln signed the Emancipation Proclamation. This proclamation made all men in our country free. Some groups soon found that being free was not enough. They were often paid low wages and were not allowed to live in certain neighborhoods. What are some ways that people can change things they think are unfair? People fighting for personal rights had different answers to that question.

In Their Own Words

Sojourner Truth, former African American slave, antislavery activist, and early equal rights supporter

" There is a great stir about colored men getting their rights, but not a word about the colored women; and if colored men get their rights, and not colored women get theirs, there will be a bad time about it. So I am for keeping the thing going while things are stirring; because if we wait till it is still, it will take a great while to get it going again. . . . "

— from a speech at the first annual meeting of the American Equal Rights Association in New York City, May 9 and 10, 1867. *Historic Speeches of African Americans*, Franklin Watts, 1993.

Sojourner Truth

Elizabeth Cady Stanton,
antislavery activist and early women's rights movement leader

Elizabeth Cady Stanton

"... if we consider her [a woman] as a citizen, as a member of a great nation, she must have the same rights as all other members, according to the fundamental principles of our Government."

— from Stanton's "The Solitude of Self" speech on January 18, 1892. *Not for Ourselves Alone: The Story of Elizabeth Cady Stanton and Susan B. Anthony*, Alfred A. Knopf, 1999.

Cesar Chavez,
founder of the United Farm Workers

"The road to social justice for the farm worker is the road to unionization. Our cause ... [is] all founded upon our deep conviction that the form of collective self-help which is unionization holds far more hope for the farm worker than any other approach..."

— from a speech delivered to the Senate Committee on Labor and Public Welfare, 1969. *The Words of César Chávez*, Texas A&M University Press, 2002.

Cesar Chavez

Dr. Martin Luther King, Jr.,
civil rights leader in the 1960s

Dr. Martin Luther King, Jr.

"... In the process of gaining our rightful place we must not be guilty of wrongful deeds.
Let us not seek to satisfy our thirst for freedom by drinking from the cup of bitterness and hatred. We must forever conduct our struggle on the high plane of dignity and discipline."

— from King's "I Have a Dream" speech given at the March on Washington on August 28, 1963. *Martin Luther King, Jr.: The Peaceful Warrior*, Pocket Books, 1968.

It's Your Turn

ANALYSIS SKILL Analyze Points of View What are the different ways these Americans believed civil rights could be won? Explain how they chose to work for civil rights.

Reading Social Studies

When you **summarize,** you restate the key points, or most important ideas, in your own words.

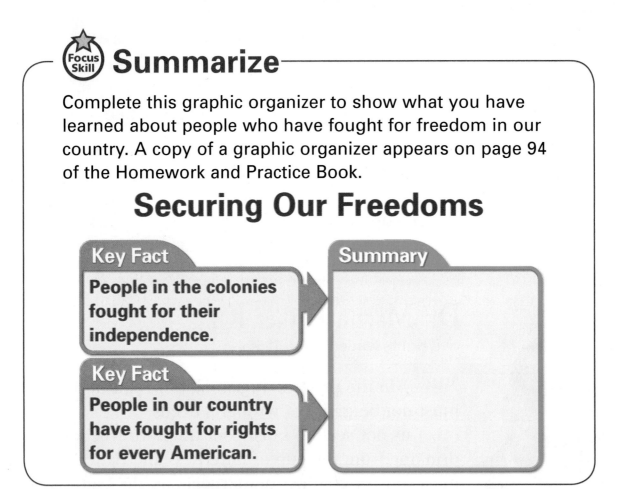

(Focus Skill) Summarize

Complete this graphic organizer to show what you have learned about people who have fought for freedom in our country. A copy of a graphic organizer appears on page 94 of the Homework and Practice Book.

Securing Our Freedoms

Key Fact

People in the colonies fought for their independence.

Key Fact

People in our country have fought for rights for every American.

Summary

California Writing Prompts

Write a Letter Imagine that you are a colonist fighting in the Revolutionary War. Write a letter telling why you are fighting in the war. Include a date, an opening, a closing, and a signature.

Write a Speech Choose one of the people from this chapter that you admire. Write a short speech telling about this person. Explain why he or she deserves an award for his or her work.

Use Vocabulary

Write the word or words that complete each sentence.

1. George Washington helped lead the ____ of the colonies.

freedom, p. 370   **revolution,** p. 372

2. Thomas Jefferson was a writer of the Declaration of ____.

Independence, p. 372 **Liberty,** p. 372

3. Freedom of religion allows us to ____ as we want.

worship, p. 381   **holiday,** p. 387

4. Susan B. Anthony worked for equal rights, or ____, for women.

equality, p. 386 **ethnic groups,** p. 387

5. Dr. Martin Luther King, Jr., worked for ____, or the rights of personal freedom, for all people.

civil war, p. 382   **civil rights,** p. 387

Apply Skills

Understand Time Periods Use the time line on pages 390 and 391 to answer the question.

6. **ANALYSIS SKILL** How many years does the time line cover?

Recall Facts

Answer these questions.

7. Why were religious leaders upset with Roger Williams and Anne Hutchinson?

8. Which President signed the Emancipation Proclamation?

Write the letter of the best choice.

9. What is one reason Americans fought the Civil War?
   A to end slavery
   B for religious freedom
   C to be free from England
   D for freedom of speech

10. What did Eleanor Roosevelt do?
   A worked as a Civil War spy
   B spoke against slavery
   C worked for human rights
   D wrote about religious freedom

Think Critically

11. **ANALYSIS SKILL** Why do you think the colonists fought against England?

12. **ANALYSIS SKILL** How do civil rights affect us today?

Monuments and Memorials in Washington, D.C.

Get Ready

A memorial is a reminder of the actions or beliefs of a person or group of people. In Washington, D.C., those who fought for our country's freedom are honored with memorials. These include the Vietnam Veterans Memorial, the Lincoln Memorial, the Washington Monument, and the Korean War Veterans Memorial. They all remind us of those who acted for our country's freedom.

Locate It
United States

Washington, D.C.

What to See

Vietnam Veterans Memorial

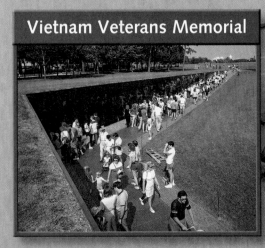

This memorial, known as "The Wall," was completed in 1982. The designer, Maya Lin, listed on it the names of more than 58,000 Americans. These people were killed or missing in action during the Vietnam War.

Lincoln Memorial

The Lincoln Memorial, built by Daniel Chester French and Henry Bacon, opened in 1922. It honors the sixteenth President of the United States, Abraham Lincoln.

Washington Monument

The Washington Monument opened in 1884 to honor George Washington, the nation's first President. It was designed by Robert Mills.

Korean War Veterans Memorial

The Korean War Veterans Memorial honors more than 54,000 men and women who fought in the Korean War. This memorial, which opened in 1955, was sculpted by Frank Gaylord and Louis Nelson.

A Virtual Tour

GO ONLINE

Visit VIRTUAL TOURS at
www.harcourtschool.com/hss

Review

☀ THE BIG IDEA

Symbols Our country's government is based on freedom. The principles we share are found in our documents, landmarks, symbols, and long-standing beliefs.

Summary

Standing United

Our patriotic symbols, such as the flag, stand for our country's beliefs. Landmarks and monuments help us remember important places and events. Our anthem, "The Star-Spangled Banner," tells how we feel about our country.

The colonies in North America fought for freedom from England. After the colonists won the war for independence, they set up a new government. One of the important new rights was freedom of religion. People in the United States have also fought for equality for all citizens.

Main Ideas and Vocabulary

Read the summary above. Then answer the questions that follow.

1. What does the word freedom mean?
   A work for the community
   B the Constitution of the United States
   C the right to make your own choices
   D a settlement ruled by another country

2. Why does our country have patriotic symbols?
   A to help pass laws
   B to stand for our beliefs
   C to tell people to follow the laws
   D to help us choose whom to vote for

Recall Facts

Answer these questions.

3. Who led the American soldiers in the Revolutionary War?

4. What did Harriet Tubman do to fight for freedom?

5. What do the Charters of Freedom explain?

6. What is the name of California's state bird?

7. What do the stars and stripes on our country's flag stand for?

Write the letter of the best choice.

8. Which is our national anthem?
   A "America"
   B "America the Beautiful"
   C "My Country 'Tis of Thee"
   D "The Star-Spangled Banner"

9. Which bird is a symbol for our country?
   A the swan
   B the crow
   C the turkey
   D the bald eagle

10. Which is a California historic site?
    A the Hoover Dam
    B Mount Rushmore
    C the Grand Canyon
    D the Cabrillo National Monument

Think Critically

11. **ANALYSIS SKILL** How was the Civil War a fight for civil rights?

12. Why do some people risk their lives to help others gain freedom?

Apply Skills

Identify State Capitals and Borders

ANALYSIS SKILL Use the map below to answer the following questions.

13. What is the state capital of California?

14. Which states border California?

15. What body of water borders western California?

Western States and Their Capitals

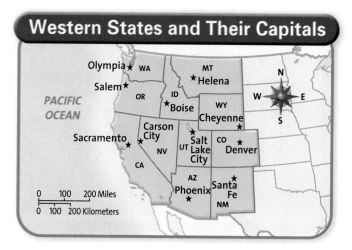

Activities

Show What You Know

Read More

■ *World Monuments*, by Susan Ring.

■ *Symbols of a Nation and California*, by Elaine Israel.

■ *Jimmy Doolittle: American Hero*, by Elaine Israel.

Unit Writing Activity

Design a Brochure Write, design, and illustrate a brochure that tells about a landmark, historic site, or monument. Tell visitors what they will see there. Explain why the landmark is important to people.

Unit Project

Patriotic Show Work with classmates to plan and perform a show that tells about our freedoms. Sing patriotic songs. Your show may include some of the following activities. Recite famous speeches. Dress as a famous freedom fighter and tell about that person. Perform a skit about a holiday, and tell why we celebrate it.

GO ONLINE Visit ACTIVITIES at **www.harcourtschool.com/hss**

Unit 6

Understanding Economics

Unit 6

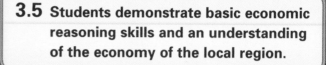

Start with the Standards

3.5 Students demonstrate basic economic reasoning skills and an understanding of the economy of the local region.

The Big Idea

Economics

People depend on one another and on other resources to produce, buy, and sell goods and services. Good decision making helps the economy of a family or a community.

What to Know

✓ How do businesses use resources from the community?

✓ Where do our goods come from, and how do they get to our community?

✓ What choices do people have for using their money?

✓ What can you do to invest in your human capital?

Show What You Know

★ Unit 6 Test

✎ Writing: An Interview

🖌 Unit Project: Make a Newspaper

Understanding Economics

Talk About

Economics

" California farmers provide many of the fruits and vegetables that we eat. "

"We get some of the goods we use from other places around the world."

"It is important to make good choices about using your money."

Vocabulary

producer   Someone who makes and sells a product.
(page 417)

business   An activity in which workers make or sell goods, or do work for others. (page 421)

human resources The workers needed to make and sell a product or service. (page 423)

consumer A person who buys a product or service. (page 418)

interdependence The way countries and states depend on one another for products and resources. (page 429)

 GO ONLINE Visit INTERNET RESOURCES at **www.harcourtschool.com/hss** to view Internet Resources.

Reading Social Studies

Generalize

To **generalize** is to make a broad statement that is based on what you know about a group of ideas.

Why It Matters

Being able to generalize can help you better understand and remember what you read.

Facts		
Information given	Information given	Information given

Generalization

General statement about that information

As you read, think about the ideas presented. Then make generalizations about what you learn. A generalization is always based on facts.

Practice the Skill

Read the paragraph. Then make a generalization.

 **Fact** People in California grow and raise many different kinds of food that are sent to other places. Vegetables such as onions, carrots, asparagus, and broccoli are exported. Meats such as beef and chicken are also exported. Californians export many fruits as well, including cherries, grapes, and oranges.

Read the paragraph. Then answer the questions.

A World Trading Center

California is a center for world trade. Part of California's success is due to its location. To California's west is the Pacific Ocean. The ocean makes it easy to trade goods with Japan, China, South Korea, and other countries. To California's east are the great markets of the United States.

California is a world leader for agriculture. A long growing season allows California to produce fruits and vegetables most of the year.

Tourism is also important to California. The state's sunny skies and beautiful cities bring in tourists from other states and countries.

California is also a center for industry. Many of the world's computers and machines are made in California factories.

Modern transportation systems help in world trade. Trains, ships, airplanes, and trucks bring products to and from California.

Focus Skill Generalize

1. What overall generalization can you make based on the selection?

2. Why is California a center for world trade?

Study Skills

CONNECT IDEAS

You can use a web organizer to show how different ideas and information are related.

- ❯ **List important themes in the web's center.**
- ❯ **Add ovals showing main ideas from the chapter that support each theme.**
- ❯ **Add bubbles for the important facts and details that support each main idea.**

Apply As You Read

Complete a web organizer like the one above as you read this chapter. Fill in each bubble by adding the facts and details that support each main idea.

California History-Social Science Standards, Grade 3

3.5 Students demonstrate basic economic reasoning skills and an understanding of the economy of the local region.

Workers and Consumers

Shoppers in Fresno, California

BOOM TOWN

by Sonia Levitin
illustrated by Cat Bowman Smith

In the mid-1800s, many people traveled west across the country to California in search of gold. This is the story of Amanda and her family. They travel to California so that her father can mine for gold. They decide to live in a cabin in town instead of in the tent cities. While her father is off mining for gold, Amanda gets very lonely and bored in this new place. One day she decides to bake some pies. It takes her many tries until she gets the gooseberry pies just right.

When Pa came home from the gold fields on Saturday night, there was a pie for him, too. "Amanda, you are the queen of the kitchen!" Pa scooped me up and whirled me around. I was proud.

The next week I made an extra pie for Pa to take with him to the gold fields.

Saturday night when he came home singing, coins jangled in his pocket.

We all ran out to ask, "Did you strike gold, Pa?"

"No," he said. "I sold Amanda's pie. The miners loved it. They paid me twenty-five cents a slice!"

After that, Pa took pies to the gold fields every week. And every week he came home with coins in his pockets. Some miners walked right to our door looking for pie. They told Ma, "You should open a bakery."

Ma said, "It's my girl Amanda who is the baker. If she wants to make pies, that's fine. But I have no time."

The cooper is a barrel maker.

The blacksmith works with iron.

The tanner works with leather.

The miller grinds wheat or corn.

I needed more pans and another bucket. One day Peddler Pete came by, and with the money I'd made I bought them.

"You're a right smart little girl," said the peddler, "being in business like this."

I thought fast and told him, "Anybody can make money out here. Folks need things all the time, and there're no stores around. If you were to settle and start one, I'll bet you'd get rich."

Peddler Pete scratched his beard. "Not a bad idea," he said. "My feet are sore from roaming. I could use this cart and build my way up to having a store."

So pretty soon we had us a real store called PEDDLER PETE'S TRADING POST. Trappers and traders and travelers appeared. After shopping at Pete's, they were good and hungry.

They came to our cabin, looking for pie. Some liked it here so well they decided to stay. Soon we had a cooper, a tanner, a miller, a blacksmith. A town was starting to grow.

A tailor came to make and mend clothes. A cobbler crafted shoes and boots. We heard the *tap tap* of his hammer and smelled the sweet leather. A barber moved in with shaving mugs, and an apothecary with herbs and healing drugs. So the town grew up all around us.

My pie business blossomed. Sometimes the line snaked clear around the house. Baby Betsy entertained the people while they waited. Billy added another shelf. Joe and Ted made a bench. We all picked berries and apples. Even Ma came to help. We had to get a bigger jar for all the money coming in.

apothecary
(uh•PAH•thuh•kair•ee)
drugstore

The money jar in our kitchen looked ready to bust. Where could we safely keep all that cash? Lucky us, one day Mr. Hooper, the banker, appeared.

"I'm building a bank," Mr. Hooper said to me. "This is getting to be a <u>boom town</u>."

"We'll use your bank," I told Mr. Hooper, "but the roads are so poor. In winter there's mud, and in summer there's dust. We need some sidewalks and better streets."

"You're a smart little lady," said Mr. Hooper, tipping his hat. "I'll see what I can do about that."

Before we knew it, the bank was built and wooden sidewalks were laid. One street was called Bank Street; the other was Main. Soon every lane and landmark had a name. Pa and my brothers built on a big room for our bakery.

One day Pa said to me, "Amanda, I'm through panning for gold. Will you let me be in business with you?"

"Sure!" I said, happily. "I'd love to work with you, Pa, and I'd also like to go to school."

So Pa turned to baking, and we all worked together. Pa sang while he rolled out the dough:

"Amanda found a skillet and berries to fill it, Made pies without a pan;

Our pies are the best in all the West. I guess I'm a lucky man."

Now Pa is with us every day. There's excitement and bustle all around. Our house sits in the middle of a boom town!

And to think it all started with me, Amanda, baking pies!

Response Corner

❶ What did Amanda say to persuade Peddler Pete to start a store?

❷ Why did people move to this California community? Why did they stay?

Working in a Community

What to Know

How do people in a community depend on one another?

✓ People work together and depend on one another.

✓ People can be both consumers and producers.

Vocabulary

goods p. 415
wage p. 415
depend p. 416
service p. 416
producer p. 417
consumer p. 418

 Generalize

California Standards
HSS 3.5, 3.5.1

In a community, people do many different jobs. Some of these people make or sell things we use every day, such as food, clothing, and shelter.

People Work Together

Think about how busy you would be if you had to make all the things you use. You would have to grow your own vegetables. If you wanted meat, eggs, and milk, you would have to raise or hunt animals. You would not be able to get water from a faucet. Instead, you would have to dig a well or take a pail to a river or lake.

⚡ Fast Fact

This Sikh farmer harvests celery in Yuba City in 1922. Many Sikhs came to California in the early 1900s to work as farmers.

► Early California workers cut trees for lumber. Some of this wood was used to build homes.

California's early settlers had to make everything they used by themselves. But as towns and then cities grew, people were able to share the work with others in their community. Some people grew and sold enough food for everyone. Some people made and sold clothing. Others gathered wood and stone for houses. They used those materials to build homes for people in the community.

In the past, people often bartered, or exchanged what they had for what they wanted. Today, most people use money to buy goods. **Goods** are things that can be bought or sold. To get money, people usually do work for someone. The money paid to a person for the work he or she does is called a **wage**.

ANALYSIS SKILL **Analyze Photographs**
❷ **How did this California family make their shelter?**

(Reading Check) ☼ **Generalize**
Why do most people today work?

Depending on One Another

Members of a community **depend**, or count on, one another. Shopkeepers, or people who own stores, depend on farmers to grow food for them to eat and to sell. Farmers, like everyone else in the community, depend on shopkeepers to sell clothes and other goods.

Members of a community depend on other kinds of workers, too. Doctors, nurses, teachers, principals, police officers, and firefighters do not sell food or goods. Instead, they provide important services for the community. A **service** is work that a person does for someone else.

Reading Check ♻ **Generalize**
Why do people in communities depend on one another?

▶ **People depend on the services doctors provide to help them stay healthy.**

People Make Things

People depend on each other to create new goods and to improve old ones. The people who create new goods depend on other people to buy them.

In 1975, Californians Steve Jobs and Steve Wozniak began making small computers. At that time, computers were really just huge calculators. Few people used them.

Soon, many people wanted the new computers because they were small and easy to use. Jobs and Wozniak started a computer company. The company became one of the world's leading computer producers. A **producer** makes and sells a product. Today, more than 10,000 people work for the company Jobs and Wozniak started.

Reading Check ⏺ **Generalize**
Why do people create and improve goods?

▶ Steve Jobs, John Sculley, and Steve Wozniak with one of their early computers

▶ People buy and sell goods at this farmer's market in Ventura County.

People Buy Things

By the 1980s, many other companies were producing computers that were easy to use. Today, people can choose from many different computers made by many different companies. Computer consumers now have far more choices than they did 30 years ago. A **consumer** is a person who buys a product or a service. Whenever you buy something, you are a consumer.

▶ **Now people can use portable computers nearly anywhere.**

Cultural Heritage

Neighborhood Shops

People come from all over the world to live and work in California. Many of them settle in the state's largest cities, in communities where people from the same place also live. Los Angeles, for example, is home to Thai Town, Little Persia, and Little Armenia. There is Koreatown, Japan Town, and Little Ethiopia. There are also large communities of people from Cambodia, El Salvador, Guatemala, Iran, Mexico, and the Philippines living in Los Angeles— more than in any other United States city. Some of the people from other countries open stores where people can buy items from their home country.

Consumers have more products to choose from all the time. Producers are always trying to make new and better cars, computers, televisions, toys, cereals, and other products.

Reading Check **Ŏ Generalize**
Who is a consumer?

Summary People in communities depend on one another for goods and services. Consumers use their wages to buy goods and services from producers.

❱ **Consumers use computers to work, play, learn, shop, and communicate.**

Review

1. How do people in a community depend on one another?

2. **Vocabulary** Explain the difference between **goods** and **services**.

3. **Your Community** Look at the advertisements in your local newspaper. How do producers try to get consumers to buy products?

Critical Thinking

4. **Make It Relevant** What jobs do you do to earn money? What goods or services have you purchased?

5. **ANALYSIS SKILL** What effects might a new company have on the people in a community?

6. **Write A Job Description** Write a description of a person who works in your community. In your description include whether the person produces a good or a service. Explain how people in your community depend on this good or service.

7. **(Focus Skill) Generalize** On a separate sheet of paper, copy and complete the graphic organizer below.

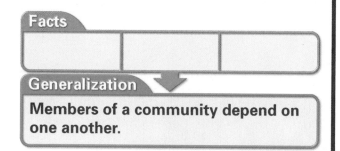

Facts

Generalization

Members of a community depend on one another.

Using Resources

 What to Know
How do businesses use resources from the community?

- ✓ Businesses depend on natural, human, and capital resources.

- ✓ Manufacturing has changed over the past century.

- ✓ New resources are being developed for the future.

Vocabulary
business p. 421
human resource p. 423
capital resource p. 423
manufacture p. 424

Focus Skill Generalize

California Standards
HSS 3.5, 3.5.1

One of California's most important natural resources is its good soil. California's farmers have used their rich farmland to make the state's agriculture famous around the world. Agriculture is the raising of crops and farm animals for sale. California's fruits, nuts, meat, and vegetables are sold in supermarkets as far away as Boston, Massachusetts, and Anchorage, Alaska.

976

GREETINGS from CHICO CALIFORNIA

3B-H1699

© CURT TEICH & CO., INC.

An Industry Starts Near Resources

Consumers all over North America enjoy the products of California's famous almond industry. Spanish priests first brought almonds to California in the mid-1700s. They planted almond trees around their missions on the California coast. But the coastal climate was too wet and often too cool for the trees.

In the 1850s, pioneer John Bidwell experimented with crops on his ranch in the warmer and drier Sacramento Valley. His work helped make almonds an important crop. Bidwell was an entrepreneur, a person who creates a new product or business. A **business** is an activity in which workers make or sell goods for others. Bidwell also founded the city of Chico on the land around his ranch.

▶ John Bidwell in about 1895

Reading Check ⓞ **Generalize**
Why do you think almonds grew better in the Sacramento Valley than they did along the coast?

Locate It

Chico

CALIFORNIA

▶ Workers process almonds at Bidwell Orchard in Chico, California.

Resources at Work

In Chico and in other California communities from the Sacramento Valley to Bakersfield, thousands of people have jobs in the almond industry. Farmers, called growers, plant orchards of almond trees. Workers care for the trees and gather the nuts at harvest time.

Processing companies hull the almonds, or remove their outer shells. Then they clean the shelled nuts and sort them by size. Other companies cut, roast, flavor, and package the almonds. Still other businesses use trucks, ships, and airplanes to send almonds to stores, where consumers buy them.

❱ An almond is the large seed inside a fruit related to the peach and plum.

A Closer Look

An Almond Factory

A factory is a building where products, such as almonds, are prepared and packaged.

❶ The almonds are collected from the field and delivered to the factory. They are dumped into a large receiving area and cleaned.

❷ The almonds are transferred by conveyor belts to hulling machines where the outer shell is removed and the inner shell is cracked open.

❸ The cracked almonds are sent to vibrating screens to separate the shells from the nut, or almond meat.

❹ The almond meats are conveyed to separating tables where the meats are sorted according to size and quality.

❺ The almond meats are packaged and are now ready for sale or additional processing.

❖ What happens after the almonds are sorted?

California's almond industry uses three kinds of resources. Land and water are the natural resources that are used to grow almonds. People are the **human resources** used to grow and sell almonds.

Finally, the industry needs **capital resources**, or money to buy factories and equipment. Entrepreneurs use capital resources to start new businesses. They may buy equipment or land to help those businesses grow.

> Maisie Jane Hurtado started a business that makes and sells flavored almonds. Her business helped save her family's farm in Chico, California.

(Reading Check) ŏ **Generalize**
On what three kinds of resources do all industries depend?

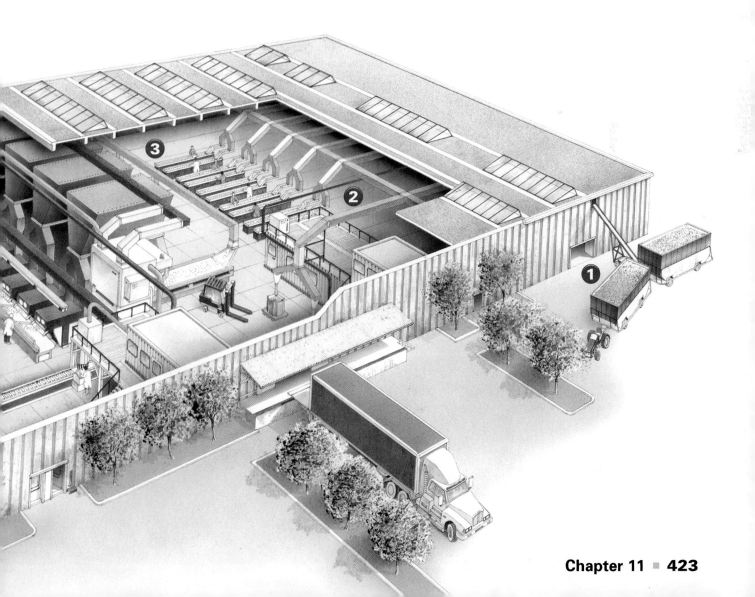

In the past, workers measured logs by hand.

Waterwheels powered machines like this one at Bale Grist Mill in Napa County.

Factories Then and Now

Food processing is just one kind of industry. Many industries are involved in manufacturing. To **manufacture** (man•yuh•FAK•chuhr) is to make something with machines. The lumber industry has been one of California's most important manufacturing industries.

Forests cover much of California. The trees in California's forests provide wood for lumber. Trees that are good for lumber include pines, Douglas firs, oaks, and redwoods. California redwoods are the world's tallest trees. In California's early days, it took many men and animals to cut the trees and haul them to the sawmill.

▶ Today, computerized machines measure logs.

▶ The Pacific Lumber Company is in Scotia.

The first lumber factories were often built near bodies of water. The water was used to float logs from the woods to the sawmill. Water also turned huge waterwheels that made the machines of the factory run.

Water resources are still used to run machines in lumber factories, but in a different way. Waterpower is now used to make the electricity that runs the machines. This is called *hydroelectric power*. The word part *hydro* means "water."

Much of the factory work that was once done by hand is now done with computers and robots. Today, many items—from lumber to airplanes to clothes and toys—are manufactured in factories.

Reading Check **Main Idea and Details**
What natural resources have been important to lumber factories both in the past and today?

Tomorrow's Resources

Water remains one of California's most important natural resources. However, additional natural resources are used to run today's factories. These resources include oil, gas, coal, sunshine, and wind power.

Another kind of natural resource is geothermal energy. This energy is produced by the heat inside Earth. California has more than 20 known geothermal resource areas.

Geography

California's Geothermal Regions

Geothermal regions form in areas where there is melted rock called magma under Earth's crust. These regions are very hot. Earthquakes move the magma and break it up, allowing water to rise to the surface. This water forms natural hot springs and geysers. Power plants that are built in geothermal regions use the water's heat to make electrical energy. This energy is a clean way to heat and cool buildings.

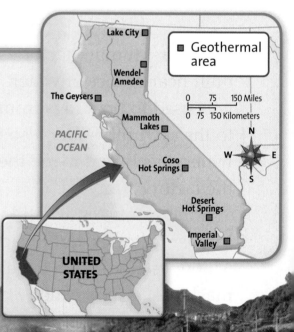

Lake City
Wendel-Amedee
The Geysers
Mammoth Lakes
PACIFIC OCEAN
Coso Hot Springs
Desert Hot Springs
Imperial Valley

■ Geothermal area

0   75   150 Miles
0   75   150 Kilometers

N W E S

UNITED STATES

As the state's population grows, more energy will be demanded by people and businesses. Californians will continue to look for new ways to provide energy for homes, cars, and businesses.

Reading Check ⚙ **Generalize**
Why is it important to look for new ways to provide energy?

Summary Businesses use natural resources, human resources, and capital resources to produce goods and provide services. The ways in which industries use these resources have changed over time and will continue to change.

▶ The California Energy Commission helps bring energy to the state's people and businesses.

Review

1. 💡 How do businesses use resources from the community?

2. **Vocabulary** Write a paragraph that describes a **business** in California.

3. **Your Community** What natural, human, and capital resources are available in your community?

Critical Thinking

4. **Make It Relevant** What are some resources you use each day?

5. **ANALYSIS SKILL** How are industries in California today similar to California industries in the past?

6. 🖌 **Make a Three-Column Chart** Choose a business described in this lesson. Make a three-column chart to show the natural, human, and capital resources the business uses in the community.

7. **Focus Skill** **Generalize** On a separate sheet of paper, copy and complete the graphic organizer below.

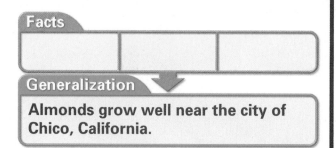

Facts		

Generalization

Almonds grow well near the city of Chico, California.

Trading with the World

Many of the products you buy come from places outside your community. They may come from other parts of California, from other states, or from other countries.

One Nation, Many Products

California has many climates and natural resources. If you live in northern California, your grocery store might sell apples grown in your community. But northern California is not good for growing all products. Stores near you may sell citrus from southern California and vegetables from central California.

❯ Consumers across the United States buy fruits and vegetables from California.

Grapes from California $ 1.99 lb.

The United States also has different climates and natural resources. People in one state use products made or grown in many other states. For example, Californians buy lobsters caught in the cold waters off the coast of Maine. People in Maine buy fruit, nuts, and vegetables grown in California. Buying and selling between states is called *interstate trade*.

Industries use interstate trade to get resources. Kansas, for example, has few forests. A construction company in Kansas might use lumber from northern California to build homes in its own state. Different states depend on each other for products and resources. This is called **interdependence**.

Reading Check 👌 **Generalize**
Why do people in different states trade with one another?

ANALYSIS SKILL Analyze Maps
❖ Regions Where in California do forest products come from?

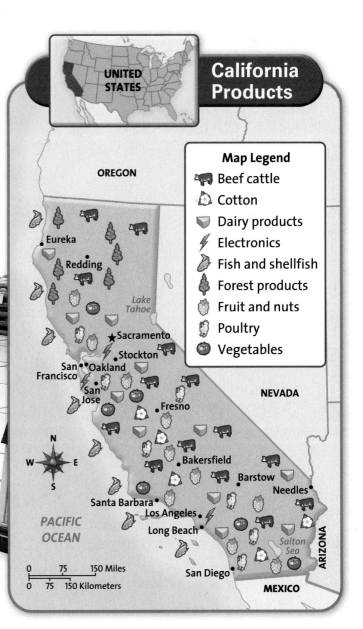

UNITED STATES

California Products

Map Legend
🐄 Beef cattle
🌱 Cotton
🥛 Dairy products
⚡ Electronics
🐟 Fish and shellfish
🌲 Forest products
🌰 Fruit and nuts
🐔 Poultry
🍅 Vegetables

OREGON

Eureka
Redding
Lake Tahoe
★Sacramento
Stockton
San Francisco • Oakland
San Jose
Fresno
Bakersfield
Barstow
Needles
Santa Barbara
Los Angeles
Long Beach
Salton Sea
San Diego

PACIFIC OCEAN

NEVADA

ARIZONA

MEXICO

0 75 150 Miles
0 75 150 Kilometers

Trade Among Countries

People in different countries depend on one another for goods and resources. Buying and selling between countries is called **international trade**.

People in countries such as the United States **import**, or bring in, products from other countries to sell. They also **export**, or ship, products to other countries to sell.

For example, tea grows well in China and India. People in those countries export tea to Britain. The British produce fine woolen goods such as sweaters and coats. People in countries around the world import them from Britain.

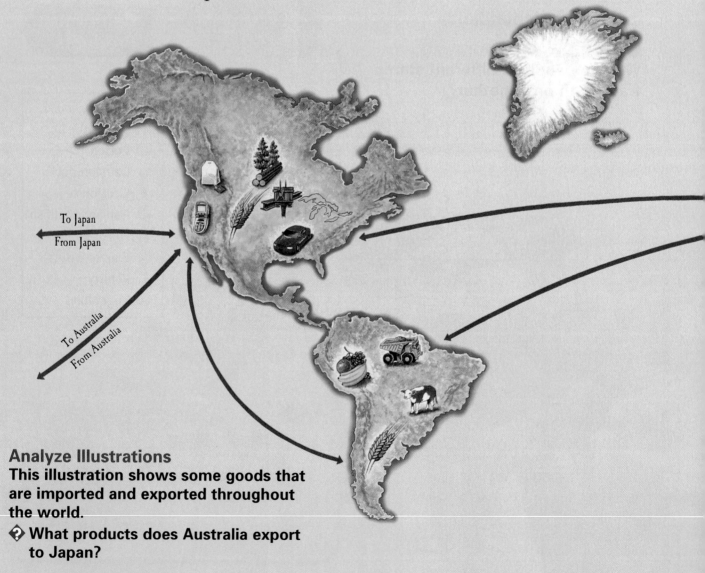

To Japan
From Japan

To Australia
From Australia

Analyze Illustrations
This illustration shows some goods that are imported and exported throughout the world.

❖ **What products does Australia export to Japan?**

People in Germany, Japan, and the United States export automobiles to people in countries in South America and Africa. Consumers in Germany, Japan, and the United States buy fruit from South American and African countries.

Countries also import and export materials that are used to make other products. For example, South Africa exports diamonds to be used in many industries. Canada is an exporter of wood.

Reading Check ⚇**Generalize**
Why is international trade important to countries?

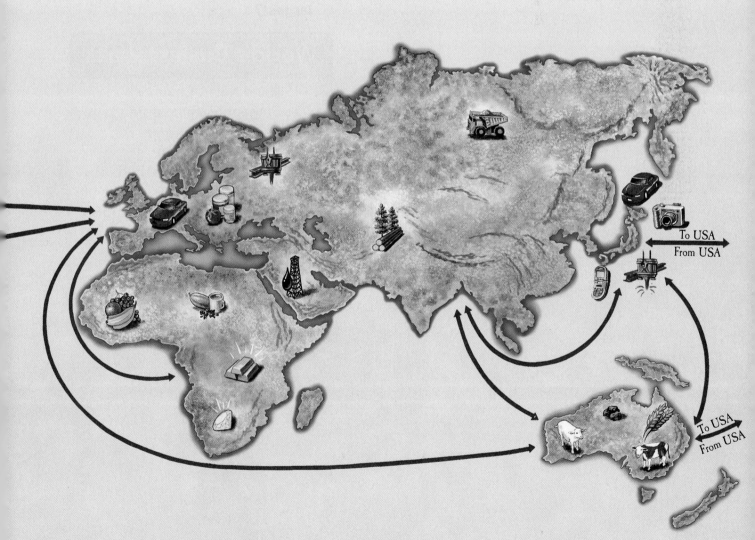

Moving Goods

How does fresh salmon from northern California reach Atlanta, Georgia, without spoiling? How are heavy logs moved from Canada to the United States? How does oil get from Venezuela to France?

Modern transportation makes it all possible. Transportation is the moving of people or things from one place to another.

▶ **Workers load goods onto a cargo plane.**

▶ **Goods travel into and out of the Port of Los Angeles at Long Beach.**

Analyze Tables

❓ **Which California ports are among the world's largest?**

World's Busiest Ports

1. Hong Kong, China
2. Singapore, Singapore
3. Pusan, South Korea
4. Kaohiung, Taiwan
5. Rotterdam, The Netherlands
6. Shanghai, China
7. Los Angeles, California, USA
8. Long Beach, California, USA
9. Hamburg, Germany
10. Antwerp, Belgium

Salmon is packed in ice and flown across the United States in a refrigerated airplane. Canada's logs travel on trucks and trains to the states that need them. Oil travels across oceans in large ships.

Reading Check ⚙️ **Generalize**
Why is transportation important to countries?

Summary Some goods and resources come from local communities. Some are transported from elsewhere in the United States. Other goods are imported from other countries.

▶ A truck carries logs along California's Interstate 5.

Review

1. 💡 Where do our goods come from, and how do they get to our community?

2. **Vocabulary** Explain the difference between **import** and **export**.

3. **Your Community** What products are made in your community and exported to other states or nations?

Critical Thinking

4. **Make It Relevant** What are some foods you eat that come from California? What are some that come from other states or countries?

5. **ANALYSIS SKILL** Why do you think people in the United States import goods, such as cars and computers, that are also made here?

6. 🖌️ **Make a Class Museum** Find three objects in your classroom—one made in California, one in another state, and one in another country. Label each object with the name of the place it comes from. Add your items to a class museum display titled "Where Do Our Goods Come From?"

7. **Focus Skill Generalize** Copy and complete the graphic organizer below.

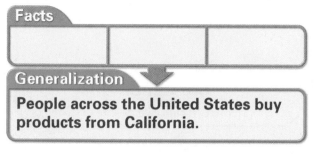

Facts		

↓

Generalization

People across the United States buy products from California.

Chapter 11 ▪ **433**

Use Latitude and Longitude

❯ Why It Matters

Mapmakers draw lines of latitude and longitude on maps and globes to form a grid system. You can give the location of any place by naming the lines of latitude and longitude closest to it.

❯ What You Need to Know

Lines of **latitude** run east and west around a globe. They measure distances in degrees (°) north and south of the equator.

Lines of latitude go from 0° at the equator to 90° at the poles. They are labeled *N* for *north* and *S* for *south*.

Lines of **longitude**, also called *meridians*, run north and south from pole to pole. They measure east and west of the prime meridian, which runs near London, England. Lines of longitude go from 0° at the prime meridian to 180° halfway around the globe. They are labeled *E* for *east* and *W* for *west*.

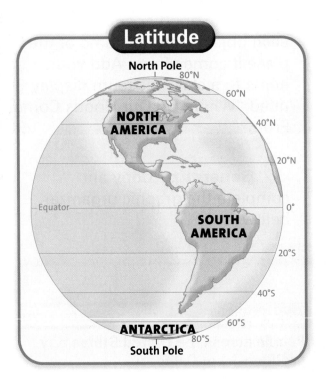

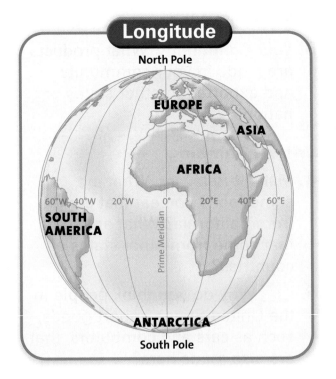

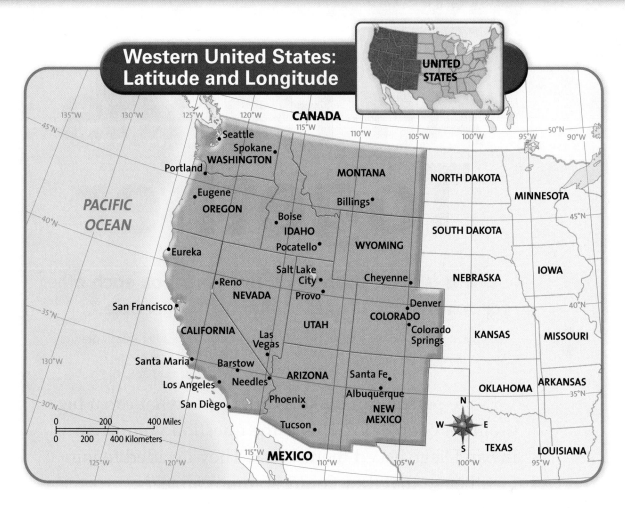

Western United States: Latitude and Longitude

UNITED STATES

CANADA

WASHINGTON
- Seattle
- Spokane
- Portland

PACIFIC OCEAN

OREGON
- Eugene

MONTANA
- Billings

NORTH DAKOTA

MINNESOTA

IDAHO
- Boise
- Pocatello

WYOMING

SOUTH DAKOTA

- Eureka

- Reno

NEVADA

Salt Lake City

Provo

Cheyenne

NEBRASKA

IOWA

San Francisco

CALIFORNIA

Las Vegas

UTAH

COLORADO
- Denver
- Colorado Springs

KANSAS

MISSOURI

- Santa Maria
- Los Angeles
- Barstow
- Needles
- San Diego

ARIZONA
- Phoenix

Santa Fe
- Albuquerque

NEW MEXICO

OKLAHOMA

ARKANSAS

- Tucson

TEXAS

LOUISIANA

MEXICO

0 200 400 Miles
0 200 400 Kilometers

❱ Practice the Skill

Answer the questions using the map above.

1 Near which line of latitude is Barstow, California?

2 Near which line of longitude is Santa Maria, California?

3 Near which lines of latitude and longitude is Eureka, California?

4 Find Needles, California. Near which lines of latitude and longitude is this city located?

❱ Apply What You Learned

ANALYSIS SKILL **Make It Relevant** Use a map or a globe to find the latitude and longitude nearest to your community. Find three cities or towns in the world with the same latitude. Then find three places with the same longitude. Share your list of world cities with a classmate.

 Practice your map and globe skills with the **GeoSkills CD-ROM.**

Map and Globe Skills

All Hands Together

"It is a good thing to be dependent on each other for something, it makes us civil and peaceable."

—Sojourner Truth, from *The History of Woman Suffrage* by Elizabeth Cady Stanton. Ayer Publishers, 1911.

If one person can make a difference, what can a big group of people do? This is the question volunteers in San Diego asked themselves. They decided to join together so that they could do more projects.

Their biggest event is called Hands On San Diego. For one week, teams of volunteers join together to help the community. The group selects projects and assigns each project to a team. In 2004, the group chose 250 projects and called on 5,000 volunteers to complete them.

Cleaning up a park

Sorting food at the food bank

Helping other citizens

The volunteers are the kinds of people you see every day. They include bankers, office workers, students, and soldiers. Family members and groups of friends also form teams. The volunteers are many different ages, from young to old, but in one way they are all alike. They all want to help others.

HANDS ON

SAN DIEGO

Poster from Hands On San Diego event.

Think About It!

Make It Relevant How do volunteers make our communities better?

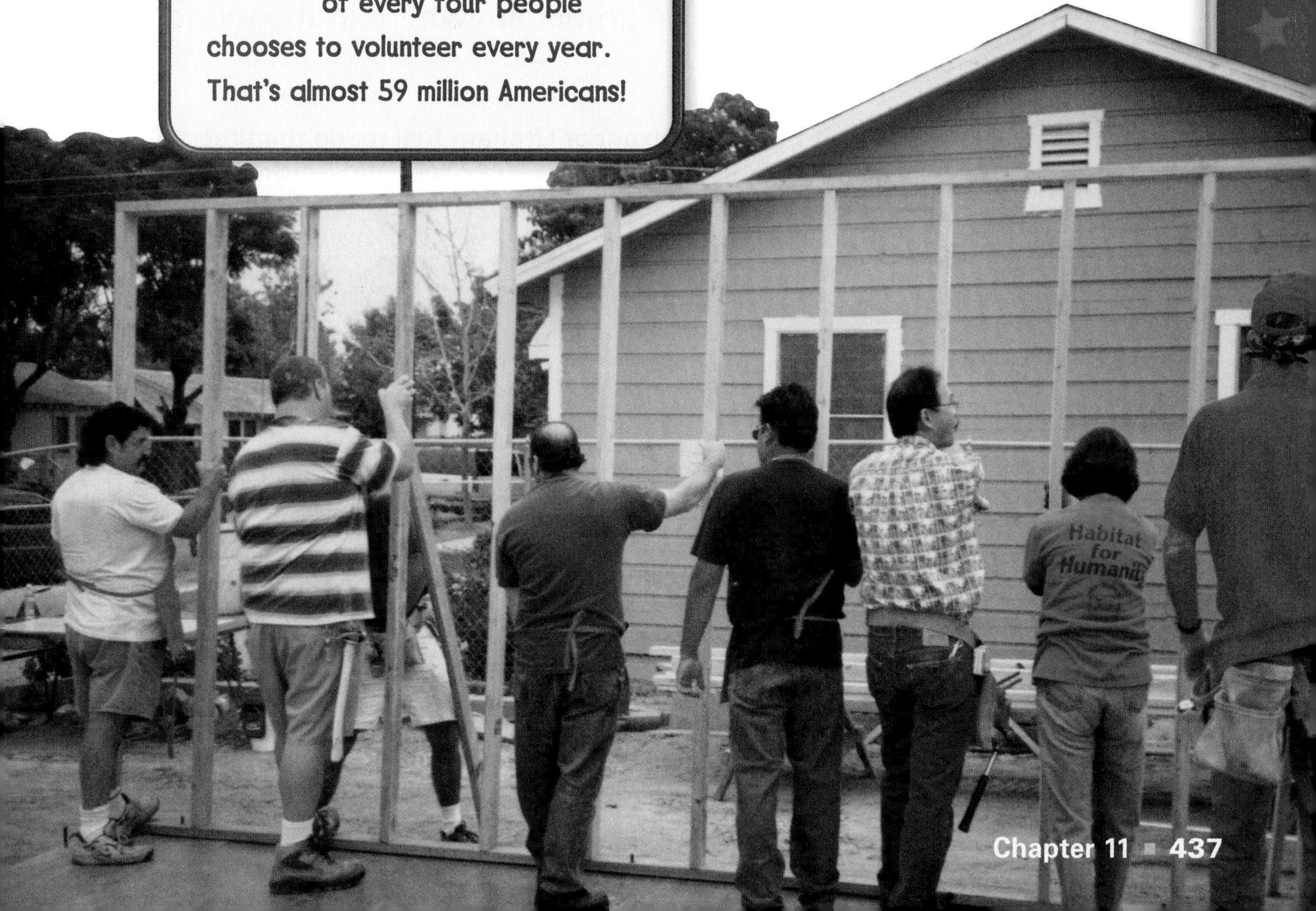

Did You Know?

Americans like to volunteer. In the United States, about one out of every four people chooses to volunteer every year. That's almost 59 million Americans!

Moving Information

What to Know

What are some ways of communicating that are used today and some that were used in the past?

✓ Technology has changed the ways we communicate.

✓ Communication links help us trade for goods.

Vocabulary
Internet p. 439
communication link p. 440

Focus Skill Generalize

California Standards
HSS 3.5

Early California settlers had few ways to communicate with people who were far away. Settlers were able to communicate with people who were far away only by mail. When Alexander Graham Bell invented the telephone, people were amazed to be able to speak directly to people far away.

Today, people use many new forms of technology to communicate. With computers, people can send messages instantly to almost anywhere in the world.

▶ In 1892, Alexander Graham Bell made the first telephone call between New York and Chicago.

Workers build computers in a Newark, California, factory.

The Information Age

In the late 1960s, computers at several California universities were connected by wires to "talk" to one another. This idea quickly grew into the Internet. The **Internet** is a system that links computers around the world. Today, people use the Internet to learn, to shop, and to send and receive electronic mail, or e-mail. We live in the information age.

As the Internet grew, California continued to be an important place for computer technology. Silicon Valley was already a place where computers and computer parts were manufactured. It quickly became a center for Internet technology as well. Leading Internet companies are still based in Silicon Valley.

Reading Check ✪ **Generalize**
What happens when improvements are made in ways to communicate?

This phone can be used to send e-mail, surf the Web, and take digital photographs.

High-Tech Buying and Selling

The Internet is a communication link. A **communication link** is a kind of technology that lets people share information instantly, even if they are separated from each other.

Communication links have made ordering and paying for goods faster and easier, too. For example, consumers often use home computers to shop on the Internet. Online buying and selling is sometimes called *e-commerce*. The word *commerce* means "business."

Analyze Flowcharts

This flowchart shows how a consumer uses a computer to order a book on the Internet.

◆ **Which steps in the process use computers?**

E-Commerce

1 A consumer places an order for a book on the Internet.

2 A worker receives the order for the book.

3 Another worker finds the book in the warehouse.

4 The order is packed to be sent.

5 A delivery person brings the book to the consumer's door.

Other communication links that are used for buying and selling products are telephones and fax machines. Many consumers pay for goods and services with debit cards or credit cards. Information from the card is sent through a communication link to a bank.

Reading Check ⚬ **Generalize**
How do communication links help businesses?

Summary Early settlers were able to communicate with people who were far away only by mail. Today, people use tools such as computers. Communication links help people order and pay for goods worldwide.

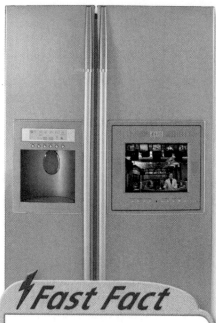

⚡ *Fast Fact*

This machine is both a refrigerator and a computer. It chills food and can also be used to shop online, send e-mail, check recipes, and much more.

Review

1. 💡 What are some ways of communicating that are used today and some that were used in the past?

2. **Vocabulary** Write a paragraph to explain how **Internet** and **communication link** are related.

3. **Your Community** Where can a person use the Internet in your community?

Critical Thinking

4. **Make It Relevant** What technology do you use to communicate?

5. **SKILL** How can communication links help families today?

6. 🖌 **Make a Time Line** Use information from this lesson to make a time line that shows how communication methods have changed over time.

7. ⭐ **Generalize** On a separate sheet of paper, copy and complete the graphic organizer below.

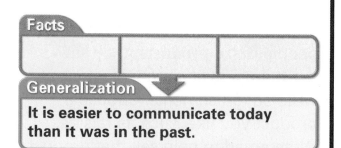

Facts

Generalization

It is easier to communicate today than it was in the past.

Reading Social Studies

When you **generalize,** you make a broad statement about the facts and details you have read.

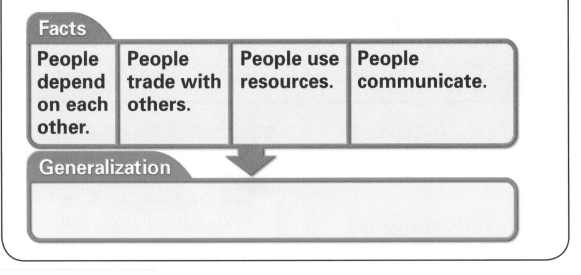Generalize

Complete this graphic organizer to make a generalization about how people work. A copy of a graphic organizer appears on page 106 of the Homework and Practice Book.

Workers and Consumers

Facts

People depend on each other.	People trade with others.	People use resources.	People communicate.

Generalization

California Writing Prompts

Create an Advertisement After people make products, they sell them. To help sell products, they write advertisements. Choose a product you like, such as raisins. Write an ad to help sell that product.

Write the Steps Choose a food you like. Find out more about how it gets to the supermarket for sale. Write and illustrate the steps on a sheet of posterboard.

Use Vocabulary

Write a definition for each word. Then use each word in a sentence that tells the meaning of each word or words.

1. **wage,** p. 415
2. **service,** p. 416
3. **capital resources,** p. 423
4. **manufacture,** p. 424
5. **export,** p. 430
6. **Internet,** p. 439
7. **communication link,** p. 440

Apply Skills

Use Latitude and Longitude Use the map on page 435 to answer the questions.

8. **ANALYSIS SKILL** Near which line of latitude is Los Angeles, California?

9. Near which lines of latitude and longitude is Reno, Nevada?

Recall Facts

Answer these questions.

10. How did people get goods from other people before they used money?

11. Why do people in countries import goods?

Write the letter of the best choice.

12. Which of the following is a natural resource?
   A money
   B a factory
   C wind power
   D a computer

13. What technology has allowed computers to "talk" to one another?
   A trains
   B Internet
   C automobiles
   D telegraph

Think Critically

14. **ANALYSIS SKILL** Why are there different industries in different places?

15. **ANALYSIS SKILL** Why do you think California exports vegetables?

Study Skills

USE AN ANTICIPATION GUIDE

An anticipation guide can help you anticipate, or predict, what you will learn as you read.

▶ **Look at the lesson titles and section titles. These are clues that tell what you will read about.**

▶ **Preview the Reading Check questions. Use what you know about the subject of each section to predict the answers.**

▶ **Read to find out whether your predictions were correct.**

Operating in a Free Market

Reading Check	Prediction	Correct?
What rights does a free market give business owners?	Business owners can make and sell any product or service.	✓

Apply As You Read

Make an anticipation guide for each lesson. Make sure you read the Reading Check question before you make your prediction. When you have finished reading, go back to see if your predictions were correct.

California History-Social Science Standards, Grade 3

3.5 Students demonstrate basic economic reasoning skills and an understanding of the economy of the local region.

Costs and Benefits

Carlos and the Carnival

by Jan Romero Stevens
illustrated by Jeanne Arnold

Carlos lives next door to his friend Gloria. Every summer, their town has a fiesta. The fiesta includes a carnival, lots of food, and a county fair where the people of the town can display things, including their best vegetables and farm animals. This year Carlos enters his pet rabbit, Gordito. Read to find out the valuable lesson Carlos learns on this visit to the carnival.

Gloria whacked the piñata as hard as she could, sending brightly colored pieces of candy scattering in all directions.

Pulling the blindfold from her eyes, she yelled, "*Feliz cumpleaños*—happy birthday, Carlos!" Carlos smiled. Suddenly he felt very grown-up. He and Gloria quickly gathered the treats that had fallen from the piñata and sat down for a piece of birthday cake. As Carlos was finishing his last bite, his father handed him a gift—two tickets for the carnival and five dollars to spend.

"Now be careful," said Papa, patting Carlos on the back. "*El tonto y su dinero se separan pronto*—a fool and his money are soon parted."

Carlos grinned at his father and sat up very straight. "Papa, did you forget? I'm older now. I know how to handle my own money."

The morning after his birthday, Carlos was up early, anxious to go with Gloria to the carnival. He crammed his pockets with all his change, the money he had earned for taking care of Señor Lopez's dog, and the five dollars his father had given him. He had ten dollars in all. Feeling rich, he left for Gloria's house.

As they walked down the dirt road to town, Carlos and Gloria were excited by the sights and sounds and smells coming from the fair. They could see the whirling Ferris wheel and hear the screams from the people on the rides. Hearing the sounds of people on the carnival rides, he coaxed Gloria to go with him on La Tormenta, a ride that jerked and twisted the riders around.

Waiting in line, Carlos felt his stomach turn over as he watched the passengers high overhead. But it was too late to turn back, so he and Gloria strapped themselves into a seat. The ride took off with a quick lurch, and Carlos and Gloria were slammed into the sides of their car and then turned upside down. Carlos was very dizzy when the ride finally slowed to a stop.

"*Qué divertido*—what fun!" Gloria shouted, skipping down the ramp from the roller coaster. "Let's go again!"

Carlos shuddered. He held onto one of the booths, feeling sick to his stomach. "Not right now," he said slowly, bravely trying to smile. He looked up at the game booths where he was standing. Hanging from the sides of the booth were a variety of colorful prizes—stuffed woolly lambs, pink giraffes, and balsa wood airplanes with red propellers that spun in the breeze.

The man at the booth shouted to them. "Two tries for a dollar. Everyone's a winner!" He reached over, gave a hard spin to a wooden wheel, and threw a dart at the twirling colored balloons. A red one popped.

"It's simple," he said, winking at Gloria. "Each balloon is worth twenty-five points. Get a hundred points, and you pick the prize of your choice."

Carlos counted up his money. He still had four dollars, which would give him eight chances to hit four balloons. It would be easy to win.

He slapped a dollar on the counter and picked up two darts. On his first try he missed the balloons entirely, but he popped one on the next throw. He handed the man another dollar and tried again.

Carlos aimed carefully, missed once, then hit a blue balloon—another twenty-five points. "*Qué suerte*—what luck!" said the man. Carlos had fifty points and two dollars left.

He eagerly handed the man another dollar and threw two more darts, popping another balloon. "Lucky again," the man said. "You're almost there."

"No problema," said Carlos, quickly adding up his score. He had seventy-five points. He only needed to pop one more balloon. He was so close to winning, but he was uncomfortable about spending all his money.

"I'll tell you what," the man said. "I like you. I'll give three tries for that dollar. You're sure to get it this time."

Nodding excitedly, Carlos handed him his last dollar. He took a deep breath, focusing on a red balloon as it spun around the wheel. He stood directly in front of the spinning balloons, squinted, and aimed carefully, but the dart landed between two balloons. On his next try, he missed the wheel entirely!

One more chance, he thought to himself. He picked up the last dart and pitched it as hard as he could. The dart brushed the edge of a balloon, but the balloon didn't pop.

"Ohhh, *qué lástima*—what a pity," the man said, shaking his head. "Oh well, everyone's a winner at this booth. We have a nice prize for you, anyway. Close your eyes and open your hand."

Carlos felt something drop into his palm. He opened his eyes. It was a black plastic spider with green eyes. Disappointed, Carlos slipped the spider into his pocket. "Let's go," he said to Gloria.

As they were leaving the carnival, Gloria wanted to stop and see the farm animals. Suddenly, Carlos remembered his pet rabbit. He and Gloria rushed to the cages where the smaller animals were kept. Gordito twitched his nose against Carlos's fingers. A large blue-and-gold ribbon marked "Best of Show" was hanging from the cage.

"*Híjole*!" Carlos shouted. "Gordito won first place!" He ran up to the woman who was in charge of the rabbits. "Can I take him home now?" he asked, and the woman nodded. Carlos returned to Gordito's cage, carefully lifted out his prize-winning rabbit, and tucked him under his arm.

"Don't forget your money for winning first prize," said the woman, and she handed a grinning Carlos the five-dollar prize.

Carlos and Gloria began walking toward the exit of the fair, past the food booths selling tamales and posole, roasted corn and sopaipillas. On the way out, a man from another game booth called to Carlos.

"Hey, big guy! Come throw the ball in the basket. Everyone's a winner!"

For a moment, Carlos hesitated. He felt the money in his pocket, and then he shook his head.

"No. *El tonto y su dinero se separan pronto*— a fool and his money are soon parted," he mumbled, remembering what his father had told him on his birthday.

And proudly patting Gordito on the head, Carlos invited Gloria back to his house for another piece of cake.

Response Corner

1 What happened to Carlos's birthday money?

2 What lesson does Carlos learn? How does Carlos show that he has learned it?

Operating in a Free Market

What to Know
How does a free market work?

- A free market allows people to decide what goods or services they will make or sell.

- Consumer demands affect what goods and services businesses supply.

- Scarcity affects prices.

Vocabulary
profit p. 452
free market p. 452
demand p. 454
supply p. 454
scarcity p. 455

Generalize

California
Standards
HSS 3.5, 3.5.3

People in the United States enjoy many freedoms. One of those freedoms is the right to start a business and to try to run that business in a way that will make a profit. A **profit** is the amount of money that is left over after all the costs of running a business have been paid.

Free Market

In the United States, people can make or sell any product or service that is allowed by law. This is called a **free market**. The government does not tell businesses what to make or sell.

▶ **A shopping mall in Costa Mesa, California**

In a free market, business owners are allowed to produce what they want. They provide goods and services that they think consumers want to buy and that they hope will make a profit. They also compete with each other to sell their goods and services. Prices must be high enough to cover their costs, but low enough to attract consumers. Business owners can also decide how much to pay people who work for them. Wages must be low enough to help business owners earn a profit, but high enough to attract workers. The government steps in only when businesses break the law.

▶ This business owner sells books.

Reading Check ✪ **Generalize**
What rights does a free market give business owners?

Children in History

Jessica Govea

Jessica Govea worked in the fields near her home in Kern County, California. Jessica, her parents, and most of the other workers were Mexican. Many were migrant workers. Workers earned very little money and were treated poorly. When Jessica was only seven years old, she helped her father organize workers into a group that asked for changes. One member of the group was Cesar Chavez.

By the age of 17, Jessica was working full-time for Chavez. She organized marches and worked in a service center that helped farm families. The organization that she helped Chavez build is called the United Farm Workers Union. It helps workers across the United States.

Supply and Demand

Business owners turn to consumers to help them decide what to make and what to sell. The wants of consumers create a **demand** for, or willingness to buy, certain goods and services. Businesses offer goods and services that consumers want to buy.

The products and services that businesses offer are the **supply**. When consumers' demand for a product is high, the business produces a greater supply of that product. For example, if a video game called Moon Walk becomes popular, the company will probably make many Moon Walk games.

It is the same with services. If there are many pets in a community, it is likely that animal hospitals and dog-walking services will open.

❯ The demand for dog-walking services keeps this woman busy.

How Supply and Demand Works		
SUPPLY	**DEMAND**	**PRICE**
High Supply +	High Demand =	Low Price
High Supply +	Low Demand =	Very Low Price
Low Supply +	High Demand =	Very High Price
Low Supply +	Low Demand =	High Price

Analyze Tables

This table shows how supply, demand, and price can change.

❓ What do high supply and low demand equal?

Prices show how scarce a product is. **Scarcity** (SKAIR•suh•tee) means that there are not enough resources to meet everyone's wants. When fruit flies destroyed California's crops, fruit became more scarce. Because of fruit's scarcity, its price went up.

At times, the demand for goods and services is low. People may choose to save their money instead of spending it. When this happens, prices go down. Also, if people want less of a certain product, it becomes less scarce, and the price of that product goes down.

▶ When fruit flies destroyed California's crops, fruit prices increased.

Reading Check ☉ **Generalize**

What happens to the price of a product or service when there is very little demand?

Summary The United States has a free market. People can choose what to sell and what to buy. Supply and demand determine these choices. When something becomes more scarce, its price may rise.

Review

1. 💡 How does a free market work?

2. **Vocabulary** Explain how **scarcity** affects price.

3. **Your Community** What businesses in your community meet new demands of people in your community?

Critical Thinking

4. **Make It Relevant** What is an item or product you would like to have that is very hard to find?

5. **ANALYSIS SKILL** What will likely happen to the price of local lumber after a forest fire? Explain.

6. ✎ **Report on a Business** Choose a local business or a business described in the lesson. Make a list of goods it might sell. In a paragraph, describe how consumers affect what it sells.

7. (Focus Skill) **Generalize** Copy and complete the graphic organizer below.

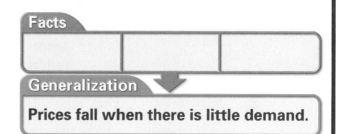

Facts		

Generalization

Prices fall when there is little demand.

Trustworthiness
Respect
Responsibility
Fairness
Caring
Patriotism

Janet Yellen

"Why are we in this business? It seems to me that it's to promote the well-being of American households."*

Why Character Counts

❖ Why is it important for someone in charge of a bank to be trustworthy?

Janet Yellen has a big job. She is president of the Federal Reserve Bank of San Francisco. This bank works with other regional Federal Reserve Banks. Together they serve as the central bank of the United States. The Federal Reserve Bank manages the nation's banks and makes decisions that affect the economy.

As a college student, Janet Yellen studied how the economy worked. She graduated from Brown University with honors in economics. Janet Yellen continued to study at Yale University, where she earned a doctoral degree in economics.

Janet Yellen

* Janet Yellen. "Interview with Janet Yellen." *The Region*, June 1995.

Later, as a professor at the University of California at Berkeley, Dr. Yellen continued to study and teach how the economy works.

When Yellen was chosen to be president of the Federal Reserve Bank of San Francisco, she was rejoining a system she knew well. She had worked as an economist at the Federal Reserve Bank in Washington, D.C. Then she worked at the White House as the head of the President's economic team, called the Council of Economic Advisers.

Dr. Yellen's job history shows that many people trust her to make important decisions. The work of the Federal Reserve Bank affects everyone who participates in the economy. People in economics are glad that Janet Yellen has this important job.

San Francisco Federal Reserve building

GO ONLINE Visit MULTIMEDIA BIOGRAPHIES at www.harcourtschool.com/hss

Bio Brief

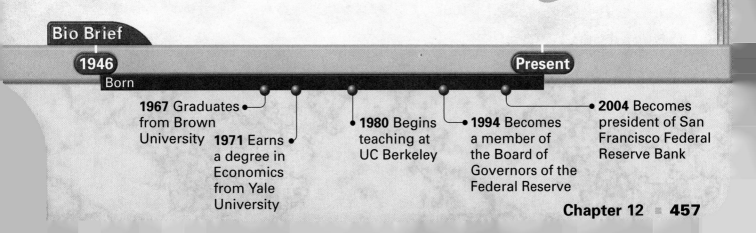

1946 Born

Present

1967 Graduates from Brown University

1971 Earns a degree in Economics from Yale University

1980 Begins teaching at UC Berkeley

1994 Becomes a member of the Board of Governors of the Federal Reserve

2004 Becomes president of San Francisco Federal Reserve Bank

Making Choices

What to Know
What choices do people have for using their money?

✓ People must make choices about how to use their money.

✓ People keep their savings in banks.

Vocabulary
income p. 458
savings p. 460
bank p. 460
deposit p. 460

 Generalize

California Standards
HSS 3.5, 3.5.3

The money people are paid for the work they do is their **income**. Most people use part of their income to buy goods and services. They may also save some of their income. Both spending and saving involve making choices.

Spending Money

Miguel Herrera (eh•REH•rah) owns a shoe store in Antioch, California. He earns his income by selling and repairing shoes.

▶ Miguel Herrera learned to make shoes in Guatemala, where he was born. Now he sells shoes made all over the world.

Locate It

CALIFORNIA

Antioch

▶ **Miguel Herrera uses part of his income to buy food for his family.**

Miguel Herrera uses most of his income to pay for things he and his family use every day. For example, a large part of his income is spent on his house payments. He also uses money to buy food and clothing for his family.

After Miguel Herrera pays for these things, he has money left over. He spends some of that money. He buys things he and his family want, such as new furniture. "I spend a lot on ballet lessons for my three daughters," he says.

Reading Check Ŏ **Generalize**
How does Miguel Herrera spend his income?

▶ **Miguel Herrera makes money selling both products and services.**

Sharing and Saving

Miguel Herrera does not spend all his income on himself and his family. He shares some with other people. He gives money to groups that help people in his community and around the world.

Miguel Herrera also saves a part of his income. The part of their income that people do not use to buy goods and services is called **savings**. Many people keep their savings in a bank. A **bank** is a business that keeps money safe.

When he can, Miguel Herrera **deposits**, or puts, money into his savings account. Miguel Herrera also uses some of his income to buy things that may grow in value.

▶ Miguel Herrera deposits some of the money he earns at his bank.

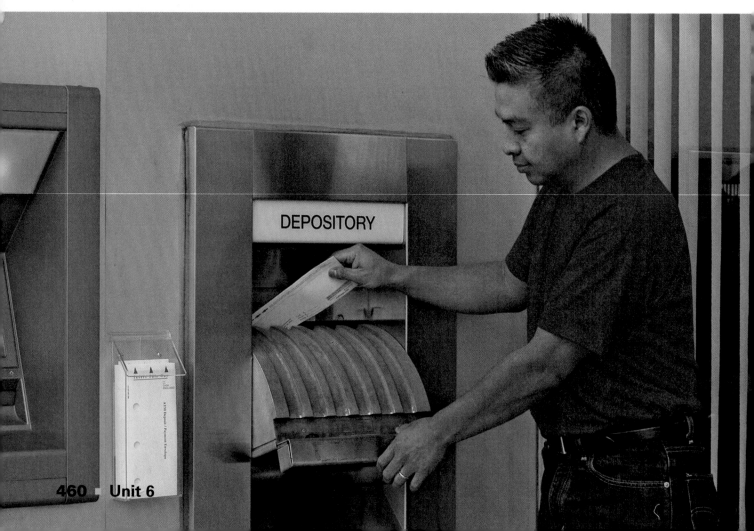

DEPOSITORY

Miguel Herrera also buys stocks. Many large businesses sell shares to the public on the stock market. People who buy shares are buying a part of a company. They hope their money will increase over time.

Reading Check ○ **Generalize**
What are some things people do with their extra income?

Summary People use most of their income to pay for things they use every day. They also use it to buy things they want. They then choose how to spend the money that is left over. People can share or save the money they do not spend.

❭ **Miguel Herrera keeps up with his checking and savings accounts online. He also uses the Internet to check the value of his stocks.**

Review

1. What choices do people have for using their money?

2. **Vocabulary** Use the terms **bank**, **savings**, and **deposit** in a paragraph.

3. **Your Community** List two banks in or near your community. Tell where they are. Compare your list with those of your classmates.

Critical Thinking

4. **Make It Relevant** Where do you keep your savings?

5. **ANALYSIS SKILL** What is the benefit of saving money?

6. **Take a Survey** Ask adults you know how they earn their income. Find out if they provide a product or a service. Share your findings with the class.

7. **Focus Skill Generalize**
On a separate sheet of paper, copy and complete the graphic organizer below.

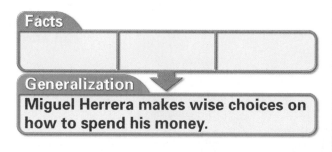

Facts

Generalization

Miguel Herrera makes wise choices on how to spend his money.

Making a Budget

What to Know
What tool can people use to help them decide how to spend their money?

✔ Making a budget helps people track their incoming and outgoing money.

✔ A budget helps people decide how to use their money.

Vocabulary
budget p. 462

Focus Skill Generalize

California Standards
HSS 3.5, 3.5.3

People cannot afford to buy everything they want. They must plan how much to spend on the things they use every day. They may decide to set aside a certain amount for saving and sharing. A person's plan for spending, saving and sharing money is called a **budget**. By using a budget, people know how much money they can spend on the things they want.

▶ **These are some of the ways Macy can earn money.**

Keeping Track of Money

Macy recently made a budget to help her keep track of her money. She used a notebook and a pencil.

On one page, she wrote the heading "Incoming Money." Under that she wrote three smaller categories—"Money Earned," "Gifts," and "Allowance."

Under "Money Earned," Macy listed the ways she earns money. Next to each chore, she wrote down the amount of money she earned from doing it. In the other sections, she listed money that she has received as gifts and her usual allowance.

On a separate page, she wrote the heading "Outgoing Money." There she also wrote three smaller categories— "Snacks," "Clothes," and "Fun." Under each category, she listed how she spends her money. She included things she often buys and how much they cost.

Reading Check ☼**Generalize**
What kinds of information do people include in a budget?

> In her notebook, Macy will record how much money she earns washing dogs.

Incoming Money	
Money Earned	
yard work	$2.00
dog washing	$4.00
Gifts	
from Grandma for birthday	$10.00
Allowance	$10.00 per week

Using a Budget

Outgoing Money

Snacks
  trail mix $4.00
Clothes
  Jeans $25.00
Fun
  movie $6.00

Ways to spend less:
  • cut down on snacks
  • do not buy new shirt

Macy thought about special things she wanted. Then she used her budget to decide what she could afford to buy.

One of the things she wanted was a bicycle. Her budget told her that she did not have enough money to buy one now. She would need to save more money for quite a while to buy the bicycle she wanted.

She began by cutting back on things listed under "Outgoing Money." She decided to spend less money on snacks. She also chose not to buy a new shirt.

Next, Macy looked at her "Incoming Money" page. She thought about how she could earn more money.

▶ Once Macy knows where her money is going, she can decide what to spend less on.

Macy decided to do some pet sitting and dog walking for her neighbors. She also thought about doing more yard work. Macy knew her mother did not like to take out the garbage. She decided to ask if that could become a new job for her.

With the help of her budget, Macy realized she could buy the bicycle in a few months. All she had to do was cut back on spending and earn a little more.

Reading Check ŎGeneralize
How can making a budget help a person reach goals?

▶ Macy pays for the bicycle with money she earned and saved. Her budget helped her reach this goal.

Summary To set up a budget, write information about incoming and outgoing money. Organize the information into categories. You can use the budget for planning and reaching goals.

Review

1. 💡 What tool can people use to help them decide how to spend their money?

2. **Vocabulary** Think about something you want to buy. Use the term **budget** in a sentence telling how you could reach your goal.

3. **Your Community** What jobs could you do at home and for your neighbors to earn money?

Critical Thinking

4. **Make It Relevant** How could having a budget make it easier for you to reach a goal?

5. **ANALYSIS SKILL** What do you think the benefits of having a budget are?

6. ⚬ **Make a Budget** Make a budget that describes how you spend money.

7. **Focus Skill** Generalize
Copy and complete the graphic organizer below.

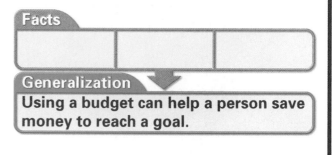

Facts		

Generalization
Using a budget can help a person save money to reach a goal.

Make an Economic Choice

❯ Why It Matters

When you buy something at a store, you are making a choice about how to spend your money. You cannot buy everything you want, so you must spend your money wisely.

❯ What You Need to Know

Here are some steps that can help you make a wise choice.

Step 1 **Think about the trade-off. To buy or do one thing, you have to give up the chance to buy or do something else. This is called a trade-off.**

Step 2 **Now think about the opportunity cost. What you give up to get what you want is an opportunity cost.**

❯ Practice the Skill

Suppose that you are going to buy a bicycle helmet. You have $25. You will have to choose which helmet to buy.

Helmet A is at the bicycle store. It is the latest style, and it comes in bright designs. It costs $25. Helmet B costs $15. It comes in solid colors only, but it gives just as much protection as Helmet A.

Helmet A

Helmet B

1. If you buy Helmet A, what is the trade-off? If you buy Helmet B, what is the trade-off?

2. What is the opportunity cost if you buy Helmet A? What is the opportunity cost if you buy Helmet B?

3. What choice will you make? Why?

❯ Apply What You Learned

ANALYSIS SKILL **Make It Relevant** Think about a recent choice you made when you bought something. What was the trade-off? What was the opportunity cost? Do you think your decision was a wise one? Explain your answer.

Investing in Yourself

What to Know
What can you do to invest in your human capital?

✔ The choices made today affect the future.

✔ Learning new things can increase human capital.

Vocabulary
human capital p. 468

 Generalize

 California Standards
HSS 3.5.4

A budget helps you plan how to spend your capital, or the money you have. You also make decisions about how to use your skills and knowledge. These things make up your **human capital**. The way you use your personal human capital now can help you plan for the future.

Planning for the Future

Emily and Alex like to talk about what they want to do when they are older. Alex loves animals. He thinks he might like to work with animals as a groomer or a veterinarian.

❯ Emily enjoys building things.

Emily likes to build things. She enjoys all sorts of building toys. Emily thinks she might like to work in construction or become an architect.

Emily and Alex do not know *exactly* what they want to do when they grow up. Yet they do have a good idea of the kind of things they would enjoy. Even as third graders, Emily and Alex can look for opportunities to become who they want to be. An opportunity is a chance to do something.

Education is an important opportunity. Learning all they can will help Emily and Alex do well in the future.

Emily and Alex work to be good students, good members of their families, and good friends to others. They also try to be good citizens of their community.

Reading Check ŏ**Generalize**
Why is it important to try to be a good student?

❯ Alex takes care of his family's pets.

❯ Doing their best in school today can give Alex and Emily better opportunities.

Using Your Human Capital

▶ Emily's time, effort, and good work habits are all part of her human capital.

▶ Alex uses his human capital to learn more about the job of a veterinarian.

At school, Alex listens closely to what the teacher is saying. He asks questions when he does not understand the lesson. Alex knows that these things will help him do well in school.

After school, Emily does her homework before playing with her friends or watching television. She has made a rule for herself: No play until after homework is done. Emily, too, is trying to develop her human capital.

Both Alex and Emily are also trying to learn more about jobs that interest them. At the library, Alex takes out books on animal care and reads stories about pets. When his parents take the family's cat for a checkup at the animal hospital, Alex goes along. The veterinarian is always happy to answer questions.

Emily has started a scrapbook of bridges that interest her. She takes photographs of bridges she especially likes. Then she searches the Internet to find out more about her favorite bridges.

Reading Check ŏ **Generalize**
How are Emily and Alex preparing for their future?

Summary School is the "work" that students do. It helps them develop their personal human capital. Education is an opportunity that can help people develop their human capital so that they can be what they want to be. Young people can prepare for their futures by learning all they can in school.

▶ **Emily reads about bridges and buildings.**

Review

1. :Q: What can you do to invest in your human capital?

2. **Vocabulary** Write a sentence using the term **human capital**.

3. **Your Community** List some of the different jobs people have in your community. Compare your list with that of a classmate.

Critical Thinking

4. **Make It Relevant** What are some examples of your human capital?

5. **ANALYSIS SKILL** How might being a good friend, family member, and citizen help you in the future?

6. ✎ **Write a Want Ad**
Choose a job you might like to have one day. Write a want ad describing the job. Include the kind of skills and knowledge you need in order to have that job one day.

7. (Focus Skill) **Generalize**
Copy and complete the graphic organizer below.

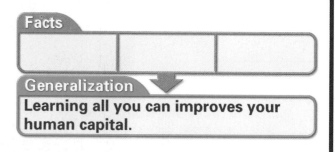

Facts		

Generalization
Learning all you can improves your human capital.

Make a Thoughtful Decision

❱ Why It Matters

People make decisions all the time. A **decision** is a choice. Some decisions are easy to make. Other decisions can be very difficult. When people make a thoughtful decision, they think carefully about the consequences before they act.

❱ What You Need to Know

Emily is a third-grade student. When she grows up, she would like to be an architect. She knows that to have this job, she must study hard and do well in school.

Today, Emily has a lot of homework. She also has a new model of a bridge she wants to build. What should she do?

To make a thoughtful decision, people usually follow these steps:

Step 1 Name the choices.

Step 2 Think about possible consequences of each choice.

Step 3 Make a choice, and act.

❱ Practice the Skill

Emily is trying to decide whether to build a model bridge or spend more time on her studies. She made a chart to help her make a thoughtful decision. Copy her chart. Then list two possible consequences of each choice.

❱ Apply What You Learned

SKILL **Make It Relevant** Think about a decision you have made recently. Make a chart that shows the choices and consequences you faced.

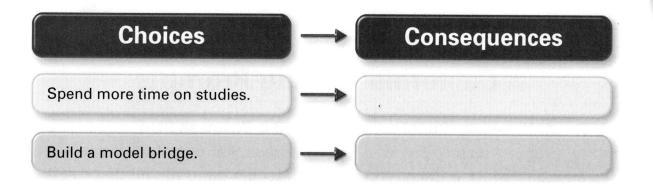

Choices	→	Consequences
Spend more time on studies.	→	
Build a model bridge.	→	

Reading Social Studies

When you **generalize**, you make a broad statement about the facts and details you have read.

 **Generalize**

Complete this graphic organizer to make a generalization about how people spend their money. A copy of a graphic organizer appears on page 116 of the Homework and Practice Book.

Costs and Benefits

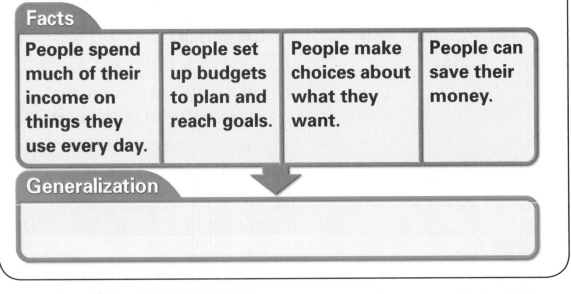

Facts

People spend much of their income on things they use every day.	People set up budgets to plan and reach goals.	People make choices about what they want.	People can save their money.

Generalization

California Writing Prompts

Write a Thank-You Note Imagine a friend or relative has just given you $25 as a gift. Write a thank-you letter telling what you did with the money and why.

Write a Business Plan Think of a business you can start. Write a plan that tells what you will do or sell, the price of your product or service, and who your customers will be.

Use Vocabulary

Write the word or words that correctly match each definition.

profit, p. 452

scarcity, p. 455

bank, p. 460

budget, p. 462

human capital, p. 468

1. your skills and knowledge

2. a business that keeps money safe

3. a plan for spending, saving, and sharing money

4. not enough resources to meet everyone's wants

5. amount of money left after all costs of running a business have been paid

Apply Skills

Make an Economic Choice

6. **ANALYSIS SKILL** One kind of chocolate milk that you know costs $.75. A new brand costs $.45. Which do you decide to buy? Why?

Recall Facts

Answer these questions.

7. How do consumers help decide what a business sells?

8. Why would someone save money?

Write the letter of the best choice.

9. Which of these is money that someone earns?
   A a cost
   B income
   C a budget
   D spending

10. Which of these is a way of investing in yourself?
   A buying snacks
   B going to college
   C spending money
   D giving away money

Think Critically

11. Why would an inventor want to live in a country that has a free market system?

12. How do you develop your human capital?

An Organic FARM

Get Ready

Consumers across the United States buy fruits and vegetables from organic farms in California. Organic farmers use natural, healthy ways to grow crops and to control the weeds and pests that harm them. Instead of spraying chemical pesticides on their crops, for example, organic growers bring in "good bugs," such as ladybugs and lacewings, which eat the "bad bugs" that attack crops.

Locate It
California

San Juan Bautista

What to See

Visitors to this farm buy freshly-picked flowers and produce and enjoy dishes from the farm's organic kitchen.

Children pick their own vegetables and learn about organic farming at the Kids' Garden.

A Virtual Tour

 GO ONLINE Visit VIRTUAL TOURS at www.harcourtschool.com/hss

Review

THE BIG IDEA

Economics People depend on one another and other resources to produce, buy, and sell goods and services. Good decision making helps the economy of a family or a community.

Understanding Economics

People work together to make and sell things we use. Businesses and people use resources to make goods and provide services. People trade with others to get the products they want. Technology has changed how we communicate.

People in the United States live in a free market. They can buy and sell whatever they want. People work to make an <u>income</u> so they can buy goods and services. Making a budget can help people decide what to do with their money. People may also decide to invest in themselves by developing their human capital.

Main Ideas and Vocabulary

Read the summary above. Then answer the questions that follow.

1. What does the word <u>income</u> mean?
   A money for work you do
   B saving money in a bank
   C the right to spend money
   D making choices about spending

2. Which of these is true about the United States?
   A People can buy and sell whatever they want.
   B Everyone has the same amount of money.
   C People sell only what the government makes.
   D People buy what the government says to buy.

Answer these questions.

3. How do people in California use the natural resource of soil?

4. When does the government get involved with how people run businesses?

5. For what reasons do people earn money?

6. Why do people use budgets?

Write the letter of the best choice.

7. Why do countries trade with each other?
    A to use the Internet
    B for interstate trade
    C to get the products they want
    D to communicate with each other

8. Which is part of your human capital?
    A where you live
    B your skills and knowledge
    C the technology you use
    D how much money you have

9. What does *free market* mean?
    A people can get free items at stores
    B people must be responsible pet owners
    C people can buy or sell whatever they want
    D people must pay property taxes

Think Critically

10. **ANALYSIS SKILL** How has technology changed the way people do business?

11. How do local businesses today use natural resources, human resources, and capital resources?

12. How are your work in the classroom and your human capital related?

Apply Skills

Use Latitude and Longitude

ANALYSIS SKILL Use the map below to answer the following questions.

13. What latitude line is the farthest south in California?

14. What state's border with California falls partly on longitude line 120°W?

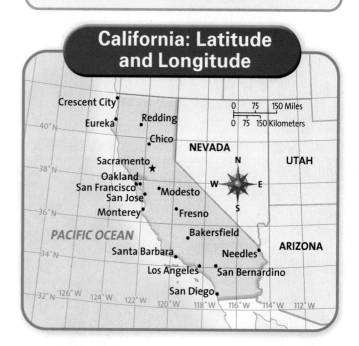

California: Latitude and Longitude

Read More

■ *Inventors and Their Inventions,* by Eleana Martin.

■ *Kids Making Money,* by Susan Ring.

■ *Wall Street,* by Susan Ring.

Show What You Know

Unit Writing Activity

Interview a Worker Think of someone whose job you might like to have some day. Interview that person. Find out what his or her job is like. Then write the interview. Put it together with other classmates' interviews to make a book.

Unit Project

Make a Newspaper Plan and develop a newspaper for your community. Some students can write articles. Others can edit the articles. Have some students take photographs or draw pictures to go with the articles. You might want to sell your newspaper in your school or community.

GO ONLINE Visit ACTIVITIES at www.harcourtschool.com/hss

For Your Reference

ATLAS

RESEARCH HANDBOOK

BIOGRAPHICAL DICTIONARY

GAZETTEER

GLOSSARY

INDEX

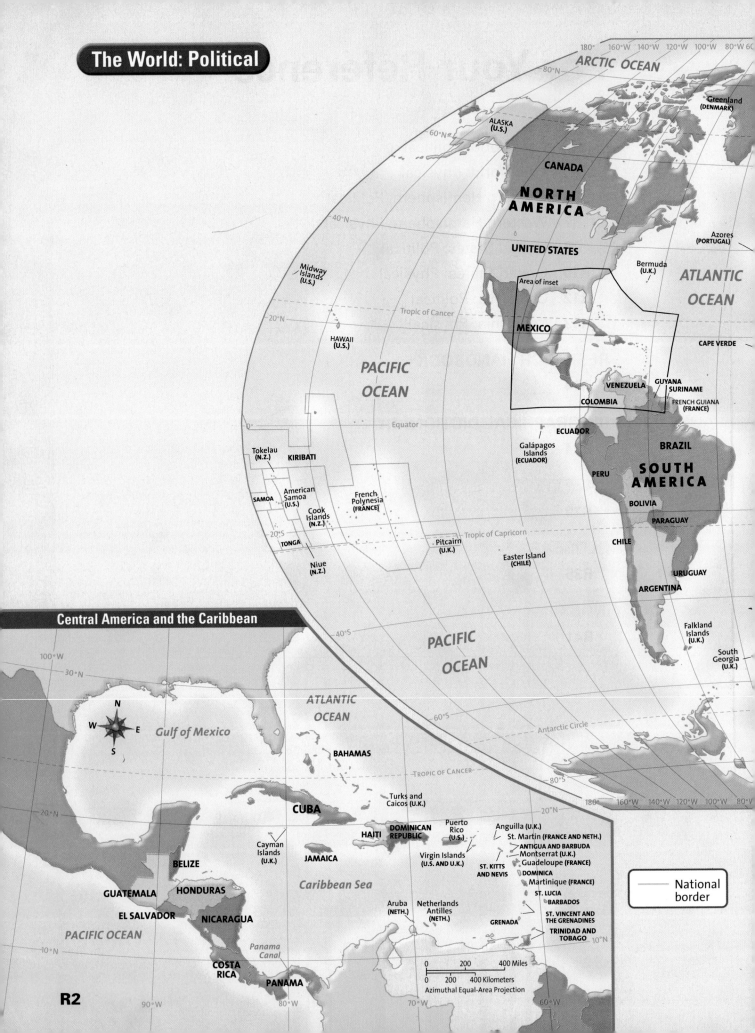

The World: Political

ARCTIC OCEAN

Greenland (DENMARK)

ALASKA (U.S.)

CANADA

NORTH AMERICA

UNITED STATES

Azores (PORTUGAL)

Bermuda (U.K.)

ATLANTIC OCEAN

Midway Islands (U.S.)

Area of inset

Tropic of Cancer

MEXICO

CAPE VERDE

HAWAII (U.S.)

PACIFIC OCEAN

VENEZUELA

GUYANA
SURINAME

COLOMBIA

FRENCH GUIANA (FRANCE)

Equator

ECUADOR

Tokelau (N.Z.)

KIRIBATI

Galápagos Islands (ECUADOR)

BRAZIL

SOUTH AMERICA

SAMOA

American Samoa (U.S.)

Cook Islands (N.Z.)

French Polynesia (FRANCE)

PERU

BOLIVIA

PARAGUAY

TONGA

Niue (N.Z.)

Pitcairn (U.K.)

Tropic of Capricorn

Easter Island (CHILE)

CHILE

URUGUAY

ARGENTINA

PACIFIC OCEAN

Falkland Islands (U.K.)

South Georgia (U.K.)

Antarctic Circle

Central America and the Caribbean

100° W

30° N

ATLANTIC OCEAN

Gulf of Mexico

BAHAMAS

20° N

CUBA

Turks and Caicos (U.K.)

TROPIC OF CANCER

20° N

Cayman Islands (U.K.)

HAITI

DOMINICAN REPUBLIC

Puerto Rico (U.S.)

Anguilla (U.K.)

St. Martin (FRANCE AND NETH.)

ANTIGUA AND BARBUDA

Montserrat (U.K.)

BELIZE

JAMAICA

Virgin Islands (U.S. AND U.K.)

ST. KITTS AND NEVIS

Guadeloupe (FRANCE)

DOMINICA

Martinique (FRANCE)

GUATEMALA

HONDURAS

Caribbean Sea

ST. LUCIA

BARBADOS

EL SALVADOR

NICARAGUA

Aruba (NETH.)

Netherlands Antilles (NETH.)

GRENADA

ST. VINCENT AND THE GRENADINES

TRINIDAD AND TOBAGO

PACIFIC OCEAN

10° N

Panama Canal

COSTA RICA

PANAMA

0   200   400 Miles

0   200   400 Kilometers

Azimuthal Equal-Area Projection

90° W

80° W

70° W

60° W

National border

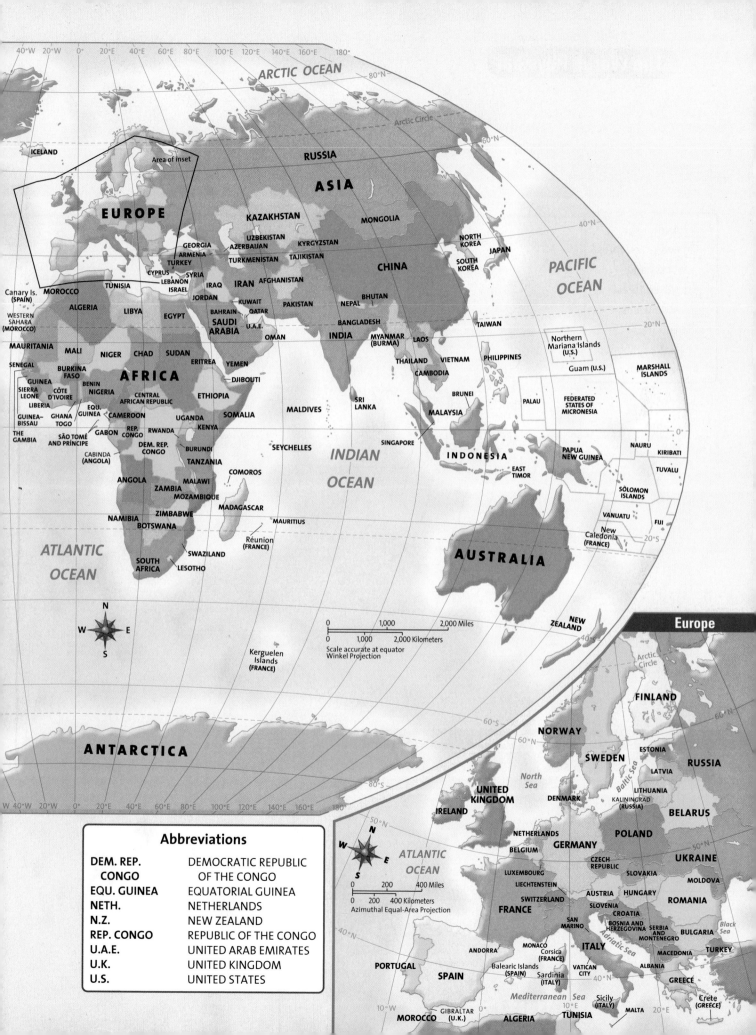

The World: Physical

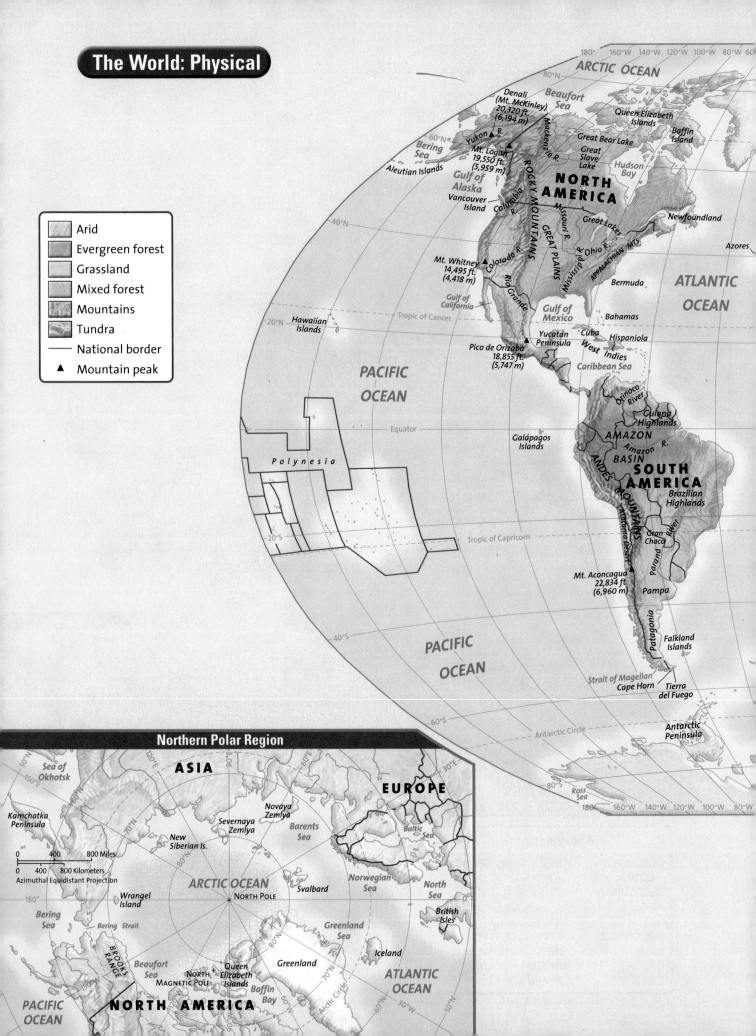

Legend
- Arid
- Evergreen forest
- Grassland
- Mixed forest
- Mountains
- Tundra
- — National border
- ▲ Mountain peak

North America / South America (main map)

ARCTIC OCEAN

Denali (Mt. McKinley) 20,320 ft. (6,194 m)

Beaufort Sea

Queen Elizabeth Islands

Baffin Island

Yukon R.

Mt. Logan 19,550 ft. (5,959 m)

Mackenzie R.

Great Bear Lake

Great Slave Lake

Hudson Bay

Bering Sea

Aleutian Islands

Gulf of Alaska

Vancouver Island

Columbia R.

ROCKY MOUNTAINS

NORTH AMERICA

Great Lakes

Missouri R.

Newfoundland

GREAT PLAINS

Azores

Mt. Whitney 14,495 ft. (4,418 m)

Colorado R.

Mississippi R.

Ohio R.

APPALACHIAN MTS.

ATLANTIC OCEAN

Rio Grande

Bermuda

Gulf of California

Gulf of Mexico

Bahamas

Tropic of Cancer

Hawaiian Islands

Pico de Orizaba 18,855 ft. (5,747 m)

Yucatán Peninsula

Cuba

Hispaniola

West Indies

Caribbean Sea

PACIFIC OCEAN

Orinoco River

Guiana Highlands

Galápagos Islands

Equator

AMAZON BASIN

Amazon R.

SOUTH AMERICA

Polynesia

ANDES MOUNTAINS

Brazilian Highlands

Atacama Desert

Tropic of Capricorn

Gran Chaco

Paraná River

Mt. Aconcagua 22,834 ft. (6,960 m)

Pampa

PACIFIC OCEAN

Patagonia

Falkland Islands

Strait of Magellan

Cape Horn

Tierra del Fuego

Antarctic Circle

Antarctic Peninsula

Ross Sea

Northern Polar Region

Sea of Okhotsk

ASIA

EUROPE

Novaya Zemlya

Barents Sea

Severnaya Zemlya

Baltic Sea

Kamchatka Peninsula

New Siberian Is.

Norwegian Sea

North Sea

ARCTIC OCEAN

NORTH POLE

Svalbard

British Isles

Wrangel Island

Bering Sea

Bering Strait

Greenland Sea

Iceland

BROOKS RANGE

Beaufort Sea

NORTH MAGNETIC POLE

Queen Elizabeth Islands

Greenland

ATLANTIC OCEAN

Baffin Bay

Arctic Circle

PACIFIC OCEAN

NORTH AMERICA

0   400   800 Miles
0   400   800 Kilometers
Azimuthal Equidistant Projection

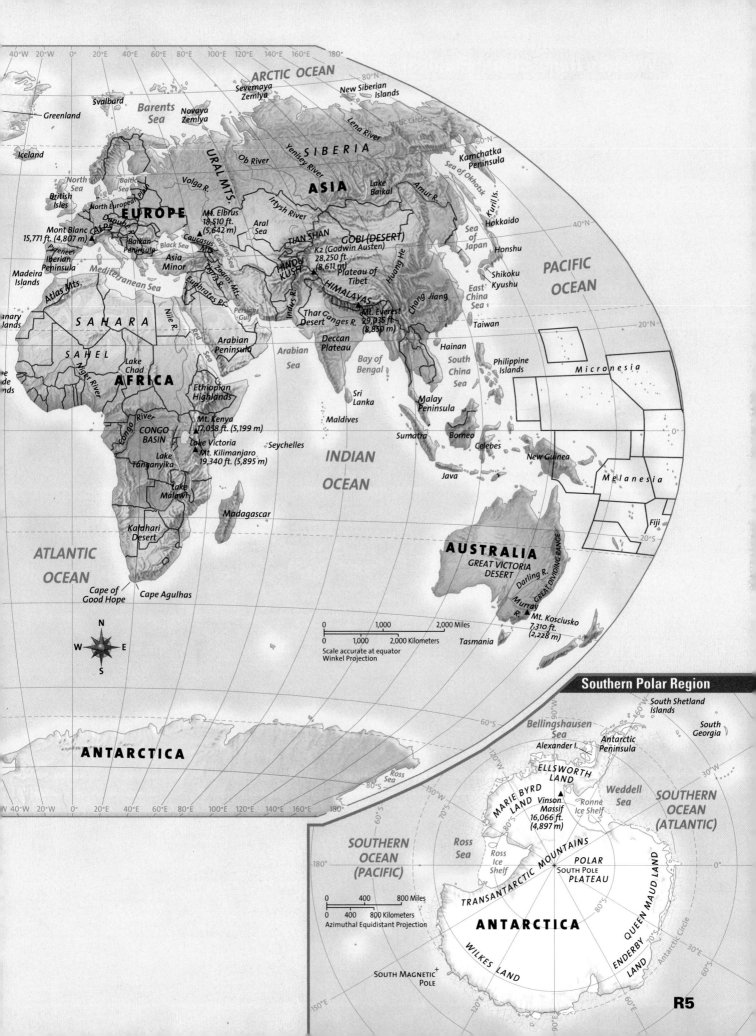

ARCTIC OCEAN

40°W 20°W 0° 20°E 40°E 60°E 80°E 100°E 120°E 140°E 160°E 180°

Greenland
Iceland
Svalbard
Severnaya Zemlya
New Siberian Islands
Novaya Zemlya
Barents Sea
80°N
Arctic Circle

North Sea
Baltic Sea
British Isles
North European Plain
EUROPE
Danube R.
ALPS
Mont Blanc 15,771 ft. (4,807 m)
Pyrenees
Iberian Peninsula
Madeira Islands
Canary Islands
Atlas Mts.
Mediterranean Sea
Balkan Peninsula
Black Sea
Asia Minor
Caspian Sea
Caucasus Mts.
Zagros Mts.
Taurus Mts.
Mt. Elbrus 18,510 ft. (5,642 m)
Volga R.
URAL MTS.
Ob River
Irtysh River
Yenisey River
Lena River
SIBERIA
ASIA
Aral Sea
TIAN SHAN
GOBI (DESERT)
K2 (Godwin Austen) 28,250 ft. (8,611 m)
HINDU KUSH
Plateau of Tibet
HIMALAYAS
Lake Baikal
Amur R.
Kamchatka Peninsula
Sea of Okhotsk
Kuril Is.
Hokkaido
Sea of Japan
60°N
40°N
PACIFIC OCEAN

SAHARA
Nile R.
Red Sea
Arabian Peninsula
Persian Gulf
Euphrates R.
Indus R.
Thar Desert
Ganges R.
Mt. Everest 29,035 ft. (8,850 m)
Deccan Plateau
Arabian Sea
Huang He
Chang Jiang
Honshu
Shikoku
Kyushu
East China Sea
Taiwan
20°N

SAHEL
Niger River
Lake Chad
AFRICA
Ethiopian Highlands
Congo River
CONGO BASIN
Mt. Kenya 17,058 ft. (5,199 m)
Lake Victoria
Mt. Kilimanjaro 19,340 ft. (5,895 m)
Lake Tanganyika
Lake Malawi
Kalahari Desert
Madagascar
Seychelles
Sri Lanka
Maldives
INDIAN OCEAN
Bay of Bengal
South China Sea
Hainan
Philippine Islands
Micronesia
0°

Sumatra
Borneo
Celebes
Malay Peninsula
Java
New Guinea
Melanesia
Fiji
20°S

ATLANTIC OCEAN
Cape of Good Hope
Cape Agulhas

AUSTRALIA
GREAT VICTORIA DESERT
Darling R.
GREAT DIVIDING RANGE
Murray R.
Mt. Kosciusko 7,310 ft. (2,228 m)
Tasmania

N W E S

0   1,000   2,000 Miles
0   1,000   2,000 Kilometers
Scale accurate at equator
Winkel Projection

ANTARCTICA

60°S
80°S

W 40°W 20°W 0° 20°E 40°E 60°E 80°E 100°E 120°E 140°E 160°E 180°

Southern Polar Region

South Shetland Islands
South Georgia
Bellingshausen Sea
Alexander I.
Antarctic Peninsula
ELLSWORTH LAND
MARIE BYRD LAND
Vinson Massif 16,066 ft. (4,897 m)
Ronne Ice Shelf
Weddell Sea
SOUTHERN OCEAN (ATLANTIC)

SOUTHERN OCEAN (PACIFIC)
Ross Sea
Ross Ice Shelf
TRANSANTARCTIC MOUNTAINS
POLAR PLATEAU
SOUTH POLE
QUEEN MAUD LAND
0°

ANTARCTICA
WILKES LAND
ENDERBY LAND
Antarctic Circle

SOUTH MAGNETIC POLE

0   400   800 Miles
0   400   800 Kilometers
Azimuthal Equidistant Projection

90°W
60°W
30°W
150°W
180°
30°E
60°E
90°E
150°E
120°E
60°S
70°S
80°S

R5

Western Hemisphere: Political

ARCTIC OCEAN

Beaufort Sea

Bering Strait

Viscount Melville Sound

Baffin Bay

Greenland (DENMARK)

Davis Strait

Foxe Basin

Arctic Circle

ALASKA (U.S.)
Yukon River
Fairbanks
Anchorage
Whitehorse
Juneau
60°N
Gulf of Alaska
Bering Sea

Mackenzie River
Great Bear Lake
Yellowknife
Great Slave Lake
Liard River
CANADA
Lake Athabasca
Peace River
Athabasca R.
Saskatchewan R.
Lake Winnipeg

Hudson Strait
Hudson Bay
James Bay

Labrador Sea

Edmonton
Calgary
Vancouver
Puget Sound
Seattle
Portland
Boise
Columbia R.
Snake R.
Saskatoon
Regina
Winnipeg
UNITED STATES
Great Lakes
Thunder Bay
St. Lawrence River
Ottawa
Toronto
Detroit
Quebec
Montreal
St. John
Albany
Boston
Cleveland
New York City
St. John's
Gulf of St. Lawrence
Halifax

Reno
San Francisco
Las Vegas
Los Angeles
San Diego
Tucson
Great Salt Lake
Salt Lake City
Denver
Colorado R.
Missouri R.
St. Louis
Memphis
Mississippi R.
Chicago
Indianapolis
Philadelphia
Washington, D.C.
Richmond
Norfolk
Atlanta
Raleigh
Charleston
Savannah
Jacksonville

Phoenix
El Paso
Dallas
Houston
New Orleans
Rio Grande
Hermosillo
Chihuahua
San Antonio
Tampa
Orlando
Miami

Gulf of California
MEXICO
Durango
Monterrey
Gulf of Mexico
Tropic of Cancer

BAHAMAS
Nassau
Havana
CUBA
HAITI
Port-au-Prince
Santo Domingo
Puerto Rico (U.S.)
DOMINICAN REPUBLIC
JAMAICA
Kingston

Honolulu
HAWAII (U.S.)

PACIFIC OCEAN

ATLANTIC OCEAN

León
Tampico
Guadalajara
Mexico City
Puebla
Veracruz
Acapulco
BELIZE
Belmopan
GUATEMALA
Guatemala City
HONDURAS
Tegucigalpa
San Salvador
EL SALVADOR
Managua
NICARAGUA
San José
COSTA RICA
PANAMA
Panama City

Maracaibo
Caracas
VENEZUELA
GUYANA
SURINAME
Georgetown
Paramaribo
Cayenne
FRENCH GUIANA (FRANCE)
Medellín
Cali
Bogotá
COLOMBIA

Galápagos Islands (ECUADOR)
Quito
Guayaquil
ECUADOR
Iquitos
Trujillo
PERU
Lima
Cuzco
Lake Titicaca
La Paz
Arequipa
BOLIVIA
Sucre

Equator
0°

Rio Negro
Manaus
Amazon R.
Belém
Fortaleza
Recife
Tapajós River
Xingu R.
Tocantins R.
BRAZIL
Brasília
Goiânia
Salvador
São Francisco R.
Belo Horizonte
Rio de Janeiro
Campo Grande
São Paulo
Curitiba

French Polynesia (FRANCE)
Papeete

Tropic of Capricorn

Antofagasta
PARAGUAY
Asunción
Salta
San Miguel de Tucumán
CHILE
Córdoba
Valparaíso
Santiago
Rosario
Buenos Aires
La Plata
URUGUAY
Montevideo
Rio de la Plata
Mar del Plata
Pôrto Alegre
Paraná R.
Paraguay R.

Concepción
Valdivia
Bahía Blanca

30°S

ARGENTINA

0   1,000   2,000 Miles
0   1,000   2,000 Kilometers
Miller Cylindrical Projection

Punta Arenas
Falkland Islands (U.K.)
South Georgia (U.K.)

N
W   E
S

National border
National capital
City

30°N

150°W   120°W   90°W   60°W   30°W

R6

Western Hemisphere: Physical

ARCTIC OCEAN

NORTH MAGNETIC POLE

Ellesmere Island

Queen Elizabeth Islands

Melville Island

Devon Island

Viscount Melville Sound

Banks Island

Baffin Bay

Greenland

Victoria Island

Bering Strait

Point Barrow

Beaufort Sea

Brooks Range

Mt. McKinley 20,320 ft. (6,194 m)

Yukon River

Yukon Plateau

Alaska Range

Mackenzie Mts.

Mackenzie River

Great Bear Lake

Great Slave Lake

Foxe Basin

Baffin Island

Davis Strait

Arctic Circle

60°N

Mt. Logan 19,550 ft. (5,959 m)

Gulf of Alaska

Kodiak Island

Liard R.

Peace River

Athabasca R.

Lake Athabasca

Hudson Strait

Hudson Bay

Labrador Sea

Cape Farewell

Alaska Peninsula

Bering Sea

Aleutian Islands

Queen Charlotte Islands

Coast Mountains

Saskatchewan River

Lake Winnipeg

James Bay

CANADIAN SHIELD

Labrador

Vancouver Island

Puget Sound

Coast Ranges

Cascade Range

ROCKY MOUNTAINS

GREAT PLAINS

NORTH AMERICA

Great Lakes

Niagara Falls

St. Lawrence R.

Gulf of St. Lawrence

Newfoundland

Snake R.

Black Hills

Missouri R.

Mississippi R.

Nova Scotia

Bay of Fundy

Sierra Nevada

Great Salt Lake

GREAT BASIN

Platte R.

Colorado R.

Arkansas R.

INTERIOR PLAINS

Ozark Plateau

Ohio R.

APPALACHIAN MTS.

Cape Cod

Long Island

Chesapeake Bay

Cape Hatteras

Mt. Whitney 14,495 ft. (4,418 m)

Death Valley (lowest point in N.A.) -282 ft. (-86 m)

Sonoran Desert

Rio Grande

Sierra Madre Occidental

Sierra Madre Oriental

COASTAL PLAIN

ATLANTIC OCEAN

30°N

Baja California

Gulf of California

Gulf of Mexico

Bahamas

Hawaiian Islands

Tropic of Cancer

Yucatán Peninsula

Cuba

Greater Antilles

Hispaniola

Puerto Rico

Lesser Antilles

Pico de Orizaba 18,855 ft. (5,747 m)

Caribbean Sea

Lake Maracaibo

PACIFIC OCEAN

Lake Nicaragua

Isthmus of Panama

Llanos

Orinoco R.

Angel Falls

Guiana Highlands

Chimborazo 20,702 ft. (6,310 m)

Galápagos Islands

Río Negro

Amazon R.

Cape São Roque

Equator

AMAZON BASIN

Line Islands

Marquesas Islands

Tuamotu Archipelago

Huascarán 22,205 ft. (6,768 m)

Tapajós River

Xingu River

Tocantins R.

São Francisco River

Cook Islands

Society Islands

Lake Titicaca

ANDES

Altiplano

Mato Grosso Plateau

Brazilian Highlands

SOUTH AMERICA

Tropic of Capricorn

Atacama Desert

Gran Chaco

Paraguay R.

Iguazú Falls

| 0 | 1,000 | 2,000 Miles |
| 0 | 1,000 | 2,000 Kilometers |

Miller Cylindrical Projection

Mt. Aconcagua 22,834 ft. (6,960 m)

MOUNTAINS

Paraná R.

Uruguay R.

Rio de la Plata

30°S

Pampa

▲ Mountain peak

▼ Point below sea level

— National border

≋ Waterfall

N

W   E

S

Patagonia

Valdés Peninsula (lowest point in S.A.) -131 ft. (-40 m)

Falkland Islands

Strait of Magellan

Tierra del Fuego

Cape Horn

150°W   120°W   90°W   60°W   30°W

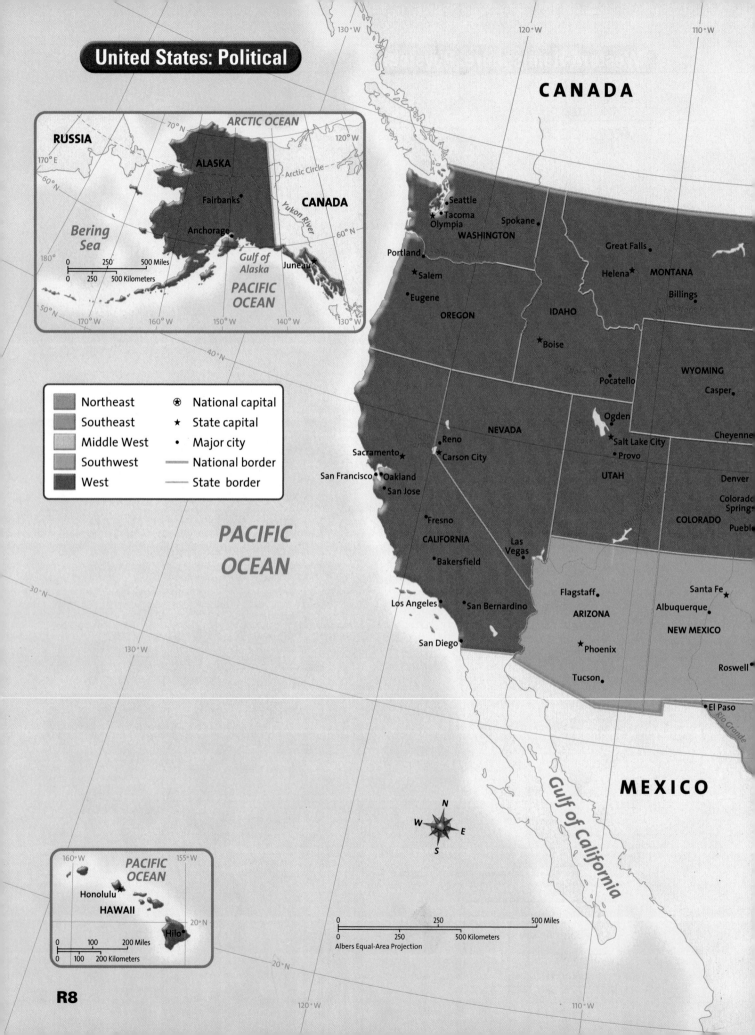

United States: Political

CANADA

RUSSIA

ARCTIC OCEAN

70° N
120° W

ALASKA

Arctic Circle

Fairbanks •

CANADA

Anchorage •

60° N

Yukon River

Bering
Sea

60° N

180°

Gulf of
Alaska

50° N

Juneau ★

PACIFIC
OCEAN

0   250   500 Miles
0   250   500 Kilometers

170° E
60° N
50° N
170° W   160° W   150° W   140° W   130° W

130° W   120° W   110° W

Seattle •
★ Tacoma
Olympia
WASHINGTON

Spokane •

Great Falls •

Portland •

Helena ★   MONTANA

★ Salem

Billings •

Eugene •

OREGON

IDAHO

★ Boise

WYOMING

40° N

Pocatello •

Casper •

Legend

	Northeast	✪	National capital
	Southeast	★	State capital
	Middle West	•	Major city
	Southwest	▬	National border
	West	▬	State border

Ogden •

Cheyenne

Reno •
Sacramento • ★
Carson City

NEVADA

★ Salt Lake City
• Provo

San Francisco •
• Oakland
• San Jose

UTAH

Denver •

Colorado
Springs

COLORADO

Pueblo •

• Fresno

PACIFIC
OCEAN

CALIFORNIA

Las
Vegas •

• Bakersfield

30° N

Los Angeles •
• San Bernardino

Flagstaff •

Santa Fe ★

Albuquerque •

ARIZONA

★ Phoenix

NEW MEXICO

San Diego •

Tucson •

Roswell •

130° W

• El Paso

Rio Grande

MEXICO

Gulf of California

160° W   155° W

PACIFIC
OCEAN

Honolulu •
HAWAII

20° N

• Hilo

0   100   200 Miles
0   100   200 Kilometers

N
W   E
S

0   250   500 Miles
0   250   500 Kilometers
Albers Equal-Area Projection

20° N

120° W   110° W

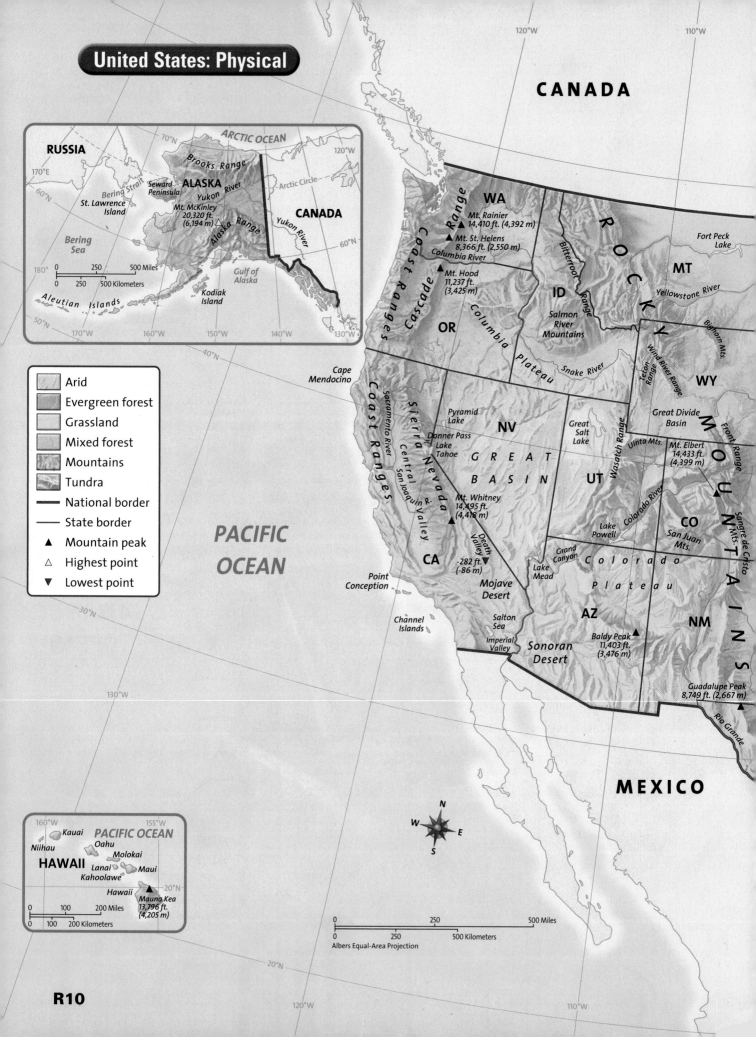

United States: Physical

RUSSIA

ARCTIC OCEAN

170°E

170°W

180°

Bering Strait

Seward Peninsula

ALASKA

Brooks Range

Yukon River

Mt. McKinley
20,320 ft.
(6,194 m) △

Alaska Range

St. Lawrence Island

Bering Sea

70°N

120°W

Arctic Circle

CANADA

Yukon River

60°N

Gulf of Alaska

Kodiak Island

Aleutian Islands

50°N

170°W 160°W 150°W 140°W 130°W

0   250   500 Miles
0   250   500 Kilometers

60°N

CANADA

120°W   110°W

40°N

Cape Mendocino

Coast Ranges

WA

Mt. Rainier
14,410 ft. (4,392 m) ▲

Mt. St. Helens
8,366 ft. (2,550 m) ▲

Columbia River

Mt. Hood
11,237 ft.
(3,425 m) ▲

Cascade Range

OR

Columbia Plateau

ID

Salmon River Mountains

Bitterroot Range

Snake River

R O C K Y

Fort Peck Lake

MT

Yellowstone River

Bighorn Mts.

Wind River Range

Teton Range

WY

Great Divide Basin

Front Range

Sacramento River

Sierra Nevada

Pyramid Lake

Donner Pass
Lake Tahoe

NV

Central Valley

San Joaquin R.

Coast Ranges

Mt. Whitney
14,495 ft.
(4,418 m) ▲

CA

Death Valley
-282 ft. ▼
(-86 m)

Mojave Desert

**G R E A T
B A S I N**

Great Salt Lake

Wasatch Range

Uinta Mts.

UT

Lake Powell

Colorado River

Grand Canyon

Lake Mead

Great Divide Basin

Mt. Elbert
14,433 ft.
(4,399 m) ▲

CO

San Juan Mts.

M O U N T A I N S

Sangre de Cristo Mts.

Colorado Plateau

AZ

Baldy Peak
11,403 ft.
(3,476 m) ▲

Salton Sea

Imperial Valley

Sonoran Desert

NM

Guadalupe Peak
8,749 ft. (2,667 m)
▲

Rio Grande

Point Conception

Channel Islands

**PACIFIC
OCEAN**

30°N

CANADA

MEXICO

130°W

120°W

110°W

Legend

- Arid
- Evergreen forest
- Grassland
- Mixed forest
- Mountains
- Tundra
- ——— National border
- ——— State border
- ▲ Mountain peak
- △ Highest point
- ▼ Lowest point

HAWAII

160°W   155°W   PACIFIC OCEAN

Kauai

Niihau

Oahu

Molokai

Lanai   Maui

Kahoolawe

Hawaii

Mauna Kea
13,796 ft.
(4,205 m) ▲

20°N

0   100   200 Miles
0   100   200 Kilometers

N
W   E
S

0   250   500 Miles
0   250   500 Kilometers

Albers Equal-Area Projection

20°N

CANADA

ME
▲ Mt. Katahdin
Moosehead 5,269 ft.
Lake (1,606 m)

Lake of
the Woods

Upper
Red Lake
Lower
Red Lake
Leech
Lake
Mille
Lacs
Lake

Isle
Royale
Keweenaw
Peninsula

Lake Superior

Mesabi
Range

Upper Peninsula

Lake Huron

St. Lawrence River

Lake
Champlain

VT
Green Mts.
NH
Mt. Washington
6,288 ft.
(1,917 m)

Cape Ann

ND

Lake Sakakawea

MN

WI

Wisconsin River

Lower Peninsula

Lake
Michigan

NY
Adirondack
Mountains

Finger
Lakes

MA
Cape
Cod

Hudson R.

CT

RI

G
R
E
A
T

Lake
Oahe

Missouri River

SD

Black
Hills

IA

Lake
Winnebago

MI
Lake
St. Clair

Niagara
Falls

Lake Ontario

Lake Erie

PA

Connecticut R.
White Mts.

NJ

Long
Island

North Platte R.

Sand Hills

NE

Platte River

South Platte R.

I
N
T
E
R
I
O
R

P
L
A
I
N
S

Illinois River

Wabash River

IL

IN

CENTRAL PLAINS

OH

Ohio River

WV

Allegheny Mts.

A
P
P
A
L
A
C
H
I
A
N

M
O
U
N
T
A
I
N
S

MD

Potomac R.

DE

Delaware
Bay

P
I
E
D
M
O
N
T

VA

James R.

Roanoke R.

Cape
Charles

Chesapeake
Bay

Albemarle
Sound

G
R
E
A
T

P
L
A
I
N
S

Smoky Hills

KS

Red Hills

Missouri River

MO

Lake of
the Ozarks

Harry S. Truman
Reservoir

Ozark Plateau

Lake of
the Ozarks

Lake
Barkley

Cumberland
Gap

KY

Cumberland R.

Mt. Mitchell
6,684 ft.
(2,037 m) ▲

NC

Cape Fear River

Cape
Hatteras

OK

Arkansas
River

Canadian River

Red River

Ouachita
Mountains

Lake
Texoma

AR

Mississippi River

TN

Tennessee R.

Stone
Mountain ▲

Clark
Hill Lake

Savannah River

SC

Oconee R.

Cape
Fear

Llano
Estacado

Sabine River

Toledo
Bend
Reservoir

LA

MS

Tombigbee R.

Alabama R.

AL

Chattahoochee R.

GA

Ocmulgee R.

Altamaha R.

Okefenokee
Swamp

C
O
A
S
T
A
L

P
L
A
I
N

TX

Pecos River

Edwards
Plateau

Brazos River

Colorado River

Sam
Rayburn
Reservoir

Lake
Maurepas

Lake
Pontchartrain

Mobile
Bay

Mississippi
Delta

St. John's River

Cape
Canaveral

Rio Grande

Galveston
Bay

Gulf of Mexico

FL

Tampa
Bay

Lake
Okeechobee

Everglades
Cape
Sable

Florida Keys

Straits of Florida

**ATLANTIC
OCEAN**

B
A
H
A
M
A
S

CUBA

California: Political

Map Legend
- ★ State capital
- • City or town
- —— National border
- —— State border

OREGON

IDAHO

NEVADA

ARIZONA

MEXICO

PACIFIC OCEAN

Crescent City
Yreka
Alturas
Eureka
Redding
Susanville
Red Bluff
Chico
Ukiah
Yuba City
Truckee
Woodland
Placerville
Sacramento
Santa Rosa
Napa
Stockton
San Francisco
Oakland
San Jose
Merced
Madera
Hollister
Salinas
Monterey
Fresno
Independence
Visalia
Tulare
Ridgecrest
Morro Bay
San Luis Obispo
Bakersfield
Santa Maria
Barstow
Needles
Lompoc
Santa Barbara
Santa Clarita
Ventura
Pasadena
San Bernardino
Oxnard
Los Angeles
Riverside
Torrance
Anaheim
Palm Springs
Long Beach
Santa Ana
Blythe
Huntington Beach
Oceanside
Escondido
San Diego
El Centro

Klamath River
Trinity River
Pit River
Goose Lake
Shasta Lake
Sacramento River
Eel River
Pyramid Lake
American River
Lake Tahoe
Stanislaus River
Mono Lake
San Joaquin River
Kings River
Salinas River
Kern River
Monterey Bay
San Francisco Bay
Lake Mead
Salton Sea
Colorado River
San Diego Bay

42°N
41°N
40°N
39°N
38°N
37°N
36°N
35°N
34°N
33°N
32°N

124°W
123°W
122°W
121°W
120°W
119°W
118°W

N
W   E
S

0   75   150 Miles
0   75   150 Kilometers
Albers Equal-Area Projection

R12

California: Physical

OREGON

IDAHO

Klamath River

Cascade Range

Mount Shasta
14,162 ft.
(4,317 m)

Goose Lake

Klamath Mountains

Warner Mts.

Clair Engle Lake

Trinity Mts.

Pit River

River

Humboldt Bay

Trinity River

Shasta Lake

Lassen Peak
10,457 ft.
(3,187 m)

Eagle Lake

Sacramento Valley

Lake Almanor

Eel River

Pyramid Lake

Coast Ranges

Lake Oroville

Feather River

River

Clear Lake

Sacramento River

Yuba River

Russian River

American River

Folsom Lake

Sierra

Lake Tahoe

Lake Berryessa

Napa Valley

NEVADA

Farallon Islands

Stanislaus River

San Joaquin River

Mono Lake

White Mountain Peak
14,246 ft.
(4,342 m)

San Francisco Bay

Merced River

Lake McClure

Nevada

North Palisade Peak
14,242 ft.
(4,341 m)

San Luis Reservoir

Monterey Bay

San Joaquin Valley

Diablo Range

San Joaquin River

Pine Flat Reservoir

Kings River

Mount Whitney
14,495 ft.
(4,418 m)

Mount Williamson
14,370 ft.
(4,380 m)

Panamint Range

Death Valley

Lake Mead

Santa Cruz Range

Salinas Valley

Coast Ranges

Salinas River

Santa Lucia Range

Lake Nacimiento

Temblor Range

Kern River

Isabella Lake

-282 ft.
(-86 m)

Lake Mohave

Mount Pinos
8,831 ft.
(2,692 m)

Cuyama R.

Tehachapi Mountains

Mojave Desert

Lake Havasu

Santa Ynez River

Santa Clara Valley

Santa Clara R.

San Gabriel Mountains

San Bernardino Mts.

Colorado River

Santa Barbara Channel

Coachella Valley

Colorado Desert

San Jacinto Mts.

Salton Sea

Alamo R.

ARIZONA

PACIFIC OCEAN

Channel Islands

Laguna Mts.

New R.

Imperial Valley

San Diego Bay

MEXICO

Legend

- —— National border
- —— State border
- ▲ Mountain peak
- ▲ Highest point
- ▽ Lowest point

N W E S

0   75   150 Miles
0   75   150 Kilometers
Albers Equal-Area Projection

Research Handbook

Before you can write a report or complete a project, you must gather information about your topic. You can find some information in your textbook. Other sources of information are technology resources, print resources, and community resources.

Technology Resources

- Internet
- Computer disk
- Television or radio

Print Resources

- Almanac
- Atlas
- Dictionary
- Encyclopedia
- Nonfiction book
- Periodical
- Thesaurus

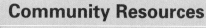

Community Resources

- Teacher
- Museum curator
- Community leader
- Older citizen

Technology Resources

The main technology resources you can use for researching information are the Internet and computer disks. Your school or local library may have CD-ROMs or DVDs that contain information about your topic. Television or radio can also be good sources of information.

Using the Internet

The Internet contains large amounts of information. By using a computer to go online, you can read documents. You can also see pictures and artworks, listen to music, or take a virtual tour of a museum. Keep in mind that some websites might contain mistakes or incorrect information. To get accurate information, be sure to visit only trusted websites, such as museum and government sites.

❯ Plan Your Search

- Identify the topic.
- Make a list of questions about your topic for which you want answers.
- List key words or groups of words that you might want to use to write or talk about your topic.
- Look for good online resources to find answers to your questions.

Use a Search Engine

A search engine is an online collection of websites. It can be sorted by entering a key word or group of words. Ask a librarian, a teacher, or a parent for suggestions about which search engine to use.

Search by Subject To search by subject, or topic, use a search engine. Choose from the list of key words that you made while planning your search. Enter a key word or group of words in the search engine field on your screen. Then click SEARCH or GO. You will see a list of websites that relate to your topic. Click on the site or sites you think will be most helpful.

Search by Address Each website has its own address, called a Uniform Resource Locator, or URL for short. To get to a website by using a URL, simply type the URL in the LOCATION/GO TO box on your screen, and hit ENTER or click GO.

Use Bookmarks The bookmark feature is an Internet tool for keeping and organizing URLs. If you find a website that seems helpful, you can save the URL. This way you can quickly return to it later. Click BOOKMARKS or FAVORITES at the top of your screen, and choose ADD. Your computer makes a copy of the URL and keeps a record of it.

Print Resources

Books in libraries are organized through a system of numbers. Every book has its own number, known as a call number. The call number tells where in the library the book can be found. Some reference books, such as encyclopedias, are usually kept in a separate section of a library. Each book there has R or RE—for *reference*—on its spine.

❱ Almanac

An almanac is a book or an electronic resource that contains facts about various subjects. The subjects are listed in alphabetical order in an index.

❱ Atlas

An atlas is a book of maps. It gives information about places. Different kinds of atlases show different places at different times. Your teacher or librarian can help you find the kind of atlas you need for your research.

❱ Dictionary

A dictionary gives the correct spelling of words and their definitions, or meanings. It also gives the words' pronunciations, or how to say the words aloud.

❯ Encyclopedia

An encyclopedia is a book or set of books that gives information about many different topics. The topics are arranged alphabetically. An encyclopedia is a good source to use when beginning your research.

❯ Nonfiction Books

A nonfiction book gives facts about real people, places, and things. All nonfiction books in a library are arranged in order and by category according to their call numbers. To find a book's call number, you use a library's card file or computer catalog. You can search for a book in the catalog by subject, by author, or by title.

❯ Periodicals

A periodical is a publication that appears each day, each week, or each month. Periodicals are good resources for current information on topics not yet recorded in books.

❯ Thesaurus

A thesaurus (thih•SAWR•uhs) lists words that mean the same or nearly the same as another word. A thesaurus also lists words that have the opposite meaning. Using a thesaurus can help you find words that better describe your topic and make your writing more interesting.

Community Resources

Often, people in your community can tell you information about your research topic. Before you talk to any of them, always ask a teacher or a parent for permission.

Listening to Find Information

It is important to plan ahead whenever you talk with people as part of your research.

❱ Before

- Find out more about the topic you want to discuss.
- List the people you want to talk to.
- Make a list of questions you want to ask.

❱ During

- Speak clearly and loudly when asking questions.
- Listen carefully. Make sure you are getting the information you need.
- Be polite. Do not talk when the other person is speaking.
- Take notes to help you remember important ideas.
- Write down the person's exact words if you think you will want to use them in your report. If possible, use a tape recorder. Be sure to ask the speaker for permission in advance.

❱ After

- Thank the person you spoke with.
- Later, write a thank-you note.

Writing to Get Information

You can also write to people in your community to gather information. You can send them an e-mail or a letter. Keep these ideas in mind as you write:

- Write neatly or use a computer.
- Say who you are and why you are writing. Check your spelling and punctuation.
- If you are writing a letter, always provide a self-addressed, stamped envelope for the person to send you a response.
- Thank the person in advance.

Reporting

❱ Written Reports

Your teacher may ask you to write a report about the information you find. Knowing how to write a report will help you make good use of the information. These tips will help you write your report.

❱ Before Writing

- Choose a main idea or topic.
- Think of questions about your topic.
- Gather information from more than one source.
- Take notes on the information you find.
- Review your notes to be sure you have the information you need. Write down ideas to put in your report.
- Use your notes to make an outline of the information you found.

❱ Citing Sources

An important part of research and writing is citing, or listing, sources. When you cite a source, you write down where you got your information. The list of sources will make up a bibliography. A bibliography is a list of the books and other sources that you used to find the information in your report.

Bibliography Card
Wyatt, Adam. *The History of California*. Philadelphia, Pennsylvania: Scenic River Publishing, 2003, page 25.
San Jose was the first state capital of California. Eventually the state government moved to Sacramento in 1854.

❱ Write a First Draft

- Use your notes and your outline to write a draft of your report. Keep in mind that your purpose is to share information.
- Write in paragraph form. Develop your topic with facts, details, and explanations. Each paragraph should focus on one idea.
- Get all your ideas down on paper.

Proofreading marks and their meanings	
Word	**Meaning**
∧	Insert word.
∧,	Insert comma.
¶	Start a new paragraph.
≡ⓒⓐⓟ	Use a capital letter.
ℯ	Delete.
ⓛⓒ	Use lowercase letter.

❱ Revise

- Read over your draft. Does it have a beginning, a middle, and an end?
- Rewrite sentences that are unclear or poorly worded. Move sentences that seem out of place.
- Add details to support your ideas.
- If too many sentences are alike, make some sentences shorter or longer to add interest.
- Check any quotations to be sure you have shown someone's exact words and that you have noted the source correctly.

Allison Cesareo
Social Studies

A History of the Capitol Building in Sacramento, California

The capitol building in Sacramento, California, is a very important place. The capitol building is the place where our government representatives make new laws. It is also where our government officials meet to talk about important issues happening in California. Many people do not know about the history of the capitol building because it was built before many of today's California citizens were born. There are many interesting historical facts about the capitol building, which is located in Sacramento, California. It is important to know where it was built, when it was built, and what happens in the capitol building today.

The capitol building in Sacramento was not always the location of our state's government offices. In 1849, the capitol of California was located in San Jose. In 1852, California's capital moved from San Jose to Vallejo, California. At that time, Vallejo was not a good place for the capitol building because work on the building took a long time and it was very expensive. In 1853, the capital of California moved to Benicia where it remained until the city of Sacramento offered its courthouse as the new capitol building. In 1854, Sacramento's courthouse became the new statehouse. The building in Sacramento that held the first state sesssion in 1854 is not the same building that served as today's California capitol building.

When the state capital was first moved to Sacramento, members of the legislature were happy to have a nice place to meet that would serve as a symbol of the great state of California. But, soon after, the city began to grow. As the population increased, so did the need for a new Capitol building.

❱ Proofread and Edit

- Proofread your report, checking for errors.
- Correct any errors in spelling, capitalization, or punctuation.

❱ Publish

- Make a neat, clean copy of your report.
- Include illustrations, maps, or other drawings to help explain your topic.

❱ Oral Presentations

Sometimes you may be asked to give an oral presentation. The purpose of an oral presentation, like that of a written report, is to share information. These tips will help you prepare an oral presentation.

- Follow the steps described in Before Writing to gather and organize information.

- Use your notes to plan and organize your presentation. Include an introduction and a conclusion in your report.

- Prepare note cards that you can refer to as you speak.

- Prepare visuals such as illustrations, diagrams, or maps to help listeners understand your topic.

- Give your audience the main idea about your topic. Support your main idea with details.

- Practice your presentation.

- Be sure to speak clearly and loudly enough. Keep your listeners interested in your report by using facial expressions and hand movements.

Biographical Dictionary

The Biographical Dictionary provides information about many of the people introduced in this book. Names are listed alphabetically by last name. Pronunciation guides are provided for hard-to-pronounce names. After each name are the birth and death dates of that person. If the person is still alive, only the year of birth appears. A brief description of the person's main achievement is then given. The page number that follows tells where the main discussion of that person appears in this book. (You can check the Index for other page references.) Guide names at the top of each page help you quickly locate the name you need to find.

A

Adams, John *(1735–1826)* [The] President of the United S[tates] [(1797–] 1801) and a signer of the [Declaration of] Independence. p. 372

Angelou, Maya (AN•juh•loo) [An] African American poet an[d writer.]

Anthony, Susan B. *(1820–19[06])* [A leader] in the women's rights move[ment. She] worked alongside Elizabeth [Cady Stanton] to earn women the right to [vote.]

Argüello y Moraga, María de la Concepción Marcela (AR•G[WAY•yoh)] *(1791–1857)* The first nun in [California] who had been born there. Sh[e was] the daughter of the commander of the presidio that became part of the city of San Francisco. p. 169

B[la...] An award-
[...] member of the Hupa [...] 118

[Borglum, Gutzon] *(18[71–1914])* An [American sculptor] who carved the [heads of four] [P]residents on Mount [Rushmore. p. 396]

[Boxer, Barbara] *(19[40–)] A United States [Senator from Califor]nia, elected in 1992.

[Breyer, Stephen Gerald] *(1938–)* An [American appointed a]s a justice of the [United States Supre]me Court. p. 271

[Buffalo Tiger] *(192[0–)* A] leader of the [Miccosukee tribe.] p. [2]1

[Bush, George W.] *(194[7–)* The forty-third President of the United States (2001–). p. 271

Bustamante, Cruz *(1953–)* The lieutenant governor of California since 1998. p. 272

B

Baca, Judy *(1946–)* An artist who is famous for her wall paintings with California themes. p. 232

Bartholdi, Frédéric–Auguste (fray•day•REEK aw•GOOST bar•TAHL•dee) *(1834–1904)* The French artist who designed the Statue of Liberty. p. 341

Bell, Alexander Graham *(1847–1922)* An American, born in Scotland, who invented the telephone in 1876. p. 438

Bell, Judy The daughter of Ray Bell. She took care of "Smokey Bear" until he went to live at the zoo. p. 335

Bidwell, John *(1819–1900)* A pioneer, entrepreneur, and political leader who founded the city of Chico, California. p. 421

C

Cabrillo, Juan Rodríguez (HWAN rohd•REE•ges kah•BREE•yoh) *(?–1543)* A sixteenth-century explorer for Spain. He was the first explorer to land in Alta California. p. 177

Carlos *(1716–1788)* An eighteenth-century Spanish king who built settlements in Alta California to protect his land there. p. 182

Carter, James "Jimmy" *(1924–)* The thirty-ninth President of the United States (1977–1981). p. 244

Chavez, Cesar *(1927–1993)* A farmworker and American leader who worked for fair treatment of all farmworkers. p. 364

Clinton, William Jefferson "Bill" (1946–) The forty-second President of the United States (1993–2001). p. 72

Coit, Lillie Hitchcock (1843–1929) An honorary member of the Knickerbocker Engine Company. She gave money to the city of San Francisco to build Coit Tower. p. 295

Columbus, Christopher (1451–1506) An Italian explorer, working for Spain, who sailed to the Americas while trying to reach Asia from Europe. p. 174

Cortés, Hernando (er•NAHN•doh kawr•TES) (1485–1547) A sixteenth-century Spanish explorer who claimed the land of Baja California for Spain. p. 176

Cortez, Edward The mayor of Pomona, California, p. 254

D

Douglass, Frederick (1817–1895) A leader and writer who was born a slave in Maryland. He escaped in 1838 and helped in the fight against slavery. p 384

Drake, Francis (1540 or 1543–1596) A sixteenth-century explorer who claimed the area that is present-day San Francisco for England. p. 178

F

Faulkner, Barry (1881–1966) An artist who painted historical murals for the Charters of Freedom display in the National Archives Building. He was known for his murals and landscapes. p. 352

Feinstein, Dianne (1933–) The first woman United States senator to represent California. She was also the first woman mayor of San Francisco. p. 270

Fillmore, Millard (1800–1874) The thirteenth President of the United States (1850–1853). He signed the bill that made California a state. p. 194

Ford, Gerald (1913–) The thirty-eighth President of the United States (1974–1977). p. 265

Franklin, Benjamin (1706–1790) An American leader, writer, and scientist. He was one of the signers of the Declaration of Independence. p. 376

Frémont, John C. (1813–1890) An American explorer who drew maps of the Oregon Trail. p. 192

G

Ghirardelli, Domingo (1817–1894) A gold rush entrepreneur who made chocolate candy. p. 209

Ginsburg, Ruth Bader (1933–) An American appointed as a justice of the United States Supreme Court in 1993. p. 271

Govea, Jessica A professor of labor education at Cornell University in New York City. As a teenager in the 1960s, she helped Cesar Chavez organize and establish the United Farm Workers Union. p. 453

Guthrie, Woody (1912–1967) An American folksinger who wrote many songs, including "This Land Is Your Land." p. 328

H

Hearst, William Randolph (1863–1951) An American newspaper publisher who lived in California. p. 199

Henry, Patrick (1736–1799) An American colonist who spoke out against Britain. He was also a Constitutional Convention delegate. p. 265

Herrera, Miguel (1967–) The owner of a shoe store in Antioch, California. p. 458

Hurtado, Maisie Jane (1976–) An entrepreneur who heads an almond farming company in Chico, California. p. 423

Hutchinson, Anne (1591–1643) A religious leader who became one of the founders of the colony of Rhode Island after she was forced to leave the Massachusetts Bay Colony. p. 379

I

Ishi *(?–1916)* The last survivor of the Yahi tribe of California. p. 140

J

Jefferson, Thomas *(1743–1826)* The third President of the United States (1801–1809). He wrote the first draft of the Declaration of Independence and presented it to Congress on July 2, 1776. p. 352

Jobs, Steve *(1955–)* An entrepreneur who helped start one of the world's leading computer companies when he was a college student. p. 417

Jones, Myldred *(1909–)* The founder of the Casa Youth Shelter in Los Alamitos, California. p. 310

Joseph *(1840?–1904)* A Nez Perce chief. p. 120

Judah, Theodore *(1826–1863)* An engineer and entrepreneur who had the idea for a transcontinental railroad to connect California to the rest of the United States. p. 210

K

Kennedy, Anthony M. *(1936–)* An American appointed as a justice of the United States Supreme Court in 1988. p. 271

Kennedy, John F. *(1917–1963)* The thirty-fifth President of the United States (1961–1963). p. 334

Key, Francis Scott *(1779–1843)* A lawyer and poet who wrote the words of "The Star-Spangled Banner." Congress adopted the song as the national anthem in 1931. p. 351

King, Dr. Martin Luther, Jr. *(1929–1968)* An American minister and civil rights leader who worked to change unfair laws. He received the Nobel Peace Prize in 1964. p. 387

L

LaVallee, Peter *(1949–)* Mayor of Eureka, California. p. 145

Lazarus, Emma *(1849–1887)* The author of the poem that is printed at the base of the Statue of Liberty. p. 341

Lincoln, Abraham *(1809–1865)* The sixteenth President of the United States (1861–1865). He was President during the Civil War. In 1863, he issued the Emancipation Proclamation, which made slavery against the law in the Confederate states. p. 382

M

Maathai, Wangari *(1940–)* The first African woman to win the Nobel Peace Prize and the first woman in eastern or central Africa to earn a doctoral degree. She founded the Green Belt Movement in Kenya. p. 73

Madison, James *(1751–1836)* The fourth President of the United States (1809–1817) and a writer of the Bill of Rights, the first ten amendments to the Constitution. p. 353

Marshall, James *(1810–1885)* A worker who found gold in 1848 in what is now Sacramento. His discovery was the beginning of the California gold rush. p. 193

Mason, George *(1725–1792)* A Virginian who wrote the Virginia Declaration of Rights. He insisted that the United States Constitution have a declaration of rights. p. 260

Milanovich, Richard The tribal chairman of the Agua Caliente Band of Cahuilla Indians. p. 151

Molina, Gloria *(1948–)* An advocate for working people and the first Hispanic elected to the Los Angeles County Board of Supervisors. p. 284

Moraga, Jose Joaquin *(1741–1785)* A Spanish military officer, explorer, and founder of a farming community called the Pueblo de San Jose de Guadalupe. p. 217

Morgan, Julia *(1872–1957)* An important architect who lived and worked in California. p. 198

Muir, John *(1838–1914)* An American naturalist, born in Scotland, who was largely responsible for the creation of many of the conservation programs in the United States. p. 42

N

Nassie, Samuel *(1988–)* A young person who helped his community of Paradise, California, by mapping a local cemetery and then researching information about each veteran buried in it. p. 312

O

Obata, Chiura *(1885–1975)* A Japanese American artist who is famous for his paintings of California. p. 24

O'Connor, Sandra Day *(1930–)* The first woman appointed as a justice of the United States Supreme Court. p. 265

P

Pantoja, José A California historian who uses primary sources in museums to research the history of his community of San Jose, California. p. 222

Parks, Rosa *(1913–2005)* An African American civil rights leader. She refused to give up her seat on a bus to a white man. p. 387

Portolá, Gaspar de (pawr•toh•LAH) *(1723–1784)* A Spanish government leader sent with Father Junípero Serra to California by King Carlos to find places to build settlements. p. 183

R

Reagan, Ronald *(1911–2004)* The fortieth President of the United States (1981–1989). He was the governor of California from 1967 to 1975. p. 245

Rehnquist, William H. *(1924–2005)* The chief justice of the United States from 1986 to 2005. He had already served as a justice from 1972 to 1986. p. 271

Romero, Gloria A California state senator for Los Angeles and the surrounding area since March 2000. p. 273

Roosevelt, Eleanor *(1884–1962)* The wife of President Franklin D. Roosevelt. She was well known for helping poor people. p. 389

Roosevelt, Franklin D. *(1882–1945)* The thirty-second President of the United States (1933–1945). He began programs and created jobs to get people working in the 1930s. p. 296

S

Satanta *(1820–1878)* A Kiowa chief. p. 121

Saubel, Katherine Siva *(1920–)* A Cahuilla Indian woman who helped start the Malki Museum at the Morongo Indian Reservation near Banning. She is the last native speaker of the Cahuilla language. p. 146

Scalia, Antonin *(1936–)* An American appointed as a justice of the United States Supreme Court in 1986. p. 271

Schwarzenegger, Arnold *(1947–)* The governor of California, sworn into office in November 2003. p. 272

Seidner, Cheryl *(1950–)* The tribal chairwoman of the Wiyot tribe and council. p. 145

Serra, Father Junípero (hoo•NEE•pay•roh SAIR•rah) *(1713–1784)* A Spanish priest who went to California to find places to build settlements and missions. p. 183

Silko, Leslie Marmon *(1948–)* An author from the Laguna Pueblo tribe. p. 121

Silverwood, F. B. A Los Angeles merchant who wrote the words to California's state song, "I Love You, California." p. 356

Sly, Larry (*1950–*) A community volunteer who began volunteering at a food bank in Contra Costa County. p. 297

Smith, Jedediah Strong (*1798–1831*) An American explorer who led a group of pioneers into California. He opened the way for other American pioneers to follow. p. 192

Souter, David Hackett (*1939–*) An American appointed as a justice of the United States Supreme Court in 1990. p. 271

Speier, Jackie A California state senator for the San Mateo/San Francisco area since 1994. p. 273

Stanton, Elizabeth Cady (*1815–1902*) A leader in the women's rights movement who worked alongside Susan B. Anthony to earn women the right to vote. p. 386

Stephens, John Paul (*1920–*) An American appointed as a justice of the United States Supreme Court in 1975. p. 271

Strauss, Levi (*1829–1902*) An entrepreneur who invented pants called blue jeans and sold them to miners during the California gold rush. p. 209

Terman, Frederick (*1900–1982*) An engineer who helped start an industrial park that today is the center of Silicon Valley. p. 220

Thiebaud, Wayne (*1920–*) A well-known California artist. Many of his paintings are of California landscapes. p. 28

Thomas, Clarence (*1948–*) An American appointed as a justice of the United States Supreme Court in 1991. p. 271

Truth, Sojourner (*1797–1883*) An African American woman who played an important role in the abolitionist and women's rights movements. p. 392

Tubman, Harriet (*1820–1913*) An escaped slave who used the Underground Railroad to lead more than 300 slaves to freedom. p. 383

Vallejo, Mariano (vah•YAY•hoh, mar•ee•AHN•oh) (*1808–1890*) A general who offered to build the California capitol in his town, Vallejo. p. 325

Vizcaíno, Sebastián (vees•kah•EE•noh) (*1550–1628*) A seventeenth-century Spanish explorer who retraced Juan Rodríguez Cabrillo's voyage. He drew maps of the coast that travelers used for nearly 200 years. p. 178

Washington, George (*1732–1799*) The first President of the United States (1789–1797). He is known as "The Father of Our Country." p. 374

Wayburn, Edgar (*1906–*) A doctor and environmentalist who has been a leader of the Sierra Club since the 1940s. p. 72

Williams, Roger (*1603?–1683*) An English colonist and minister who was the founder of the colony of Rhode Island and a pioneer of religious liberty. p. 379

Wilson, Samuel (*1766–1854*) A Massachusetts man who became known as "Uncle Sam," the symbol of the United States. p. 359

Wozniak, Steve (*1950–*) One of the founders of one of the world's leading computer companies. p. 417

Yellen, Janet (*1946–*) The head of the San Francisco Federal Reserve Bank since 2004. p. 456

Gazetteer

The Gazetteer is a geographical dictionary that can help you locate places discussed in this book. Place-names are listed alphabetically. Hard-to-pronounce names are followed by pronunciation guides. A description of the place is then given. The page number that follows tells where each place is shown on a map. Guide words at the top of each page help you locate the place-name you need to find.

A

Africa The second-largest continent. p. 181

Alaska A state of the United States, in the northwestern corner of North America. pp. 348–349

Alta California The area that is now the state of California. p. 176

Alturas A city in Modoc County, California. p. 61

American River A main tributary of the Sacramento River. p. 31

Antarctica The continent located at the South Pole, covered by an ice cap. p. 181

Arizona A state in the southwestern United States. pp. 348–349

Asia The largest continent. p. 181

Atlanta The capital of Georgia. pp. 348–349

Atlantic Ocean The body of water that separates North and South America from Europe and Africa. p. 181

B

Baja California A part of the country of Mexico. p. 176

Bakersfield A city in south-central California in the San Joaquin Valley. p. 15

Berkeley A city in Alameda County, California. p. 37

Big Basin Redwoods State Park The oldest state park in California. p. 346

Boise The capital of Idaho. pp. 348–349

Boston The capital of Massachusetts. pp. 348–349

C

Cabrillo National Monument A landmark honoring explorer Juan Rodríguez Cabrillo, located in San Diego, California. p. 177

Calexico A city in Imperial County, California, separated from Mexico only by a fence. p. 215

California A state in the western United States. p. 15

Canada A country in North America. pp. 348–349

Cascade Range A part of the Pacific mountain system that runs from Lassen Peak, California, through Oregon and Washington. p. 33

Central Valley A valley in California running along the Pacific coast. It is almost completely surrounded by mountains. p. 32

Central Valley Region One of California's four geographic regions. p. 31

Chico A city, founded by John Bidwell, located in Butte County, California, in the Sacramento River valley. p. 15

Coast Ranges A mountain chain that runs along the western side of California. p. 22

Coast Region One of California's four geographic regions. p. 32

Coastal Plains Lowland areas along a seacoast or an ocean. p. 23

Colorado A state in the western United States. pp. 348–349

Colorado Desert Part of the Sonoran Desert, stretching from southeastern California to the Colorado River delta. p. 33

Colorado River A river in the southwestern United States. p. 61

Colorado Springs A city in Colorado. p. 435

Contra Costa County A county in California. p. 282

Coso Hot Springs A geothermal area of California. p. 426

D

Dallas A city in northeastern Texas. p. 22

Death Valley A basin in southeastern California that is the lowest, hottest, driest place in North America. p. 31

Denver The capital of Colorado. pp. 348–349

Desert Hot Springs A geothermal area of California. p. 426

Desert Region One of California's four geographic regions. p. 33

E

Eastern Hemisphere (heh•muh•sfir) The eastern half of Earth. p. 434

Eureka A port city in northern California. p. 61

F

Farallon Islands A group of islands located in the Pacific Ocean off the coast of San Francisco. p. 31

Feather River A main tributary of the Sacramento River. p. 61

Florida A state in the southeastern United States. pp. 348–349

Fresno A city in central California in the San Joaquin Valley. p. 61

G

Georgia A state in the southeastern United States. pp. 348–349

Geysers, The A geothermal area of California. p. 426

Golden Gate Bridge A human-made landmark that connects San Francisco Bay with the Pacific Ocean. p. 344

Great Basin A low area in the western United States. p. 22

Gulf of Mexico A body of water on the southeastern coast of North America. pp. 348–349

H

Hawaii A state made up of a string of volcanic islands in the north-central Pacific Ocean. pp. 348–349

Honolulu The capital of Hawaii. pp. 348–349

I

Idaho A state in the northwestern United States. pp. 348–349

Illinois A state in the Middle West region of the United States. pp. 348–349

Imperial Valley An irrigated part of the Colorado Desert and a geothermal area of California. p. 426

Indian Island An island near Eureka, California, preserved by the Wiyot Indians. p. 145

Indian Ocean The smallest of the world's three major oceans, stretching between the southern tips of Africa and Australia. p. 181

GAZETTEER

J

Joshua Tree National Park A national park located in Southern California, known for its unusual desert plants. p. 20

K

Kansas A state in the central United States. pp. 348–349

Klamath River A river that begins in Oregon and runs into northern California. p. 32

L

Lake County A county in the north-central area of California. p. 282

Lake City A geothermal area of California. p. 426

Lake Oroville A lake in northern California created by the building of Oroville Dam. p. 62

Lake Tahoe A freshwater lake on the California-Nevada border in the northern Sierra Nevada. p. 61

Las Vegas A city in Nevada, one of California's bordering states. p. 435

Lassen Peak A volcanic peak located at the southern end of the Cascade Range in northern California. p. 31

Long Beach A port city in southwestern California on San Pedro Bay. p. 31

Los Angeles A city in southern California. It is the second-most populated city and metropolitan area in the United States. p. 33

Louisiana A state in the southeastern United States. pp. 348–349

M

Maine A state in the northeastern United States. pp. 348–349

Mammoth Lakes A geothermal area of California. p. 426

Mariposa County A county in California. p. 282

Massachusetts A state in the northeastern United States. pp. 348–349

Mendocino County A county along the north-central coast of California. p. 282

Mexico A country in southern North America that borders on the Pacific Ocean and the Gulf of Mexico. Mexico is on California's southern border. pp. 348–349

Minneapolis A city in Minnesota. p. 22

Minnesota A state in the north-central United States. pp. 348–349

Missouri A state in the central United States. pp. 348–349

Modesto A city in Stanislaus County, California, in the San Joaquin Valley. p. 61

Modoc County A county in California. p. 282

Mojave Desert (moh•HAH•vee) An arid region of southeastern California and portions of Nevada, Arizona, and Utah. p. 33

Montana A state in the northwestern United States. pp. 348–349

Monterey A city in Monterey County, California. p. 61

Morongo Indian Reservation A Cahuilla Indian reservation near Banning, California. p. 139

Morro Bay A fishing village located on the coast of central California. p. 54

Mount Shasta A peak of the Cascade Range in California that used to be an active volcano. p. 33

Mount Whitney The highest peak in the continental United States. It is part of the Sierra Nevada. p. 33

Mountain Region One of California's four geographic regions. p. 33

GAZETTEER

N

Nebraska A state in the central United States. pp. 348–349

Nevada A state in the western United States. pp. 348–349

New Mexico A state in the southwestern United States. pp. 348–349

New Orleans A city in Louisiana located on the Gulf of Mexico. p. 22

New York A state in the northeastern United States. pp. 348–349

New York Colony One of the original 13 American colonies. p. 371

New York Harbor The harbor located at the mouth of the Hudson River. Home of Staten Island and the Statue of Liberty. p. 340

North America The continent that includes the United States, Canada, Mexico, and some countries of Central America. p. 10

Northern Hemisphere The northern half of Earth. p. 434

O

Oregon A state in the northwestern United States and California's neighbor to the north. p. 23

Oregon Trail An early pioneer trail running from Independence, Missouri, to the Colorado River. p. 192

Orlando A city in Florida. p. 23

Oroville A community near the Feather River in California. p. 63

Oroville Dam A dam on the Feather River in California. It is one of the highest earthen dams in the world. p. 62

P

Pacific Ocean The body of water that separates North America and South America from Australia and Asia. pp. 348–349

Palm Springs A city in Riverside County, California. p. 15

Pasadena A city in Los Angeles County, California. p. 215

Pennsylvania A state in the northeastern United States. pp. 348–349

Phoenix The capital of Arizona. pp. 348–349

Pigeon Point Light Station State Historic Park A historical site in the San Francisco Bay area of California that has one of the tallest lighthouses in the Americas. p. 346

Pittsburgh A city in Pennsylvania. p. R9

Plymouth Colony A colony in the United States, now Plymouth, Massachusetts. p. 378

Porterville A city in south-central California. p. 134

Providence An early colonial settlement, now the capital of Rhode Island. p. 349

R

Redding A city in the Sacramento Valley in northern California. p. 61

Rhode Island A state in the northeastern United States. pp. 348–349

Russian River A river in northern California. p. 61

GAZETTEER

S

Sacramento The capital of California. pp. 348–349

Sacramento River A river that begins near Mount Shasta in northern California and flows into San Francisco Bay. p. 61

Sacramento Valley The northern area of California's Central Valley. p. 31

Salem The capital of Oregon. pp. 348–349

Salton Sea A lake in the California Desert. p. 31

San Diego A port city in southern California. p. 33

San Francisco A large port city in California. p. 33

San Francisco Bay A large inlet of the Pacific Ocean in west-central California. p. 61

San Gregorio State Beach A sandy beach on California's coast. p. 346

San Joaquin River A river in California that begins in the Sierra Nevada and flows into the Sacramento River. p. 32

San Joaquin Valley The southern area of California's Central Valley. p. 31

San Jose A city that lies in the Santa Clara Valley in west-central California. p. 61

San Manuel Reservation The reservation of the San Manuel of the Band of Mission Indians near Highland, California. p. 139

San Mateo County A county in California. p. 282

Santa Barbara A city that lies along the Pacific coast in southwestern California. p. 61

Santa Clara River A river in southern California. p. 31

Santa Clara Valley A California valley that lies between the Santa Cruz Mountains and the Diablo Range. p. 219

Santa Cruz A city in Santa Cruz County, California, on the northern shore of Monterey Bay. p. 215

Saratoga A city in Santa Clara County, California. p. 346

Sierra Nevada (see•a ir •ah neh•va h •dah) An enormous mountain range running along the eastern edge of California. p. 33

Silicon Valley An area around San Francisco Bay, known as a center for the development and manufacture of computers and computer parts. Silicon Valley includes northwestern Santa Clara County as far inland as San Jose, as well as parts of Alameda and San Mateo Counties. p. 219

Sonoma A county that lies along the north-central coast of California. p. 282

Sonoran Desert (soh•nawr •ahn) A desert in the Desert Region of California. p. 33

Southern Hemisphere The southern half of Earth. p. 434

Stockton A city that lies along the San Joaquin River in central California. p. 61

T

Texas A state in the southern United States. pp. 348–349

Trinity River The largest tributary of the Klamath River in northern California. p. 61

Tule River Reservation A Yokuts Indian Reservation located near Porterville, California. p. 134

U

United States A country on the continent of North America. pp. 348-349

Utah A state in the western United States. pp. 348–349

V

Virginia A state in the southern United States. pp. 348–349

W

Washington A state in the northwestern United States. pp. 348–349

Washington, D.C. The capital of the United States. pp. 348–349

Weaverville A community in the Trinity Mountains of northern California. p. 12

Wendel-Amedee A geothermal area of California. p. 426

Western Hemisphere The western half of Earth. p. 434

Wyoming A state in the northwestern United States. p. 348

Y

Yosemite National Park (yoh•SEH•muh•tee) A national landmark in the Sierra Nevada. p. 344

Glossary

The Glossary contains important social studies words and their definitions, listed in alphabetical order. Each word is respelled as it would be in a dictionary. When you see this mark ´ after a syllable, pronounce that syllable with more force. The page number at the end of the definition tells where the word is first used in this book. Guide words at the top of each Glossary page help you quickly locate the word you need to find.

add, āce, câre, pälm; end, ēqual; it, īce; odd, ōpen, ôrder; took, pool; up, bûrn; yoo as u in fuse; oil; pout; ə as a in above, e in sicken, i in possible, o in melon, u in circus; check; ring; thin; this; zh as in vision

adapt (ə•dapt´) To change as the environment changes. p. 66

agriculture (a´gri•kəl•chər) The growing of crops and the raising of farm animals for sale. p. 47

amendment (ə•mend´mənt) A change in the Constitution. p. 261

ancestor (an´ses•tər) Someone in a person's family who lived long ago. p. 226

anthem (an´thəm) A patriotic song. p. 351

appoint (ə•point´) To choose. p. 271

aqueduct (a´kwə•dukt) A large pipe or canal that carries water from one place to another. p. 50

artifact (är´tə•fakt) An object that was used by people in the past. p. I2

ballot (ba´lət) A list of the choices in an election. p. 303

bank (bangk) A business that keeps money safe. p. 460

bar graph (bär graf) A kind of graph that uses bars to show amounts and numbers of things. p. 274

barter (bär´tər) To trade without using money. p. 110

bay (bā) A body of water that is part of a sea or an ocean and is partly enclosed by land. p. 55

Bill of Rights (bil əv rīts) The first ten amendments to the Constitution that list the freedoms and rights that the people of the United States will always have. p. 261

biography (bī•ä´gru•fē) The story of a person's life. p. I2

border (bôr´dər) On a map, a line that shows where a state or a nation ends. p. 11

boundary (boun´drē) A line that shows state or national borders. p. 349

budget (bu´jət) A plan for spending, saving, and sharing money. p. 462

business (biz´nəs) An activity in which workers make or sell goods for others. p. 421

canal (kə•nal´) A human-made waterway. p. 50

candidate (kan´də•dāt) A person who wants to be elected as a leader. p. 306

capital resource (ka´pə•təl rē´sôrs) Money to start a new business. p. 423

capitol (ka´pə•təl) The government building in a capital city. p. 272

cardinal directions (kär´də•nəl di•rek´shənz) The main directions north, south, east, and west. p. I13

century (sen´chrē) A period of 100 years. p. 390

character trait (kar´ik•tər trāt) A quality that a person has, such as caring, fairness, responsibility, and respect. p. 295

citizen (sit´ə•zən) A person who lives in and belongs to a community. p. 254

civil rights (si´vəl rīts) Rights of personal freedom. p. 387

civil war (si´vəl wôr) A war in which the people of a country fight each other. p. 382

claim (klām) To say that something belongs to you. p. 175

climate (klī´mət) Weather that a place has over a long period of time. p. 20

coastal plain (kōs´təl plān) A lowland plain that lies along a seacoast or along an ocean. p. 18

colonist (kä´lə•nist) A person who lives in a colony. p. 371

colony (kä´lə•nē) A settlement that is ruled by another country. p. 371

common good (kä´mən good) Something that is good for everyone. p. 309

communication (kə•myōō•nə•kā´shən) The sharing of information. p. 210

communication link (kə•myōō•nə•kā´shən lingk) A kind of technology that lets people who are far apart share information instantly. p. 440

community (kə•myōō´nə•tē) A group of people who live in the same place. p. 10

compass rose (kum´pəs rōz) A drawing on a map that shows cardinal directions to help people use the map. p. I13

compromise (käm´prə•mīz) Each person's giving up of some of what he or she wants. p. 256

conflict (kän´flikt) A disagreement. p. 256

Congress (kän´grəs) The legislative branch of the national government. p. 270

consequence (kän´sə•kwens) Something that happens because of what a person does. p. 253

conservation (kän•sər•vā´shən) Protecting resources to make them last longer. p. 70

constitution (kän•stə•tōō´shən) A written set of laws that describe how a government is to work. p. 150

consumer (kən•sōō´mər) A person who buys a product or service. p. 418

continent (kon´tə•nənt) One of the largest land areas on Earth. p. I10

cooperate (kō•ä´pə•rāt) To work together. p. 252

council (koun´səl) A group of people chosen to make laws. p. 278

county (koun´tē) Part of a state. p. 282

county seat (koun´tē sēt) A town or city where the county government meets. p. 283

court (kôrt) A place where a jury makes decisions about the law. p. 255

culture (kul´chər) A way of life shared by members of a group. p. 142

custom (kus´təm) A way of doing something. p. 114

cutaway diagram (kut´ə•wā dī´ə•gram) A picture that shows both the inside and the outside of an object at the same time. p. 108

D

dam (dam) An earthen or concrete structure that enables workers to control the flow of water and to prevent floods. p. 62

decade (de´kād) A period of 10 years. p. 390

decision (di•si´zhən) A choice. p. 472

demand (di•mand´) The wants and needs of consumers. p. 454

democracy (di•mä´krə•sē) The form of government of the United States, in which each adult citizen has the right to vote. p. 306

depend (di•pend´) To rely on one another. p. 416

deposit (di•pä´zət) To put money in a bank account. p. 460

desert (de´zərt) A place with a hot, dry climate. p. 21

disaster (di•zas´tər) An event that causes great harm or damage. p. 66

E

economy (i•kä´nə•mē) The ways a country or community makes and uses goods and services. p. 110

elder (el´dər) An older, respected member of a tribe. p. 144

elect (i•lekt´) To choose by voting. p. 254

election (i•lek´shən) A time set aside when citizens vote. p. 302

energy (e´nər•jē) A power that makes electricity. p. 58

entrepreneur (än•trə•prə•nûr´) Someone who starts and runs a business. p. 209

environment (in•vī´rən•mənt) The physical and human features that make up a place. p. 62

equality (i•kwä´lə•tē) Equal rights. p. 386

equator (i•kwā´•tər) On a map or a globe, a line that appears halfway between the North Pole and the South Pole. p. I11

ethnic group (eth´nik grōōp) A group of people who share the same language, culture, and way of life. p. 387

exact location (ig•zakt´ lō•kā•shən) The point where two grid lines meet, or cross, on a map. p. 36

executive branch (ig•ze´kyə•tiv branch) The branch of government that sees that the laws are obeyed. p. 267

explorer (ik•splôr´ər) A person who goes to find out about a place. p. 174

export (ek•spôrt´) To ship products and resources to other countries to sell. p. 430

fact (fakt) A statement that can be proved. p. 358

fiction (fik´shən) A story that is made up. p. 358

flowchart (flō´chärt) A drawing that shows the steps it takes to do something. p. 300

folklore (fō´klôr) The history, beliefs, and customs of a group as told in its stories. p. 116

free market (frē mär´kət) The freedom to make and sell any product or service that is allowed by law. p. 452

freedom (frē´dəm) The right to make your own choices. p. 370

fuel (fyool) A natural resource that is burned to make heat or electricity. p. 49

G

geography (jē•ä´grə•fē) The study of Earth's surface and the ways people use it. p. I8

globe (glōb) A model of the Earth. p. I10

goods (goodz) Things that can be bought or sold. p. 415

government (gu´vərn•mənt) A group of people that makes rules and solves problems for a community. p. 112

government service (gu´vərn•mənt sûr´vəs) Work that is done by the government for everyone in a city or town. p. 280

governor (gu´vən•ər) The elected leader of a state's government. p. 272

grid system (grid sis´təm) A set of lines that cross each other to form boxes. p. 36

H

harbor (här´bər) A place with deep water that allows ships to come close to the shore. p. 178

hemisphere (he´mə•sfir) Half of the globe when it is divided into either northern and southern halves or eastern and western halves. p. I11

heritage (her´ə•tij) A set of values and traditions handed down from those who lived earlier. p. 226

hero (hir´ō) A brave person who sets an example. p. 299

historian (hi•stôr´e•an) A person whose work is to study the past. p. I2

historic site (hi•stôr´ik sīt) A place that is important in history. p. 228

historical society (hi•stôr´i•kəl sə•sī´ə•tē) An organization of people who are interested in the history of their community. p. 230

history (his´tə•rē) The story of what has happened in a place in the past. p. I2

history map (his´tə•rē map) A map that shows how a place looked in an earlier time. p. 138

holiday (hä´lə•dā) A day set aside for remembering a special person or event. p. 387

human capital (hyoo´mən ka´pə•təl) A person's skills and knowledge. p. 468

human resources (hyoo´mən rē´sôr•səz) The people needed to grow or make and sell a product or provide a service. p. 423

human rights (hyoo´mən rīts) The rights of human beings, such as to have food, clean water, and a safe place to live. p. 388

human-made feature (hyoo´mən mād fē´chər) Something that people add to a landscape, such as a bridge, a wall, or a building. p. 26

hybrid (hī´brəd) A car that conserves resources by sometimes using electricity instead of gas. p. 70

I

immigrant (im´ə•grənt) A person who comes to live in a country from somewhere else in the world. p. 211

import (im´pôrt) To bring in products and resources from other countries to sell them. p. 430

income (in´kum) Money that people are paid for the work they do. p. 458

independence (in•də•pen´dəns) Freedom from another country's control. p. 372

industry (in´dəs•trē) Companies that make the same product or provide the same service. p. 219

inset map (in´set map) A small map within a larger map. p. I12

interdependence (in•tər•də•pen´dəns) The reliance of different states or countries on each other for products and resources they need. p. 429

GLOSSARY

intermediate directions (in•tər•mē´dē•ət də•rek´shənz) The in-between directions, northeast, southeast, northwest, and southwest, that give more exact information about location. p. 14

international trade (in•tər•nash´nəl trād) Buying and selling between countries. p. 430

Internet (in´tər•net) A system that links computers around the world. p. 439

invention (in•ven´shən) Something that has been made for the first time. p. 212

irrigation (ir•ə•gā´shən) Moving of water to dry areas. p. 51

J

judge (juj) A person from the community who is chosen to work as a leader in the courts. p. 255

judicial branch (jŏŏ•di´shəl branch) The branch of government that decides whether laws are fair. p. 267

jury (jûr´ē) A group of 6 to 12 citizens who decide if a person has broken the law. p. 304

justice (jus´təs) Fairness. p. 294

L

landform (land´fôrm) A physical feature, such as a mountain, a valley, a plain, or a hill. p. 16

landform map (land´fôrm map) A map that shows a place's physical features, such as mountains, hills, plains, plateaus, lakes, rivers, and oceans. p. 22

landmark (land´märk) An important human or natural feature that helps people find their way. p. 340

language (lang´gwij) The group of sounds and words people use to communicate. p. 93

latitude (la´tə•tŏŏd) Lines that run east and west around a globe. p. 434

laws (lô) Rules that a community makes. p. 253

legend (le´jənd) A story that helps explain something. p. 88

legislative branch (le´jəs•lā•tiv branch) The branch of government that makes laws. p. 267

liberty (li´bər•tē) Freedom. p. 372

line graph (līn graf) A graph that uses a line to show patterns formed over time. p. 196

location (lō•kā´shən) The place where something is found. p. 11

locator (lō•kā•tər) A small map or picture of a globe that shows where an area on the main map is found in a state, on a continent, or in the world. p. I12

longitude (län´jə•tŏŏd) Lines that run north and south on a globe, from pole to pole. p. 434

M

majority rule (mə•jôr´ə•tē rŏŏl) Accepting the thing or person that more than half the people vote for. p. 263

manufacture (man•yə•fak´chər) To make something with machines. p. 424

map (map) A picture that shows the location of things. p. I3

map legend (map le´jənd) A box on a map in which map symbols are explained; also called a map key. p. I12

map scale (map skāl) A part of a map that compares a distance on the map to a distance in the real world. p. I12

map title (map tī´təl) A title that tells what a map is about. p. I12

mayor (mā´ər) A leader of a community government. p. 254

mediator (mē´dē•ā•tər) A person who helps other people settle a disagreement. p. 256

memorial (mə•môr´ē•əl) Something that keeps a memory alive. p. 342

mineral (min´ər•əl) A kind of natural resource found in the ground, such as iron or gold. p. 48

minority rights (mə•nôr´ə•tē rīts) The rights kept by a smaller group that did not vote for the same thing or person most people voted for. p. 263

mission (mi´shən) A religious community. p. 132

monument (män´yə•mənt) Something built to honor or remember a person or an event in history. p. 342

mountain range (moun´tən rānj) A large chain of mountains. p. 17

museum (myŏŏ•zē´əm) A place that keeps and displays objects. p. 143

GLOSSARY

N

natural resource (na´chə•rəl rē´sôrs) Something from nature that people can use, such as trees, water, animals, or soil. p. 46

O

opportunity cost (ä•pər•tōō´nə•tē cost) What you give up to get what you want. p. 466

oral history (ôr´əl his´tə•rē) Spoken history. p. 117

P

patriotic symbol (pā•trē•ä´tik sim´bəl) A symbol of a country, such as a flag, that stands for the ideas that people believe in. p. 332

patriotism (pā´trē•ə•ti•zəm) A feeling of pride in one's country. p. 332

physical feature (fi´zi•kəl fē´chər) A feature of a place's land, water, climate, or plant life. p. 16

physical map (fi´zi•kəl map) A map that shows kinds of land and bodies of water. p. I12

picture graph (pik´chər graf) A graph that uses pictures or symbols to stand for the numbers of things. p. 52

pioneer (pī•ə•nir´) A person who helps settle a new land. p. 192

plateau (pla•tō´) A landform with steep sides and a flat top. p. 17

political map (pə•li´ti•kəl map) A map that shows cities, states, and countries. p. I12

pollution (pə•lōō´shən) Anything that makes a natural resource dirty or unsafe to use. p. 69

population (pä•pyə•lā´shən) The total number of people in a place. p. 34

population density (pä•pyə•lā´shən den´sə•tē) The number of people living in an area of a certain size. p. 214

port (port) A place where ships dock to take on goods or passengers. p. 213

preserve (pri•zərv´) To keep something safe. p. 143

President (pre´zə•dənt) The title given to the leader of the United States of America. He leads the executive branch of the national government. p. 271

presidio (prā•sē´dē•ō) A fort built to protect missions from enemy attacks. p. 185

primary sources (prī´mer•ē sôr´səz) Records written by people who saw or took part in an event. p. 222

Prime Meridian (prīm mə•ri´dē•ən) The line that divides Earth into Eastern and Western Hemispheres. p. I11

private property (prī´vət prä´pər•tē) Property such as a home or a business that belongs to one person or to a group of people. p. 217

producer (prə•dōō´sər) Someone who makes and sells a product. p. 417

profit (prä´fət) The amount of money that is left over after all the costs of running a business have been paid. p. 452

public property (pu´blik prä´pər•tē) Property that is used by all the people of a community. p. 217

public service (pu´blik sər´vəs) Work for the good of the community. p. 308

public works (pu´blik wurks) A department of a community government that provides services to meet day-to-day needs. p. 281

pueblo (pwe´blō) A village. p. 186

R

rancheria (ran•chər•ee´ə) A small reservation. p. 135

ranchero (ran•cher´ō) A man who owns a rancho. p. 191

recreation (re•krē•ā´shən) Any activity, hobby, or sport done for enjoyment. p. 280

recycle (rē•sī´kəl) To reuse resources. p. 71

reference works (ref´runce werkz) Sources of facts. p. 225

region (rē´jən) A large area with at least one feature that makes it different from other areas. p. 30

relative location (re´lə•tiv lō•kā´shən) The location of a place in relation to another place. p. I12

religion (ri•li´jən) A set of ideas a person has about gods or spirits. p. 114

representative (re•pri•zen´tə•tiv) A person chosen by a group of people to act or speak for them. p. 262

GLOSSARY

reservation (re•zər•vā´shən) An area of land set aside for American Indians. p. 133

reservoir (re´zə•vwär) A human-made lake used for collecting and storing water. p. 63

resource map (rē´sôrs map) A map that uses symbols and color to show different natural resources and land uses. p. 60

responsibility (ri•spon•sə•bil´ə•tē) Something a person should do because it is necessary and important. p. 294

revolution (re•və•lōō´shən) A fight for a change in a government. p. 372

rights (rīts) Freedoms. p. 260

route (rōōt) A path or direction a person takes to get somewhere. p. 180

rural (rûr´əl) Having to do with an area that has countryside and small towns. p. 35

savings (sā´vings) The money that people save. p. 460

scarcity (sker´sə•tē) Very low supply. p. 455

secondary sources (se´kən•der•ē sôrs•əz) Records written by people who were not present at an event. p. 223

service (sûr´vəs) Work that someone does for someone else. p. 416

settlement (se´təl•mənt) A new community. p. 182

settler (set´lər) A person who lives in a new community. p. 182

shaman (shä´mən) In some cultures, a curing doctor who helps cure the sick. p. 114

shelter (shel´tər) A home or building that protects from the weather. p. 94

slave (slāv) A person who is forced to work for another person without pay. p. 383

sovereign (sä´vrən) Separate from the federal, state, and local government. p. 150

strait (strāt) A narrow water passage that connects two bodies of water. p. 175

suburban (sə•bûr´bən) Having to do with smaller communities around cities. p. 34

supply (sə•plī´) The amount of available products and services. p. 454

Supreme Court (sə•prēm´ kôrt) A part of the judicial branch of the national government; the most important court in the U.S. p. 271

table (tā´bəl) A graphic organizer used to organize information. p. 98

tax (taks) The money that citizens pay to run the government and to obtain its services. p. 281

technology (tek•nä´lə•jē) The inventions people use in everyday life. p. 220

time line (tīm līn) A drawing that shows when and in what order events took place. p. 188

tool (tōōl) An instrument used to do work. p. 101

trade (trād) To exchange one thing for another. p. 27

trade-off (trād´ôf) The giving up of one thing in return for something else. p. 466

tradition (trə•di´shən) A custom, or way of doing something, that is passed on to others. p. 144

transcontinental (trans•kän•tən•en´təl) Going across a continent. p. 210

transportation (trans•pər•tā´shən) The moving of people, goods, and ideas from one place to another. p. 29

treaty (trē´tē) An agreement between groups or countries. p. 152

tribal council (trī´bəl koun´səl) A group of leaders elected by tribe members. p. 151

tribe (trīb) A group of American Indians who share some common ways of life. p. 92

urban (ûr´bən) Having to do with cities. p. 34

V

valley (va´lē) A lowland that lies between hills or mountains. p. 18

volunteer (vä•lən•tir´) A person who chooses to work without getting paid. p. 297

voyage (voi´ij) A journey by water. p. 175

W

wage (wāj) Money paid to a worker for the work he or she does. p. 415

worship (wûr´shəp) To take part in a church service. p. 381

GLOSSARY

Index

Page references for illustrations are set in italic type. An italic "m" indicates a map. Page references set in boldface type indicate the pages on which vocabulary terms are defined.

INDEX

INDEX

M

INDEX

For permission to reprint copyrighted material, grateful acknowledgment is made to the following sources:

Carus Publishing Company, 30 Grove Street, Suite C, Peterborough, NH 03458: From "Young Cesar E. Chavez: The Early Years of an American Hero" by Rebecca Valbuena in *Appleseeds: Cesar E. Chavez,* February 2002. Text © 2002 by Cobblestone Publishing Company.

Chronicle Books LLC, San Francisco, CA, www. ChronicleBooks.com: From *Fire Race: A Karuk Coyote Tale,* retold by Jonathan London, illustrated by Sylvia Long. Text copyright © by Jonathan London, illustrations copyright © by Julian Lang.

Dial Books for Young Readers, a Division of Penguin Young Readers Group, A Member of Penguin Group (USA) Inc., 345 Hudson Street, New York, NY 10014: "Walk Lightly" from *A World of Wonders: Geographic Travels in Verse and Rhyme* by J. Patrick Lewis, illustrated by Alison Jay. Text copyright © 2002 by J. Patrick Lewis; illustrations copyright © 2002 by Alison Jay.

Fulcrum Publishing: From *John Muir: America's Naturalist* by Thomas Locker. Copyright © 2003 by Thomas Locker.

Harcourt, Inc.: From *Rachel's Journal: The Story of A Pioneer Girl* by Marissa Moss. Copyright © 1998 by Marissa Moss.

Little, Brown and Company, (Inc.): Illustrations by Kathy Jakobsen from *This Land Is Your Land* by Woody Guthrie. Illustrations copyright © 1998 by Kathy Jakobsen.

Ludlow Music, Inc.: Lyrics from "This Land Is Your Land" by Woody Guthrie. TRO - © - copyright 1956 (Renewed), 1958 (Renewed), 1970 and 1972 by Ludlow Music, Inc. Published by TRO-Ludlow Music, Inc.

Mary Laychak, on behalf of Northland Publishing, Flagstaff, AZ: From *Carlos and the Carnival* by Jan Romero Stevens, illustrated by Jeanne Arnold. Text copyright © 1999 by Jan Romero Stevens, illustrations copyright © 1999 by Jeanne Arnold.

Scholastic Inc.: From *Boom Town* by Sonia Levitin, illustrated by Cat Bowman Smith. Text copyright © 1998 by Sonia Levitin; illustration copyright © 1998 by Cat Bowman Smith. Published by Orchard Books/Scholastic Inc.

PHOTO CREDITS

Placement key: (t) top; (b) bottom; (l) left; (r) right; (c) center; (bg) background; (fg) foreground; (i) inset.

COVER

Peter Bennett/Alamy Images (Aqua Caliente Indian Statue); age Fotostock/Robert Glusic (El Capitan); Roberto M. Arakaki/ Imagestate (Transamerica Building).

ENDSHEET

Inga Spence/Index Stock (Zinfandel grapes); Peter Bennett/Alamy Images (Aqua Caliente Indian Statue); age Fotostock/Robert Glusic (El Capitan).

FRONTMATTER

blind Panoramic Images; I2 (l) Macduff Everton/Corbis; (r) Bettman/Corbis; I3 (b) Robert Landau/Corbis; (t)Library of Congress.

UNIT 1

1 Larry Ulrich Photography; 2 (t) Robert Harding World Imagery/Getty Images; (b) Getty Images; 3 (b) Tom McHugh/Photo Researchers, Inc.; (cl) Mark Gibson/Index Stock Imagery; (t) Royalty-Free/Corbis; (cr) Superstock; 5 (b) Paul Edmondson/ Corbis; (t) Royalty-Free/Corbis; 6-7 David Muench Photography; 12 Mark E. Gibson; 16 (b) Joseph Sohm/Visions of America/ PictureQuest; 17 (t) Bob Krist/Corbis; 19 (t) SuperStock; 20 (b) Bill Hatcher; 21 (t) Chuck Mitchell; 24 (tl),(tr) Courtesy of the Obata Family Collection; 26 (b) Mike Mullen/Event Photography; 27 (t) Getty Images; 28 LeBaron's Fine Art/Wayne Thiebaud; Urban Freeways, 1979/Licensed by VAGA; New York; NY; 29 Ron Watts/ Corbis; 31 (t) Roy Ooms/Masterfile; (b) Chuck Place; (bc) David Barber/PhotoEdit; (tc) Terry W. Eggers/Corbis; 32 (bl) Tim Barnett/Masterfile; (br) Mark E. Gibson Photography; 33 (bl) Getty Images; (br) Mark Gibson; 34 (b) Royalty-Free/Corbis; (inset) Damir Frkovic/Masterfile; 35 Chuck Place; 40-41 Nik Wheeler Photography; 46 Stock Solution/Index Stock Imagery; 47 (t) Larry Ulrich Photography; (b) Grant Heilman Photography; 48 (t) Maximilian Stock Ltd/Science Photo Library/Photo Researchers; (b) The Bancroft Library; 49 Kim Kulish/Corbis; 51 Larry Ulrich Photography; 54 (b) Mark E. Gibson; 55 (inset) Richard Herrmann Photography; 56 (br) David Young-Wolff/PhotoEdit; (bl) Richard Hamilton Smith/Corbis; 57 (br) Craig Lovell/Corbis; (bl) Craig Lovell/ Corbis; 58 Woody Wooden/SuperStock; 59 (t) Tony Freeman/PhotoEdit; 62 (b) Office of Water Education, California Dept. of Water Resources; 63 (r) Office of Water Education, California Dept. of Water Resources; 64 (b) William Manning/Corbis; (cl) Golden Gate Bridge, Highway and Transportation District; (tl) Bettmann/Corbis; 66 (t) Charles O. Cecil/Words & Pictures/PictureQuest; 66 (b) Bettmann/Corbis; 67 Getty Images; 68 (t) Nik Wheeler; 69 (t) Grant Heilman Photography; 70 (t) Design by Gregory Berger, Pomegranate Design (c)2004 Sacramento Area Earth Day Network; (b) Kathy Ries/Sacramento Area Earth Day Network; 71 HondaMotor/Handout/ Reuters/Corbis; 72 J. Scott Applewhite/AP/ Wide World Photos; (b) Tree Musketeers/ www.treemusketeers.org 72 (t) Karen Prinsloo/AP/Wide World Photos; 76-77 (bg) Terry W. Eggers/Corbis; 76 (b) Lawrence Migdale/www.migdale.com; 77 (t),(cl),(b) Lawrence Migdale/www.migdale.com.

UNIT 2

80-81 Larry Ulrich Photography; 82 (t) Phoebe A. Hearst Museum of Anthropology; (br) Denis Poroy/AP/Wide World Photos; 83 (tl), (tr) Marilyn "Angel" Wynn/Nativestock. com; (c) Michael Newman/Photo Edit;

(b) Spencer Grant/PhotoEdit; 85 (t) Getty Images; (b) Timothy H. O'Sullivan/ Corbis; 86 Library of Congress; 92 Robert B. Honeyman, Jr./Collection of Early Californian and Western American Pictorial Material/The Bancroft Library; 100 Edward S. Curtis, 1924/Plate No. 489/Library of Congress; 101 (l) Edward S. Curtis, 1924/ Plate No. 481/The Library of Congress; (r) The Bridgeman Art Library; 102 (t) John Bigelow Taylor/Art Resource, NY; (b) The Field Museum,#CSA9518; 103 The Field Museum,#CSA1912; 104 (t) Courtesy Southwest Museum; (b) Kayte Deioma Photography; 105 (r) Southwest Museum; (bl) Antelope Valley Indian Museum; (c) Bruce W. Miller/Courtesy Southwest Museum; 106 (b) Denver Public Library; (t) Logan Museum of Anthropology; 107 (t) Northwestern University Library;108 John Elk, III; 110 Gift; State Historical Society of Colorado; 1949/Library of Congress; 111 (b) Oakland Museum; (r) C. Hart Merriam Collection of Native American Photographs, ca. 1890-1938/The Bancroft Library; (l) Oakland Museum; 112 (t) Library of Congress Prints & Photographs Division; (b) Smithsonian American Art Museum, Washington, D.C./Art Resource, NY; 114 San Diego Museum of Man; 115 G. Ballard Studio; 116 Bob Rowan; Progressive Image/ Corbis; 118 (t) Bettman/Corbis; (b) Lawrence Migdale/www.migdale.com; 119 Logan Museum of Anthropology; 120 Picture History, LLC; 121 (t) W.S. Soule/Picture History, LLC; (b) Marilyn "Angel" Wynn/ nativestock.com; (c) Courtesy of Texas State University; 124 Nik Wheeler Photography; 126-131 Lawrence Migdale/www.migdale. com; 130 (c) Al Kroeber Collection at Phoebe Hearst Museum of Anthropolog; 132 Santa Barbara Mission Archive Library; 133 Corbis; 134 Lawrence Migdale/www.migdale.com; 135 (t) Lawrence Migdale/www. migdale.com; (b) Marilyn "Angel" Wynn/ Nativestock; 136 (t) Robert Landau/Corbis; (b) David Young-Wolff/PhotoEdit; (c) Bob Rowan; Progressive Image/Corbis; (inset) Lawrence Migdale/www.migdale.com; 137 Marilyn "Angel" Wynn/nativestock. com; 140 The Phoebe A. Hearst Museum of Anthropology; 141 (tc) Phoebe A. Hearst Museum of Anthropology; (tl) The Phoebe A. Hearst Museum of Anthropology; (tr) The Bancroft Library, University of California, Berkeley; 142 Marilyn "Angel" Wynn/native-stock.com; 143 (inset) AP Photo/Damian Dovarganes; 144 (b) California Department of Water Resources; (inset) Kate Hedges; 145 AP Photo/Ben Margot; 146 (t),(b) Courtesy of DQ University; 147 (t) Malki Museum; 148-149 Oakland Museum of California History Department; 148 (t) Lee Foster/ Lonely Planet Images; 150 (b) Courtesy of the Agua Caliente Tribal Council; 151 (b) Dennis Poroy/AP/Wide World Photos; 152 (b) Bettmann/Corbis; 153 Ken James/Corbis; 156 (bg) California Department of Parks and Recreation; (b) Robert Holmes Photography; 157 (tl) Marilyn "Angel" Wynn/nativestock. com; (inset) Darrell Gulin/Corbis; (cl) Marilyn "Angel" Wynn; (tr) Robert Holmes Photography.

UNIT 3

160-161 John Elk III; 162 (t) Corbis; (br) Newberry Library, Chicago/Superstock

163 (c) Mark Richards/PhotoEdit; (bl) Robert Landau/Corbis; (tl) Bettmann/Corbis; (tr) STR/AFP/Getty Images; 165 (t) Simi Valley Historical Society; (b) Simi Valley Historical Society; 166 Marc Muench/David Muench Photography; 174 Corbis;175 (t) National Maritime Museum; 176 (inset) Library of Congress; John Warden / Index Stock Imagery; 178 (t) Bridgeman Art Library; (b) Mary Evans Picture Library; 179 Larry Ulrich; 184 (t) Courtesy of Santa Barbara Mission; (b) Mark Gibson Photography; 185 Mark E. Gibson Photography; 186 (inset) Mark E. Gibson Photography; (r) Mark E. Gibson Photography; 190 (b) Robert B. Honeyman, Jr. Collection of Early Californian and Western American Pictorial Material/The Bancroft Library; 191 (t) Seaver Center for Western History Research, Los Angeles County Museum of Natural History; 192 Ewing Galloway/Index Stock; 193 (inset) Corbis; 194 The Bancroft Library; 195 The Bancroft Library; 198 Special Collections Dept./Robert E. Kennedy Library; 199 (tl) Bison Archives/ Marc Wanamaker; (cr) Special Collections Dept./Robert E. Kennedy Library, Cal Poly University; (tr) Joseph Sohm; ChromoSohm/ Corbis; 202 Mark E. Gibson Photography; 208 Hulton Archives/Getty Images; 209 (t) AP/Wide World Photos; (b) Hulton Archive/ Getty Images; 210 (t) California State Railroad Museum Library (b) Bettmann/ Corbis; 211 (t) The Bancroft Library; (b) California State Library Foundation; 212 (b) Orange Public Library History Collection; 213 San Pedro Bay Historical Archives; 216 David Sanger Photography; 217-218 Courtesy, History San Jose; 218 (t) The Bancroft Library, University of California, Berkeley; (b) Arbuckle Collection/California Room, San Jose Public Library; 219 Gary Crabbe/Enlightened Images Photography; 220 (bl), (br) Courtesy, History San Jose; 220 (t) Hewlett Packard Company; 225 (t) PictureNet/Corbis; 226 (b) Greg Probst/ Panoramic Images; 228 Library of Congress; (inset) Douglas Peebles/Corbis; 229 Library of Congress; 230 (b) Robert Holmes/Corbis; 232 Social and Public Art Resource Center; 233 (b) Social and Public Art Resource Center; 233 (t) Social and Public Art Resource Center; 236 Gerald L. French; 237 (tl) John Elk III; (inset) Spencer Grant/Photo Edit; (bl) John Elk III; (tr) Gibson Stock Photography; (inset) Andrea Wells Photography; (cr) Christine Pemberton/ Omni-Photo Communications, Inc.

UNIT 4

240-241 John Elk III; 242 (br) Mark Richards/ PhotoEdit; 243 (tl) David Butow/Corbis SABA; 243 (c) Getty Images; (b) Getty Images; (tr) William Whitehurst/Corbis; 245 Wally McNamee/Corbis; 246 Richard Cummins Photography; 253 (t) Kayte M. Deioma/PhotoEdit; 254 (t), (b) City of Pomona; 255 Michael Newman/PhotoEdit; 258 The Granger Collection, New York; 259 (br) Joseph Sohm/Visions of America/Corbis; 260 (t) The Granger Collection, New York; (b) Lee Celano/AP/Wide World Photos; 261 (t) Ron Fehling/Masterfile; 262 (t) Jim Ruymen/ Reuters/Corbis; (b) Mike Blake/Corbis; 263 Jim Ruymen/Reuters/Corbis; 264 (bl) Atwater Kent Museum of Philadelphia, Courtesy of Historical Society of Pennsylvania Collection/ www.bridgeman.co.uk; (br) Todd A. Gipstein/ Corbis; 265 (c) Corbis; 265 (b) Brooks Kraft/ Corbis; 265 (t) The Granger Collection, New York; 266 Michael Newman/PhotoEdit; 267 (cr) Index Stock Imagery; 268 Mark Gibson Photography; 270 (t) Mark Wilson/Getty Images; (b) Ron Sachs/Corbis; 271 (t) Richard Strauss/Collection of the Supreme Court of the Unites States; 272 (t) Justin Sullivan/Getty Images; (b) Index Stock Imagery; 273 Rich Pedroncelli/Associated Press, AP Wide World; 276 Gary Moon; 277 Lawrence Migdale/www. migdale.com; 278 Spencer Grant/Photo Edit; 279 City Council, City of Los Angeles; 280 Adams/Hansen Photography; 281 (t) Michael Newman/PhotoEdit; 281 (b) David Young-Wolff/ Photo Edit; 284-285 Gloria Molina/County of Los Angeles; 288 Getty Images; 294 David Schmidt/Masterfile; 295 (b) California State Library; (t) The Shreveport Times, Shane Bevel/AP/Wide World Photos; 296 (t) Alex Wong/Newsmakers/Getty Images; 296 (b) Bettmann/Corbis; 297 (t) Food Bank of Contra Costa; 297 (b) Food Bank of Contra Costa; 298 (t) Associated Press, AP Photographer PATSY LYNCH, Stringer; (b) Reuters/Corbis; 299 Press-Enterprise, Tracy Lee Silveria/AP/Wide World Photos; 301 (t) Associated Press, AP Photographer REED SAXON, Staff; (cr) Lawrence Migdale/www. migdale.com; (br) Michael Newman/Photo Edit; (bl) Jack Kurtz/The Image Works; (cl) Associated Press, AP Photographer ELISE AMENDOLA, Staff; 302 Spencer Grant/Photo Edit; 303 Joseph Sohm/Visions of America/ Corbis; 304 John Neubauer/PhotoEdit; 305 Philip Rostron/Masterfile; 308 Direct Relief International/Juliana Minsky/SurfMediaR Communications; 309 (b) Lakeshore Elementary School; 309 Mark Richards/ PhotoEdit; 310 (t) Casa Youth Shelter; Lydia Fitzgerald; (b) Casa Youth Shelter; Lydia Fitzgerald; 311 (inset) Armando Arorizo/ ZUMA/Corbis; (t) Shirley Hammond/ California Rescue Dog Association; 312 (r) 2004 Prudential Spirit of Community National Honoree; (l) Sacramento Bee/Jay Mather; 313 Michael Newman/PhotoEdit; 316 (b) Tim Moore; 316 (inset) Tim Moore; 317 (bl) Ariane Wilson; (br) Photo Courtesy of Ariane Wilson; (tl), (tr) The Fresno Bee.

UNIT 5

320-321 Joseph Sohm /Pan America Image/ PictureQuest; 322 (br) Gary Conner/ PhotoEdit; (t) Bill Ross/Corbis; 323 (b) Bettmann/Corbis; (tl) Francis Miller/Time Life Pictures/Getty Images; (c) David Young-Wolff/PhotoEdit; (tr) Ted Spiegel/ Corbis; 325 Dave G. Houser/Corbis; 326 AP Photo/U.S. Navy, Charles P. Cavanaugh; 333 Rob Crandall/Stock Boston; 334 Frans Lanting/Minden Pictures; 335 (b) Smokey Bear Historical Park; 335 Bettmann/Corbis; 337 Getty Images; 339 (tr) ART on File/ Corbis; (tl) Stephen Saks Photography; 340 (inset) Corbis; Index Stock Imagery; 341 (t) Brown Brothers; 342 National Geographic Society; 343 (tl) Guy Crittenden / Index Stock Imagery; 346 Getty Images; 347 (t) David Boyer/National Geographic Image Collection; 350 The Granger Collection, New York; 351 (t) Brown Brothers; 352 (b) National Archives; 353 (t) National Archives; 354 (t) John Huling/Courtesy of Colton Hall Museum; (bl) California State Archives; 354 (br) California State Archives; 355 (b) James Randklev/Visions of America/Corbis; 356 (l) (r) The Bancroft Library; 357 Courtesy of the Obata Family Collection; 358 Superstock; 359 (inset) Photo Courtesy of James D. Julia, Inc., Auctioneers, Fairfield, ME; 362 Lynn Seldon; 370 Royalty-free/Corbis; 372 Bettmann/ Corbis; 373 (inset) Bettmann/Corbis; (b) Gala/ Superstock; 374 (b) The Historical Society of Pennsylvania; (t) Bettmann/Corbis; 375 Bill Freeman/PhotoEdit; 376 (l) The Granger Collection, New York; 376 (r) The Granger Collection, New York; 377 (l) Courtesy of the Historical Society of Pennsylvania; (r) The Granger Collection, New York; 378 Dave G. Houser/Corbis; 379 (inset) Burstein Collection/Corbis; 380 (cl) Christine Pemberton/Omni-Photo Communications; 380 (bl) Mike Mullen Event Photography; (cr) Robert Campbell/Superstock; (tr) John Elk III; 382 The Granger Collection, New York; 383 Library of Congress; 384 (r), (l) Courtesy of The University of North Carolina at Chapel Hill; 385 (b) National Archives ; 385 Douglass, Frederick and Delany, Martin, editors. "North Star, June 2, 1848." 1848. African American Odyssey: A Quest for Full Citizenship, Library of Congress.; 386 (c) California Historical Society; (l) National Museum of Women's History; 387 (b) Bettmann/Corbis; (t) Bettmann/Corbis; 388 Victor Aleman/ Black Star Publishing/ PictureQuest; 389 (t) Bettmann/Corbis; 392 Bettmann/Corbis; 393 (c) Nailah Feanny/Corbis; (t) Bettmann/ Corbis; 393 (b) Bettmann/Corbis; 396 (l) J.Blank/H.Armstrong Roberts; (b) Adam Woodfitt/Woodfin Camp & Associates; 397 (t) Royalty-Free/Corbis; (b) Gayna Hoffman/ Stock Boston/PictureQuest.

UNIT 6

401 John Elk, III; 402 (br) Getty Images; (t) Getty Images; 403 (cr) SW Production/ Index Stock Imagery; (bl) Getty Images; (tl) Spencer Grant/PhotoEdit; 405 Damian Dovarganes/AP/Wide World Photos; 406 Associated Press/Fresno Bee/David Hunter; 414 Courtesy of the Uppal Family/University of California, Berkley; 415 (t) Fresno County Historical Society; (inset) C.C. Curtis/Annand Collection; 416 (b) Alamy Images; (t) Barbara Stitzer/PhotoEdit; 417 (t) Bettmann/Corbis; 418 (b) Lawrence Migdale/www.migdale.com; (t) Arni Katz / Index Stock Imagery; 420 (b) Photographer: Burr McIntosh Photographs, Donor: CSU Chico, Meriam Library, Special Collections/California State University, Chico, Meriam Library, Special Collections; (inset) Lake County Museum/Corbis; 421 (t) Photographer: O.H. Reichling, Chico, California, Donor: Bidwell Mansion State Historic Park/California State University, Chico, Meriam Library, Special Collections; 422 George D. Lepp/Corbis; Maisie Jane's California Sunshine Products; 424 (b) John Elk, III; (t) From the Eastman's Originals Collection, Department of Special Collections, General Library, University of California, Davis; 425 (inset) Alamy Images; (t) John Elk, III; 426 Inga Spence/Index Stock Imagery; 427 (t) Christopher J. Morris/Corbis; (inset) California Energy Commission; 432 (t) Alamy Images; (b) Alamy Images; 433 Gibson Stock Photography; (c) Tony Freeman/PhotoEdit; (r) David Young-Wolff/PhotoEdit; 436 (l) David Young-Wolff/PhotoEdit; 437 (t) Courtesy of Volunteer San Diego; 437 (b) Tim Moore; 438 Hulton-Deutsch Collection/Corbis; 439 (b) Getty Images ; 439 (t) Mark Richards/ PhotoEdit; 440 (tr) Ed Wheeler/Corbis; (br) AP Photo/Scott Sady; (bc) Chuck Savage/Corbis;